U·X·L
Encyclopedia
of Science

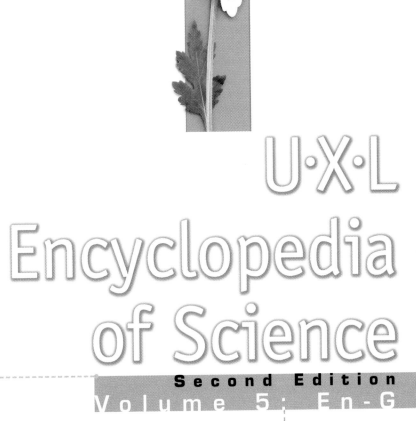

U·X·L
Encyclopedia
of Science

Second Edition

Volume 5: En-G

Rob Nagel, Editor

U·X·L

GALE GROUP

THOMSON LEARNING

Detroit • New York • San Diego • San Francisco
Boston • New Haven, Conn. • Waterville, Maine
London • Munich

U·X·L Encyclopedia of Science
Second Edition

Rob Nagel, *Editor*

Staff

Elizabeth Shaw Grunow, *U·X·L Editor*

Julie Carnagie, *Contributing Editor*

Carol DeKane Nagel, *U·X·L Managing Editor*

Thomas L. Romig, *U·X·L Publisher*

Shalice Shah-Caldwell, *Permissions Associate (Pictures)*

Robyn Young, *Imaging and Multimedia Content Editor*

Rita Wimberley, *Senior Buyer*

Pamela A. E. Galbreath, *Senior Art Designer*

Michelle Cadorée, *Indexing*

GGS Information Services, *Typesetting*

On the front cover: Nikola Tesla with one of his generators, reproduced by permission of the Granger Collection.

On the back cover: The flow of red blood cells through blood vessels, reproduced by permission of Phototake.

Library of Congress Cataloging-in-Publication Data

U-X-L encyclopedia of science.—2nd ed. / Rob Nagel, editor
p.cm.
Includes bibliographical references and indexes.
Contents: v.1. A-As — v.2. At-Car — v.3. Cat-Cy — v.4. D-Em — v.5. En-G — v.6. H-Mar — v.7. Mas-O — v.8. P-Ra — v.9. Re-St — v.10. Su-Z.
Summary: Includes 600 topics in the life, earth, and physical sciences as well as in engineering, technology, math, environmental science, and psychology.
ISBN 0-7876-5432-9 (set : acid-free paper) — ISBN 0-7876-5433-7 (v.1 : acid-free paper) — ISBN 0-7876-5434-5 (v.2 : acid-free paper) — ISBN 0-7876-5435-3 (v.3 : acid-free paper) — ISBN 0-7876-5436-1 (v.4 : acid-free paper) — ISBN 0-7876-5437-X (v.5 : acid-free paper) — ISBN 0-7876-5438-8 (v.6 : acid-free paper) — ISBN 0-7876-5439-6 (v.7 : acid-free paper) — ISBN 0-7876-5440-X (v.8 : acid-free paper) — ISBN 0-7876-5441-8 (v.9 : acid-free paper) — ISBN 0-7876-5775-1 (v.10 : acid-free paper)

1. Science-Encyclopedias, Juvenile. 2. Technology-Encyclopedias, Juvenile. [1. Science-Encyclopedias. 2. Technology-Encyclopedias.] I. Title: UXL encyclopedia of science. II. Nagel, Rob.
Q121.U18 2001
503-dc21

2001035562

Table of Contents

Reader's Guide vii

Entries by Scientific Field ix

Volume 1: A-As 1
    Where to Learn More xxxi
    Index xxxv

Volume 2: At-Car 211
    Where to Learn More xxxi
    Index xxxv

Volume 3: Cat-Cy 413
    Where to Learn More xxxi
    Index xxxv

Volume 4: D-Em 611
    Where to Learn More xxxi
    Index xxxv

Volume 5: En-G 793
    Where to Learn More xxxi
    Index xxxv

Volume 6: H-Mar 1027
    Where to Learn More xxxi
    Index xxxv

Volume 7: Mas-O 1235
    Where to Learn More xxxi
    Index xxxv

Contents

Volume 8: P-Ra **1457**
    Where to Learn More . . . . **xxxi**
    Index . . . . **XXXV**

Volume 9: Re-St **1647**
    Where to Learn More . . . . **xxxi**
    Index . . . . **XXXV**

Volume 10: Su-Z **1829**
    Where to Learn More . . . . **xxxi**
    Index . . . . **XXXV**

Reader's Guide

Demystify scientific theories, controversies, discoveries, and phenomena with the *U•X•L Encyclopedia of Science,* Second Edition.

This alphabetically organized ten-volume set opens up the entire world of science in clear, nontechnical language. More than 600 entries—an increase of more than 10 percent from the first edition—provide fascinating facts covering the entire spectrum of science. This second edition features more than 50 new entries and more than 100 updated entries. These informative essays range from 250 to 2,500 words, many of which include helpful sidebar boxes that highlight fascinating facts and phenomena. Topics profiled are related to the physical, life, and earth sciences, as well as to math, psychology, engineering, technology, and the environment.

In addition to solid information, the *Encyclopedia* also provides these features:

- "Words to Know" boxes that define commonly used terms
- Extensive cross references that lead directly to related entries
- A table of contents by scientific field that organizes the entries
- More than 600 color and black-and-white photos and technical drawings
- Sources for further study, including books, magazines, and Web sites

Each volume concludes with a cumulative subject index, making it easy to locate quickly the theories, people, objects, and inventions discussed throughout the *U•X•L Encyclopedia of Science,* Second Edition.

Suggestions

We welcome any comments on this work and suggestions for entries to feature in future editions of *U•X•L Encyclopedia of Science.* Please write: Editors, *U•X•L Encyclopedia of Science,* U•X•L, Gale Group, 27500 Drake Road, Farmington Hills, Michigan, 48331-3535; call toll-free: 800-877-4253; fax to: 248-699-8097; or send an e-mail via www.galegroup.com.

Entries by Scientific Field

Boldface indicates volume numbers.

Acoustics

Acoustics	**1:**17
Compact disc	**3:**531
Diffraction	**4:**648
Echolocation	**4:**720
Magnetic recording/ audiocassette	**6:**1209
Sonar	**9:**1770
Ultrasonics	**10:**1941
Video recording	**10:**1968

Aerodynamics

Aerodynamics	**1:**39
Fluid dynamics	**5:**882

Aeronautical engineering

Aircraft	**1:**74
Atmosphere observation	**2:**215
Balloon	**1:**261
Jet engine	**6:**1143
Rockets and missiles	**9:**1693

Aerospace engineering

International Ultraviolet Explorer	**6:**1120
Rockets and missiles	**9:**1693
Satellite	**9:**1707
Spacecraft, manned	**9:**1777
Space probe	**9:**1783
Space station, international	**9:**1788
Telescope	**10:**1869

Agriculture

Agriculture	**1:**62
Agrochemical	**1:**65
Aquaculture	**1:**166
Biotechnology	**2:**309
Cotton	**3:**577
Crops	**3:**582
DDT (dichlorodiphenyl-trichloroethane)	**4:**619
Drift net	**4:**680
Forestry	**5:**901
Genetic engineering	**5:**973
Organic farming	**7:**1431
Slash-and-burn agriculture	**9:**1743
Soil	**9:**1758

Anatomy and physiology

Anatomy	**1:**138
Blood	**2:**326

Entries by Scientific Field

Brain	2:337
Cholesterol	3:469
Chromosome	3:472
Circulatory system	3:480
Digestive system	4:653
Ear	4:693
Endocrine system	5:796
Excretory system	5:839
Eye	5:848
Heart	6:1037
Human Genome Project	6:1060
Immune system	6:1082
Integumentary system	6:1109
Lymphatic system	6:1198
Muscular system	7:1309
Nervous system	7:1333
Physiology	8:1516
Reproductive system	9:1667
Respiratory system	9:1677
Skeletal system	9:1739
Smell	9:1750
Speech	9:1796
Taste	10:1861
Touch	10:1903

Anesthesiology

| Alternative medicine | 1:118 |
| Anesthesia | 1:142 |

Animal husbandry

Agrochemical	1:65
Biotechnology	2:309
Crops	3:582
Genetic engineering	5:973
Organic farming	7:1431

Anthropology

Archaeoastronomy	1:171
Dating techniques	4:616
Forensic science	5:898
Gerontology	5:999
Human evolution	6:1054
Mounds, earthen	7:1298
Petroglyphs and pictographs	8:1491

Aquaculture

Aquaculture	1:166
Crops	3:582
Drift net	4:680
Fish	5:875

Archaeology

Archaeoastronomy	1:171
Archaeology	1:173
Dating techniques	4:616
Fossil and fossilization	5:917
Half-life	6:1027
Nautical archaeology	7:1323
Petroglyphs and pictographs	8:1491

Artificial intelligence

| Artificial intelligence | 1:188 |
| Automation | 2:242 |

Astronomy

Archaeoastronomy	1:171
Asteroid	1:200
Astrophysics	1:207
Big bang theory	2:273
Binary star	2:276
Black hole	2:322
Brown dwarf	2:358
Calendar	2:372
Celestial mechanics	3:423
Comet	3:527
Constellation	3:558
Cosmic ray	3:571

Cosmology   3:574
Dark matter   4:613
Earth (planet)   4:698
Eclipse   4:723
Extrasolar planet   5:847
Galaxy   5:941
Gamma ray   5:949
Gamma-ray burst   5:952
Gravity and gravitation 5:1012
Infrared astronomy   6:1100
International Ultraviolet
    Explorer   6:1120
Interstellar matter   6:1130
Jupiter (planet)   6:1146
Light-year   6:1190
Mars (planet)   6:1228
Mercury (planet)   7:1250
Meteor and meteorite   7:1262
Moon   7:1294
Nebula   7:1327
Neptune (planet)   7:1330
Neutron star   7:1339
Nova   7:1359
Orbit   7:1426
Pluto (planet)   8:1539
Quasar   8:1609
Radio astronomy   8:1633
Red giant   9:1653
Redshift   9:1654
Satellite   9:1707
Saturn (planet)   9:1708
Seasons   9:1726
Solar system   9:1762
Space   9:1776
Spacecraft, manned   9:1777
Space probe   9:1783
Space station,
    international   9:1788
Star   9:1801
Starburst galaxy   9:1806
Star cluster   9:1808
Stellar magnetic fields 9:1820

Sun   10:1844
Supernova   10:1852
Telescope   10:1869
Ultraviolet astronomy   10:1943
Uranus (planet)   10:1952
Variable star   10:1963
Venus (planet)   10:1964
White dwarf   10:2027
X-ray astronomy   10:2038

Astrophysics

Astrophysics   1:207
Big bang theory   2:273
Binary star   2:276
Black hole   2:322
Brown dwarf   2:358
Celestial mechanics   3:423
Cosmic ray   3:571
Cosmology   3:574
Dark matter   4:613
Galaxy   5:941
Gamma ray   5:949
Gamma-ray burst   5:952
Gravity and gravitation 5:1012
Infrared astronomy   6:1100
International Ultraviolet
    Explorer   6:1120
Interstellar matter   6:1130
Light-year   6:1190
Neutron star   7:1339
Orbit   7:1426
Quasar   8:1609
Radio astronomy   8:1633
Red giant   9:1653
Redshift   9:1654
Space   9:1776
Star   9:1801
Starburst galaxy   9:1806
Star cluster   9:1808
Stellar magnetic fields 9:1820
Sun   10:1844

Entries by
Scientific Field

Supernova   **10**:1852
Ultraviolet astronomy   **10**:1943
Uranus (planet)   **10**:1952
Variable star   **10**:1963
White dwarf   **10**:2027
X-ray astronomy   **10**:2038

Atomic/Nuclear physics

Actinides   **1**:23
Alkali metals   **1**:99
Alkali earth metals   **1**:102
Alternative energy sources   **1**:111
Antiparticle   **1**:163
Atom   **2**:226
Atomic mass   **2**:229
Atomic theory   **2**:232
Chemical bond   **3**:453
Dating techniques   **4**:616
Electron   **4**:768
Half-life   **6**:1027
Ionization   **6**:1135
Isotope   **6**:1141
Lanthanides   **6**:1163
Mole (measurement)   **7**:1282
Molecule   **7**:1285
Neutron   **7**:1337
Noble gases   **7**:1349
Nuclear fission   **7**:1361
Nuclear fusion   **7**:1366
Nuclear medicine   **7**:1372
Nuclear power   **7**:1374
Nuclear weapons   **7**:1381
Particle accelerators   **8**:1475
Quantum mechanics   **8**:1607
Radiation   **8**:1619
Radiation exposure   **8**:1621
Radiology   **8**:1637
Subatomic particles   **10**:1829
X ray   **10**:2033

Automotive engineering

Automobile   **2**:245
Diesel engine   **4**:646
Internal-combustion
  engine   **6**:1117

Bacteriology

Bacteria   **2**:253
Biological warfare   **2**:287
Disease   **4**:669
Legionnaire's disease   **6**:1179

Ballistics

Ballistics   **2**:260
Nuclear weapons   **7**:1381
Rockets and missiles   **9**:1693

Biochemistry

Amino acid   **1**:130
Biochemistry   **2**:279
Carbohydrate   **2**:387
Cell   **3**:428
Cholesterol   **3**:469
Enzyme   **5**:812
Fermentation   **5**:864
Hormones   **6**:1050
Human Genome Project   **6**:1060
Lipids   **6**:1191
Metabolism   **7**:1255
Nucleic acid   **7**:1387
Osmosis   **7**:1436
Photosynthesis   **8**:1505
Proteins   **8**:1586
Respiration   **9**:1672
Vitamin   **10**:1981
Yeast   **10**:2043

Biology

Adaptation   1:26
Algae   1:91
Amino acid   1:130
Amoeba   1:131
Amphibians   1:134
Anatomy   1:138
Animal   1:145
Antibody and antigen   1:159
Arachnids   1:168
Arthropods   1:183
Bacteria   2:253
Behavior   2:270
Biochemistry   2:279
Biodegradable   2:280
Biodiversity   2:281
Biological warfare   2:287
Biology   2:290
Biome   2:293
Biophysics   2:302
Biosphere   2:304
Biotechnology   2:309
Birds   2:312
Birth   2:315
Birth defects   2:319
Blood   2:326
Botany   2:334
Brain   2:337
Butterflies   2:364
Canines   2:382
Carbohydrate   2:387
Carcinogen   2:406
Cell   3:428
Cellulose   3:442
Cetaceans   3:448
Cholesterol   3:469
Chromosome   3:472
Circulatory system   3:480
Clone and cloning   3:484
Cockroaches   3:505
Coelacanth   3:508
Contraception   3:562

Coral   3:566
Crustaceans   3:590
Cryobiology   3:593
Digestive system   4:653
Dinosaur   4:658
Disease   4:669
Ear   4:693
Embryo and embryonic
   development   4:785
Endocrine system   5:796
Enzyme   5:812
Eutrophication   5:828
Evolution   5:832
Excretory system   5:839
Eye   5:848
Felines   5:855
Fermentation   5:864
Fertilization   5:867
Fish   5:875
Flower   5:878
Forestry   5:901
Forests   5:907
Fungi   5:930
Genetic disorders   5:966
Genetic engineering   5:973
Genetics   5:980
Heart   6:1037
Hibernation   6:1046
Hormones   6:1050
Horticulture   6:1053
Human Genome Project   6:1060
Human evolution   6:1054
Immune system   6:1082
Indicator species   6:1090
Insects   6:1103
Integumentary system   6:1109
Invertebrates   6:1133
Kangaroos and wallabies   6:1153
Leaf   6:1172
Lipids   6:1191
Lymphatic system   6:1198
Mammals   6:1222

Entries by Scientific Field

Mendelian laws of inheritance	**7:**1246
Metabolism	**7:**1255
Metamorphosis	**7:**1259
Migration (animals)	**7:**1271
Molecular biology	**7:**1283
Mollusks	**7:**1288
Muscular system	**7:**1309
Mutation	**7:**1314
Nervous system	**7:**1333
Nucleic acid	**7:**1387
Osmosis	**7:**1436
Parasites	**8:**1467
Photosynthesis	**8:**1505
Phototropism	**8:**1508
Physiology	**8:**1516
Plague	**8:**1518
Plankton	**8:**1520
Plant	**8:**1522
Primates	**8:**1571
Proteins	**8:**1586
Protozoa	**8:**1590
Puberty	**8:**1599
Rain forest	**8:**1641
Reproduction	**9:**1664
Reproductive system	**9:**1667
Reptiles	**9:**1670
Respiration	**9:**1672
Respiratory system	**9:**1677
Rh factor	**9:**1683
Seed	**9:**1729
Sexually transmitted diseases	**9:**1735
Skeletal system	**9:**1739
Smell	**9:**1750
Snakes	**9:**1752
Speech	**9:**1796
Sponges	**9:**1799
Taste	**10:**1861
Touch	**10:**1903
Tree	**10:**1927
Tumor	**10:**1934
Vaccine	**10:**1957
Vertebrates	**10:**1967
Virus	**10:**1974
Vitamin	**10:**1981
Wetlands	**10:**2024
Yeast	**10:**2043

Biomedical engineering

Electrocardiogram	**4:**751
Radiology	**8:**1637

Biotechnology

Biotechnology	**2:**309
Brewing	**2:**352
Fermentation	**5:**864
Vaccine	**10:**1957

Botany

Botany	**2:**334
Cellulose	**3:**442
Cocaine	**3:**501
Cotton	**3:**577
Flower	**5:**878
Forestry	**5:**901
Forests	**5:**907
Horticulture	**6:**1053
Leaf	**6:**1172
Marijuana	**6:**1224
Photosynthesis	**8:**1505
Phototropism	**8:**1508
Plant	**8:**1522
Seed	**9:**1729
Tree	**10:**1927

Cartography

Cartography	**2:**410
Geologic map	**5:**986

Cellular biology

Amino acid	**1**:130
Carbohydrate	**2**:387
Cell	**3**:428
Cholesterol	**3**:469
Chromosome	**3**:472
Genetics	**5**:980
Lipids	**6**:1191
Osmosis	**7**:1436
Proteins	**8**:1586

Chemistry

Acids and bases	**1**:14
Actinides	**1**:23
Aerosols	**1**:43
Agent Orange	**1**:54
Agrochemical	**1**:65
Alchemy	**1**:82
Alcohols	**1**:88
Alkali metals	**1**:99
Alkaline earth metals	**1**:102
Aluminum family	**1**:122
Atom	**2**:226
Atomic mass	**2**:229
Atomic theory	**2**:232
Biochemistry	**2**:279
Carbon dioxide	**2**:393
Carbon family	**2**:395
Carbon monoxide	**2**:403
Catalyst and catalysis	**2**:413
Chemical bond	**3**:453
Chemical w\arfare	**3**:457
Chemistry	**3**:463
Colloid	**3**:515
Combustion	**3**:522
Composite materials	**3**:536
Compound, chemical	**3**:541
Crystal	**3**:601
Cyclamate	**3**:608
DDT (dichlorodiphenyl-trichloroethane)	**4**:619
Diffusion	**4**:651
Dioxin	**4**:667
Distillation	**4**:675
Dyes and pigments	**4**:686
Electrolysis	**4**:755
Element, chemical	**4**:774
Enzyme	**5**:812
Equation, chemical	**5**:815
Equilibrium, chemical	**5**:817
Explosives	**5**:843
Fermentation	**5**:864
Filtration	**5**:872
Formula, chemical	**5**:914
Halogens	**6**:1030
Hormones	**6**:1050
Hydrogen	**6**:1068
Industrial minerals	**6**:1092
Ionization	**6**:1135
Isotope	**6**:1141
Lanthanides	**6**:1163
Lipids	**6**:1191
Metabolism	**7**:1255
Mole (measurement)	**7**:1282
Molecule	**7**:1285
Nitrogen family	**7**:1344
Noble gases	**7**:1349
Nucleic acid	**7**:1387
Osmosis	**7**:1436
Oxidation-reduction reaction	**7**:1439
Oxygen family	**7**:1442
Ozone	**7**:1450
Periodic table	**8**:1486
pH	**8**:1495
Photochemistry	**8**:1498
Photosynthesis	**8**:1505
Plastics	**8**:1532
Poisons and toxins	**8**:1542
Polymer	**8**:1563
Proteins	**8**:1586
Qualitative analysis	**8**:1603
Quantitative analysis	**8**:1604

Entries by Scientific Field

Reaction, chemical	**9:**1647
Respiration	**9:**1672
Soaps and detergents	**9:**1756
Solution	**9:**1767
Transition elements	**10:**1913
Vitamin	**10:**1981
Yeast	**10:**2043

Civil engineering

Bridges	**2:**354
Canal	**2:**376
Dam	**4:**611
Lock	**6:**1192

Climatology

Global climate	**5:**1006
Ice ages	**6:**1075
Seasons	**9:**1726

Communications/ Graphic arts

Antenna	**1:**153
CAD/CAM	**2:**369
Cellular/digital technology	**3:**439
Compact disc	**3:**531
Computer software	**3:**549
DVD technology	**4:**684
Hologram and holography	**6:**1048
Internet	**6:**1123
Magnetic recording/ audiocassette	**6:**1209
Microwave communication	**7:**1268
Petroglyphs and pictographs	**8:**1491
Photocopying	**8:**1499
Radio	**8:**1626
Satellite	**9:**1707
Telegraph	**10:**1863
Telephone	**10:**1866
Television	**10:**1875
Video recording	**10:**1968

Computer science

Artificial intelligence	**1:**188
Automation	**2:**242
CAD/CAM	**2:**369
Calculator	**2:**370
Cellular/digital technology	**3:**439
Compact disc	**3:**531
Computer, analog	**3:**546
Computer, digital	**3:**547
Computer software	**3:**549
Internet	**6:**1123
Mass production	**7:**1236
Robotics	**9:**1690
Virtual reality	**10:**1969

Cosmology

Astrophysics	**1:**207
Big Bang theory	**2:**273
Cosmology	**3:**574
Galaxy	**5:**941
Space	**9:**1776

Cryogenics

Cryobiology	**3:**593
Cryogenics	**3:**595

Dentistry

Dentistry	**4:**626
Fluoridation	**5:**889

Ecology/Environmental science

Acid rain	**1:**9
Alternative energy sources	**1:**111
Biodegradable	**2:**280
Biodiversity	**2:**281

Bioenergy 2:284
Biome 2:293
Biosphere 2:304
Carbon cycle 2:389
Composting 3:539
DDT (dichlorodiphenyl-
trichloroethane) 4:619
Desert 4:634
Dioxin 4:667
Drift net 4:680
Drought 4:682
Ecology 4:725
Ecosystem 4:728
Endangered species 5:793
Environmental ethics 5:807
Erosion 5:820
Eutrophication 5:828
Food web and food chain 5:894
Forestry 5:901
Forests 5:907
Gaia hypothesis 5:935
Greenhouse effect 5:1016
Hydrologic cycle 6:1071
Indicator species 6:1090
Nitrogen cycle 7:1342
Oil spills 7:1422
Organic farming 7:1431
Paleoecology 8:1457
Pollution 8:1549
Pollution control 8:1558
Rain forest 8:1641
Recycling 9:1650
Succession 10:1837
Waste management 10:2003
Wetlands 10:2024

Electrical engineering

Antenna 1:153
Battery 2:268
Cathode 3:415
Cathode-ray tube 3:417
Cell, electrochemical 3:436
Compact disc 3:531
Diode 4:665
Electric arc 4:734
Electric current 4:737
Electricity 4:741
Electric motor 4:747
Electrocardiogram 4:751
Electromagnetic field 4:758
Electromagnetic induction 4:760
Electromagnetism 4:766
Electronics 4:773
Fluorescent light 5:886
Generator 5:962
Incandescent light 6:1087
Integrated circuit 6:1106
LED (light-emitting diode) 6: 1176
Magnetic recording/
audiocassette 6:1209
Radar 8:1613
Radio 8:1626
Superconductor 10:1849
Telegraph 10:1863
Telephone 10:1866
Television 10:1875
Transformer 10:1908
Transistor 10:1910
Ultrasonics 10:1941
Video recording 10:1968

Electronics

Antenna 1:153
Battery 2:268
Cathode 3:415
Cathode-ray tube 3:417
Cell, electrochemical 3:436
Compact disc 3:531
Diode 4:665
Electric arc 4:734
Electric current 4:737
Electricity 4:741
Electric motor 4:747

Electromagnetic field   4:758
Electromagnetic induction   4:760
Electronics   4:773
Generator   5:962
Integrated circuit   6:1106
LED (light-emitting diode) 6:1176
Magnetic recording/
   audiocassette   6:1209
Radar   8:1613
Radio   8:1626
Superconductor   10:1849
Telephone   10:1866
Television   10:1875
Transformer   10:1908
Transistor   10:1910
Ultrasonics   10:1941
Video recording   10:1968

Embryology

Embryo and embryonic
   development   4:785
Fertilization   5:867
Reproduction   9:1664
Reproductive system   9:1667

Engineering

Aerodynamics   1:39
Aircraft   1:74
Antenna   1:153
Automation   2:242
Automobile   2:245
Balloon   1:261
Battery   2:268
Bridges   2:354
Canal   2:376
Cathode   3:415
Cathode-ray tube   3:417
Cell, electrochemical   3:436
Compact disc   3:531
Dam   4:611

Diesel engine   4:646
Diode   4:665
Electric arc   4:734
Electric current   4:737
Electric motor   4:747
Electricity   4:741
Electrocardiogram   4:751
Electromagnetic field   4:758
Electromagnetic induction   4:760
Electromagnetism   4:766
Electronics   4:773
Engineering   5:805
Fluorescent light   5:886
Generator   5:962
Incandescent light   6:1087
Integrated circuit   6:1106
Internal-combustion
   engine   6:1117
Jet engine   6:1143
LED (light-emitting diode) 6: 1176
Lock   6:1192
Machines, simple   6:1203
Magnetic recording/
   audiocassette   6:1209
Mass production   7:1236
Radar   8:1613
Radio   8:1626
Steam engine   9:1817
Submarine   10:1834
Superconductor   10:1849
Telegraph   10:1863
Telephone   10:1866
Television   10:1875
Transformer   10:1908
Transistor   10:1910
Ultrasonics   10:1941
Video recording   10:1968

Entomology

Arachnids   1:168
Arthropods   1:183

Butterflies 2:364
Cockroaches 3:505
Insects 6:1103
Invertebrates 6:1133
Metamorphosis 7:1259

Epidemiology
Biological warfare 2:287
Disease 4:669
Ebola virus 4:717
Plague 8:1518
Poliomyelitis 8:1546
Sexually transmitted
  diseases 9:1735
Vaccine 10:1957

Evolutionary biology
Adaptation 1:26
Evolution 5:832
Human evolution 6:1054
Mendelian laws of
  inheritance 7:1246

Food science
Brewing 2:352
Cyclamate 3:608
Food preservation 5:890
Nutrition 7:1399

Forensic science
Forensic science 5:898

Forestry
Forestry 5:901
Forests 5:907
Rain forest 8:1641
Tree 10:1927

General science
Alchemy 1:82
Chaos theory 3:451
Metric system 7:1265
Scientific method 9:1722
Units and standards 10:1948

Genetic engineering
Biological warfare 2:287
Biotechnology 2:309
Clone and cloning 3:484
Genetic engineering 5:973

Genetics
Biotechnology 2:309
Birth defects 2:319
Cancer 2:379
Carcinogen 2:406
Chromosome 3:472
Clone and cloning 3:484
Genetic disorders 5:966
Genetic engineering 5:973
Genetics 5:980
Human Genome Project 6:1060
Mendelian laws of
  inheritance 7:1246
Mutation 7:1314
Nucleic acid 7:1387

Geochemistry
Coal 3:492
Earth (planet) 4:698
Earth science 4:707
Earth's interior 4:708
Glacier 5:1000
Minerals 7:1273
Rocks 9:1701
Soil 9:1758

Geography

Africa	**1**:49
Antarctica	**1**:147
Asia	**1**:194
Australia	**2**:238
Biome	**2**:293
Cartography	**2**:410
Coast and beach	**3**:498
Desert	**4**:634
Europe	**5**:823
Geologic map	**5**:986
Island	**6**:1137
Lake	**6**:1159
Mountain	**7**:1301
North America	**7**:1352
River	**9**:1685
South America	**9**:1772

Geology

Catastrophism	**3**:415
Cave	**3**:420
Coal	**3**:492
Coast and beach	**3**:498
Continental margin	**3**:560
Dating techniques	**4**:616
Desert	**4**:634
Earthquake	**4**:702
Earth science	**4**:707
Earth's interior	**4**:708
Erosion	**5**:820
Fault	**5**:855
Geologic map	**5**:986
Geologic time	**5**:990
Geology	**5**:993
Glacier	**5**:1000
Hydrologic cycle	**6**:1071
Ice ages	**6**:1075
Iceberg	**6**:1078
Industrial minerals	**6**:1092
Island	**6**:1137
Lake	**6**:1159

Minerals	**7**:1273
Mining	**7**:1278
Mountain	**7**:1301
Natural gas	**7**:1319
Oil drilling	**7**:1418
Oil spills	**7**:1422
Petroleum	**8**:1492
Plate tectonics	**8**:1534
River	**9**:1685
Rocks	**9**:1701
Soil	**9**:1758
Uniformitarianism	**10**:1946
Volcano	**10**:1992
Water	**10**:2010

Geophysics

Earth (planet)	**4**:698
Earth science	**4**:707
Fault	**5**:855
Plate tectonics	**8**:1534

Gerontology

Aging and death	**1**:59
Alzheimer's disease	**1**:126
Arthritis	**1**:181
Dementia	**4**:622
Gerontology	**5**:999

Gynecology

Contraception	**3**:562
Fertilization	**5**:867
Gynecology	**5**:1022
Puberty	**8**:1599
Reproduction	**9**:1664

Health/Medicine

Acetylsalicylic acid	**1**:6
Addiction	**1**:32
Attention-deficit hyperactivity disorder (ADHD)	**2**:237

Depression	**4**:630	Hallucinogens	**6**:1027
AIDS (acquired immunod-eficiency syndrome)	**1**:70	Immune system	**6**:1082
		Legionnaire's disease	**6**:1179
Alcoholism	**1**:85	Lipids	**6**:1191
Allergy	**1**:106	Malnutrition	**6**:1216
Alternative medicine	**1**:118	Marijuana	**6**:1224
Alzheimer's disease	**1**:126	Multiple personality disorder	**7**:1305
Amino acid	**1**:130		
Anesthesia	**1**:142	Nuclear medicine	**7**:1372
Antibiotics	**1**:155	Nutrition	**7**:1399
Antiseptics	**1**:164	Obsession	**7**:1405
Arthritis	**1**:181	Orthopedics	**7**:1434
Asthma	**1**:204	Parasites	**8**:1467
Attention-deficit hyperactivity disorder (ADHD)	**2**:237	Phobia	**8**:1497
		Physical therapy	**8**:1511
Birth defects	**2**:319	Plague	**8**:1518
Blood supply	**2**:330	Plastic surgery	**8**:1527
Burn	**2**:361	Poliomyelitis	**8**:1546
Carcinogen	**2**:406	Prosthetics	**8**:1579
Carpal tunnel syndrome	**2**:408	Protease inhibitor	**8**:1583
Cholesterol	**3**:469	Psychiatry	**8**:1592
Cigarette smoke	**3**:476	Psychology	**8**:1594
Cocaine	**3**:501	Psychosis	**8**:1596
Contraception	**3**:562	Puberty	**8**:1599
Dementia	**4**:622	Radial keratotomy	**8**:1615
Dentistry	**4**:626	Radiology	**8**:1637
Depression	**4**:630	Rh factor	**9**:1683
Diabetes mellitus	**4**:638	Schizophrenia	**9**:1716
Diagnosis	**4**:640	Sexually transmitted diseases	**9**:1735
Dialysis	**4**:644		
Disease	**4**:669	Sleep and sleep disorders	**9**:1745
Dyslexia	**4**:690	Stress	**9**:1826
Eating disorders	**4**:711	Sudden infant death syndrome (SIDS)	**10**:1840
Ebola virus	**4**:717		
Electrocardiogram	**4**:751	Surgery	**10**:1855
Fluoridation	**5**:889	Tranquilizers	**10**:1905
Food preservation	**5**:890	Transplant, surgical	**10**:1923
Genetic disorders	**5**:966	Tumor	**10**:1934
Genetic engineering	**5**:973	Vaccine	**10**:1957
Genetics	**5**:980	Virus	**10**:1974
Gerontology	**5**:999	Vitamin	**10**:1981
Gynecology	**5**:1022	Vivisection	**10**:1989

Horticulture

Horticulture	**6:**1053
Plant	**8:**1522
Seed	**9:**1729
Tree	**10:**1927

Immunology

Allergy	**1:**106
Antibiotics	**1:**155
Antibody and antigen	**1:**159
Immune system	**6:**1082
Vaccine	**10:**1957

Marine biology

Algae	**1:**91
Amphibians	**1:**134
Cetaceans	**3:**448
Coral	**3:**566
Crustaceans	**3:**590
Endangered species	**5:**793
Fish	**5:**875
Mammals	**6:**1222
Mollusks	**7:**1288
Ocean zones	**7:**1414
Plankton	**8:**1520
Sponges	**9:**1799
Vertebrates	**10:**1967

Materials science

Abrasives	**1:**2
Adhesives	**1:**37
Aerosols	**1:**43
Alcohols	**1:**88
Alkaline earth metals	**1:**102
Alloy	**1:**110
Aluminum family	**1:**122
Artificial fibers	**1:**186
Asbestos	**1:**191
Biodegradable	**2:**280

Carbon family	**2:**395
Ceramic	**3:**447
Composite materials	**3:**536
Dyes and pigments	**4:**686
Electrical conductivity	**4:**731
Electrolysis	**4:**755
Expansion, thermal	**5:**842
Fiber optics	**5:**870
Glass	**5:**1004
Halogens	**6:**1030
Hand tools	**6:**1036
Hydrogen	**6:**1068
Industrial minerals	**6:**1092
Minerals	**7:**1273
Nitrogen family	**7:**1344
Oxygen family	**7:**1442
Plastics	**8:**1532
Polymer	**8:**1563
Soaps and detergents	**9:**1756
Superconductor	**10:**1849
Transition elements	**10:**1913

Mathematics

Abacus	**1:**1
Algebra	**1:**97
Arithmetic	**1:**177
Boolean algebra	**2:**333
Calculus	**2:**371
Chaos theory	**3:**451
Circle	**3:**478
Complex numbers	**3:**534
Correlation	**3:**569
Fractal	**5:**921
Fraction, common	**5:**923
Function	**5:**927
Game theory	**5:**945
Geometry	**5:**995
Graphs and graphing	**5:**1009
Imaginary number	**6:**1081
Logarithm	**6:**1195
Mathematics	**7:**1241

Multiplication   7:1307
Natural numbers   7:1321
Number theory   7:1393
Numeration systems   7:1395
Polygon   8:1562
Probability theory   8:1575
Proof (mathematics)   8:1578
Pythagorean theorem   8:1601
Set theory   9:1733
Statistics   9:1810
Symbolic logic   10:1859
Topology   10:1897
Trigonometry   10:1931
Zero   10:2047

Metallurgy

Alkali metals   1:99
Alkaline earth metals   1:102
Alloy   1:110
Aluminum family   1:122
Carbon family   2:395
Composite materials   3:536
Industrial minerals   6:1092
Minerals   7:1273
Mining   7:1278
Precious metals   8:1566
Transition elements   10:1913

Meteorology

Air masses and fronts   1:80
Atmosphere, composition and
   structure   2:211
Atmosphere observation   2:215
Atmospheric circulation   2:218
Atmospheric optical
   effects   2:221
Atmospheric pressure   2:225
Barometer   2:265
Clouds   3:490
Cyclone and anticyclone   3:608
Drought   4:682

El Niño   4:782
Global climate   5:1006
Monsoon   7:1291
Ozone   7:1450
Storm surge   9:1823
Thunderstorm   10:1887
Tornado   10:1900
Weather   10:2017
Weather forecasting   10:2020
Wind   10:2028

Microbiology

Algae   1:91
Amoeba   1:131
Antiseptics   1:164
Bacteria   2:253
Biodegradable   2:280
Biological warfare   2:287
Composting   3:539
Parasites   8:1467
Plankton   8:1520
Protozoa   8:1590
Yeast   10:2043

Mineralogy

Abrasives   1:2
Ceramic   3:447
Industrial minerals   6:1092
Minerals   7:1273
Mining   7:1278

Molecular biology

Amino acid   1:130
Antibody and antigen   1:159
Biochemistry   2:279
Birth defects   2:319
Chromosome   3:472
Clone and cloning   3:484
Enzyme   5:812
Genetic disorders   5:966

Genetic engineering	**5:**973
Genetics	**5:**980
Hormones	**6:**1050
Human Genome Project	**6:**1060
Lipids	**6:**1191
Molecular biology	**7:**1283
Mutation	**7:**1314
Nucleic acid	**7:**1387
Proteins	**8:**1586

Mycology

Brewing	**2:**352
Fermentation	**5:**864
Fungi	**5:**930
Yeast	**10:**2043

Nutrition

Diabetes mellitus	**4:**638
Eating disorders	**4:**711
Food web and food chain	**5:**894
Malnutrition	**6:**1216
Nutrition	**7:**1399
Vitamin	**10:**1981

Obstetrics

Birth	**2:**315
Birth defects	**2:**319
Embryo and embryonic development	**4:**785

Oceanography

Continental margin	**3:**560
Currents, ocean	**3:**604
Ocean	**7:**1407
Oceanography	**7:**1411
Ocean zones	**7:**1414
Tides	**10:**1890

Oncology

Cancer	**2:**379
Disease	**4:**669
Tumor	**10:**1934

Ophthalmology

Eye	**5:**848
Lens	**6:**1184
Radial keratotomy	**8:**1615

Optics

Atmospheric optical effects	**2:**221
Compact disc	**3:**531
Diffraction	**4:**648
Eye	**5:**848
Fiber optics	**5:**870
Hologram and holography	**6:**1048
Laser	**6:**1166
LED (light-emitting diode)	**6:**1176
Lens	**6:**1184
Light	**6:**1185
Luminescence	**6:**1196
Photochemistry	**8:**1498
Photocopying	**8:**1499
Telescope	**10:**1869
Television	**10:**1875
Video recording	**10:**1968

Organic chemistry

Carbon family	**2:**395
Coal	**3:**492
Cyclamate	**3:**608
Dioxin	**4:**667
Fermentation	**5:**864
Hydrogen	**6:**1068
Hydrologic cycle	**6:**1071
Lipids	**6:**1191

Natural gas   7:1319
Nitrogen cycle   7:1342
Nitrogen family   7:1344
Oil spills   7:1422
Organic chemistry   7:1428
Oxygen family   7:1442
Ozone   7:1450
Petroleum   8:1492
Vitamin   10:1981

Orthopedics

Arthritis   1:181
Orthopedics   7:1434
Prosthetics   8:1579
Skeletal system   9:1739

Paleontology

Dating techniques   4:616
Dinosaur   4:658
Evolution   5:832
Fossil and fossilization   5:917
Human evolution   6:1054
Paleoecology   8:1457
Paleontology   8:1459

Parasitology

Amoeba   1:131
Disease   4:669
Fungi   5:930
Parasites   8:1467

Pathology

AIDS (acquired immunode-
   ficiency syndrome)   1:70
Alzheimer's disease   1:126
Arthritis   1:181
Asthma   1:204
Attention-deficit hyperactivity
   disorder (ADHD)   2:237

Bacteria   2:253
Biological warfare   2:287
Cancer   2:379
Dementia   4:622
Diabetes mellitus   4:638
Diagnosis   4:640
Dioxin   4:667
Disease   4:669
Ebola virus   4:717
Genetic disorders   5:966
Malnutrition   6:1216
Orthopedics   7:1434
Parasites   8:1467
Plague   8:1518
Poliomyelitis   8:1546
Sexually transmitted
   diseases   9:1735
Tumor   10:1934
Vaccine   10:1957
Virus   10:1974

Pharmacology

Acetylsalicylic acid   1:6
Antibiotics   1:155
Antiseptics   1:164
Cocaine   3:501
Hallucinogens   6:1027
Marijuana   6:1224
Poisons and toxins   8:1542
Tranquilizers   10:1905

Physics

Acceleration   1:4
Acoustics   1:17
Aerodynamics   1:39
Antiparticle   1:163
Astrophysics   1:207
Atom   2:226
Atomic mass   2:229
Atomic theory   2:232
Ballistics   2:260

Entries by Scientific Field

Battery	**2:**268	Gases, properties of	**5:**959
Biophysics	**2:**302	Generator	**5:**962
Buoyancy	**2:**360	Gravity and gravitation	**5:**1012
Calorie	**2:**375	Gyroscope	**5:**1024
Cathode	**3:**415	Half-life	**6:**1027
Cathode-ray tube	**3:**417	Heat	**6:**1043
Celestial mechanics	**3:**423	Hologram and holography	**6:**1048
Cell, electrochemical	**3:**436	Incandescent light	**6:**1087
Chaos theory	**3:**451	Integrated circuit	**6:**1106
Color	**3:**518	Interference	**6:**1112
Combustion	**3:**522	Interferometry	**6:**1114
Conservation laws	**3:**554	Ionization	**6:**1135
Coulomb	**3:**579	Isotope	**6:**1141
Cryogenics	**3:**595	Laser	**6:**1166
Dating techniques	**4:**616	Laws of motion	**6:**1169
Density	**4:**624	LED (light-emitting diode)	**6:**1176
Diffraction	**4:**648	Lens	**6:**1184
Diode	**4:**665	Light	**6:**1185
Doppler effect	**4:**677	Luminescence	**6:**1196
Echolocation	**4:**720	Magnetic recording/	
Elasticity	**4:**730	audiocassette	**6:**1209
Electrical conductivity	**4:**731	Magnetism	**6:**1212
Electric arc	**4:**734	Mass	**7:**1235
Electric current	**4:**737	Mass spectrometry	**7:**1239
Electricity	**4:**741	Matter, states of	**7:**1243
Electric motor	**4:**747	Microwave communication	**7:**1268
Electrolysis	**4:**755	Molecule	**7:**1285
Electromagnetic field	**4:**758	Momentum	**7:**1290
Electromagnetic induction	**4:**760	Nuclear fission	**7:**1361
Electromagnetic spectrum	**4:**763	Nuclear fusion	**7:**1366
Electromagnetism	**4:**766	Nuclear medicine	**7:**1372
Electron	**4:**768	Nuclear power	**7:**1374
Electronics	**4:**773	Nuclear weapons	**7:**1381
Energy	**5:**801	Particle accelerators	**8:**1475
Evaporation	**5:**831	Periodic function	**8:**1485
Expansion, thermal	**5:**842	Photochemistry	**8:**1498
Fiber optics	**5:**870	Photoelectric effect	**8:**1502
Fluid dynamics	**5:**882	Physics	**8:**1513
Fluorescent light	**5:**886	Pressure	**8:**1570
Frequency	**5:**925	Quantum mechanics	**8:**1607
Friction	**5:**926	Radar	**8:**1613
Gases, liquefaction of	**5:**955	Radiation	**8:**1619

Radiation exposure	**8:**1621
Radio	**8:**1626
Radioactive tracers	**8:**1629
Radioactivity	**8:**1630
Radiology	**8:**1637
Relativity, theory of	**9:**1659
Sonar	**9:**1770
Spectroscopy	**9:**1792
Spectrum	**9:**1794
Subatomic particles	**10:**1829
Superconductor	**10:**1849
Telegraph	**10:**1863
Telephone	**10:**1866
Television	**10:**1875
Temperature	**10:**1879
Thermal expansion	**5:**842
Thermodynamics	**10:**1885
Time	**10:**1894
Transformer	**10:**1908
Transistor	**10:**1910
Tunneling	**10:**1937
Ultrasonics	**10:**1941
Vacuum	**10:**1960
Vacuum tube	**10:**1961
Video recording	**10:**1968
Virtual reality	**10:**1969
Volume	**10:**1999
Wave motion	**10:**2014
X ray	**10:**2033

Primatology

Animal	**1:**145
Endangered species	**5:**793
Mammals	**6:**1222
Primates	**8:**1571
Vertebrates	**10:**1967

Psychiatry/Psychology

Addiction	**1:**32
Alcoholism	**1:**85
Attention-deficit hyperactivity disorder (ADHD)	**2:**237
Behavior	**2:**270
Cognition	**3:**511
Depression	**4:**630
Eating disorders	**4:**711
Multiple personality disorder	**7:**1305
Obsession	**7:**1405
Perception	**8:**1482
Phobia	**8:**1497
Psychiatry	**8:**1592
Psychology	**8:**1594
Psychosis	**8:**1596
Reinforcement, positive and negative	**9:**1657
Savant	**9:**1712
Schizophrenia	**9:**1716
Sleep and sleep disorders	**9:**1745
Stress	**9:**1826

Radiology

Nuclear medicine	**7:**1372
Radioactive tracers	**8:**1629
Radiology	**8:**1637
Ultrasonics	**10:**1941
X ray	**10:**2033

Robotics

Automation	**2:**242
Mass production	**7:**1236
Robotics	**9:**1690

Seismology

Earthquake	**4:**702
Volcano	**10:**1992

Sociology

Adaptation	**1:**26
Aging and death	**1:**59

Alcoholism   **1:**85
Behavior   **2:**270
Gerontology   **5:**999
Migration (animals)   **7:**1271

Technology

Abrasives   **1:**2
Adhesives   **1:**37
Aerosols   **1:**43
Aircraft   **1:**74
Alloy   **1:**110
Alternative energy sources   **1:**111
Antenna   **1:**153
Artificial fibers   **1:**186
Artificial intelligence   **1:**188
Asbestos   **1:**191
Automation   **2:**242
Automobile   **2:**245
Balloon   **1:**261
Battery   **2:**268
Biotechnology   **2:**309
Brewing   **2:**352
Bridges   **2:**354
CAD/CAM   **2:**369
Calculator   **2:**370
Canal   **2:**376
Cathode   **3:**415
Cathode-ray tube   **3:**417
Cell, electrochemical   **3:**436
Cellular/digital technology   **3:**439
Centrifuge   **3:**445
Ceramic   **3:**447
Compact disc   **3:**531
Computer, analog   **3:**546
Computer, digital   **3:**547
Computer software   **3:**549
Cybernetics   **3:**605
Dam   **4:**611
Diesel engine   **4:**646
Diode   **4:**665
DVD technology   **4:**684

Dyes and pigments   **4:**686
Fiber optics   **5:**870
Fluorescent light   **5:**886
Food preservation   **5:**890
Forensic science   **5:**898
Generator   **5:**962
Glass   **5:**1004
Hand tools   **6:**1036
Hologram and holography   **6:**1048
Incandescent light   **6:**1087
Industrial Revolution   **6:**1097
Integrated circuit   **6:**1106
Internal-combustion engine   **6:**1117
Internet   **6:**1123
Jet engine   **6:**1143
Laser   **6:**1166
LED (light-emitting diode)   **6:**1176
Lens   **6:**1184
Lock   **6:**1192
Machines, simple   **6:**1203
Magnetic recording/
  audiocassette   **6:**1209
Mass production   **7:**1236
Mass spectrometry   **7:**1239
Microwave communication   **7:**1268
Paper   **8:**1462
Photocopying   **8:**1499
Plastics   **8:**1532
Polymer   **8:**1563
Prosthetics   **8:**1579
Radar   **8:**1613
Radio   **8:**1626
Robotics   **9:**1690
Rockets and missiles   **9:**1693
Soaps and detergents   **9:**1756
Sonar   **9:**1770
Space station, international **9:**1788
Steam engine   **9:**1817
Submarine   **10:**1834
Superconductor   **10:**1849
Telegraph   **10:**1863
Telephone   **10:**1866

Television	**10**:1875
Transformer	**10**:1908
Transistor	**10**:1910
Vacuum tube	**10**:1961
Video recording	**10**:1968
Virtual reality	**10**:1969

Virology

AIDS (acquired immuno-deficiency syndrome)	**1**:70
Disease	**4**:669
Ebola virus	**4**:717
Plague	**8**:1518
Poliomyelitis	**8**:1546
Sexually transmitted diseases	**9**:1735
Vaccine	**10**:1957
Virus	**10**:1974

Weaponry

Ballistics	**2**:260
Biological warfare	**2**:287
Chemical warfare	**3**:457
Forensic science	**5**:898
Nuclear weapons	**7**:1381
Radar	**8**:1613
Rockets and missiles	**9**:1693

Wildlife conservation

Biodiversity	**2**:281
Biome	**2**:293
Biosphere	**2**:304
Drift net	**4**:680
Ecology	**4**:725
Ecosystem	**4**:728
Endangered species	**5**:793
Forestry	**5**:901
Gaia hypothesis	**5**:935
Wetlands	**10**:2024

Zoology

Amphibians	**1**:134
Animal	**1**:145
Arachnids	**1**:168
Arthropods	**1**:183
Behavior	**2**:270
Birds	**2**:312
Butterflies	**2**:364
Canines	**2**:382
Cetaceans	**3**:448
Cockroaches	**3**:505
Coelacanth	**3**:508
Coral	**3**:566
Crustaceans	**3**:590
Dinosaur	**4**:658
Echolocation	**4**:720
Endangered species	**5**:793
Felines	**5**:855
Fish	**5**:875
Hibernation	**6**:1046
Indicator species	**6**:1090
Insects	**6**:1103
Invertebrates	**6**:1133
Kangaroos and wallabies	**6**:1153
Mammals	**6**:1222
Metamorphosis	**7**:1259
Migration (animals)	**7**:1271
Mollusks	**7**:1288
Plankton	**8**:1520
Primates	**8**:1571
Reptiles	**9**:1670
Snakes	**9**:1752
Sponges	**9**:1799
Vertebrates	**10**:1967

En

Endangered species

An endangered species is any animal or plant species whose very survival is threatened to the point of extinction. Once extinct, a species is no longer found anywhere on Earth. Once gone, it is gone forever.

Throughout Earth's geological history species have become extinct naturally. However, in modern times species and their natural habitats are mostly threatened by human activities. Humans have already caused the extinction of many species, and large numbers of many other species are currently endangered and may soon become extinct.

Causes of extinction and endangerment

Most of the species that have ever lived on Earth are now extinct. Extinction and endangerment can occur naturally. It can be the result of a catastrophic disturbance, such as the collision of an asteroid with Earth some 65 million years ago. The impact brought about the extinction of almost 50 percent of plant species and 75 percent of animals species then living on Earth, including the dinosaurs. Disease, a change in climate, and competition between species also can result in natural extinction.

However, since humans became Earth's dominant species, there has been a dramatic increase in the number of endangered or extinct species. The overhunting of wild animals (for their hides or meat or to protect livestock) and the destruction of natural habitats are the human activities most responsible. A wave of extinctions began in North America about 11,000 years ago, at about the time when people first migrated across a land bridge from Siberia to present-day Alaska. Probably within only a

Words to Know

Biodiversity: The wide range of organisms—plants and animals—that exist within any given geographical region.

Endangered: When a species is vulnerable to extinction.

Extinct: When no members of a species are found anywhere on Earth.

Threatened: When a species is capable of becoming endangered in the near future.

few centuries, species such as the mastodon, mammoth, and saber-toothed tiger had become extinct on the continent.

In modern times, overhunting has caused the extinction of such species as the dodo (1681), great auk (1844), and passenger pigeon (1914). In 2000, for the first time in about 300 years, a member of the primate order (the group of mammals that includes monkeys, apes, and humans) became extinct. The vanished primate was Miss Waldron's red colobus, a red-cheeked monkey. Scientists said its extinction was brought about by overhunting and the destruction of its habitat in the rain forest canopy in the African countries of Ghana and Ivory Coast.

How many endangered species are there?

Scientists readily agree that the rate at which species are becoming extinct around the world is increasing rapidly. At present, they believe extinctions caused by humans are taking place at 100 to 1,000 times nature's normal rate between great extinction episodes. It is hard, however, to put a figure on the actual number of endangered species. Researchers are able to document the endangerment of large and well-known animal and plant species. But it is impossible to measure the total number of species going extinct because scientists have described and named only a small percentage of the world's species. Only about 1.4 million species—out of an estimated 10 million to 100 million—have been described to date.

There is an enormously large number of endangered species living in tropical rain forests, and most of these have not yet been "discovered" by scientists. Because rain forests are quickly being converted to farmland and human settlements, many of these species are becoming extinct before humans know anything about them.

Conservation organizations around the world have taken on the task of trying to catalog as many of the world's endangered species as possible. At the beginning of 2001, it was estimated that there were more than 1,200 endangered or threatened (those capable of becoming endangered) species in the United States and more than 1,800 worldwide. Because most of Earth's biodiversity (the number of species in a given habitat) is not yet discovered and cataloged, it is likely that there are perhaps several million endangered species on Earth.

Why are endangered species important?

It is critical that humans act to preserve endangered species and their natural habitats. These species are important and worthwhile for many reasons. First, and most important, all species have value simply because they are living organisms on Earth. Second, many species have a known value to humans. Food is provided by domestic plants and animals raised on farms, as well as certain animals, birds, and fish hunted in the wild. Humans also benefit from the role many species play in the environment. This includes cleansing the air and water, controlling erosion, providing atmospheric oxygen, and maintaining the food chain. Third, many species have a presently unknown value to humans, such as undiscovered medicinal plants.

The endangered hooded parakeet. *(Reproduced by permission of Field Mark Publications.)*

Various actions have been taken to protect endangered species. In 1973, the U.S. Congress passed the Endangered Species Act. It established a list of endangered species and prohibited their trade (the list is updated periodically). The Convention on International Trade in Endangered Species (CITES, pronounced SIGH-tees) is a multinational agreement that took effect in 1975. Its aim is to prevent the international trade of endangered or threatened animal and plant species and the products made from them (by the end of 2000, 152 nations had signed the agreement). In 1992, the United Nations Conference on Environment and Development (also known as the Earth Summit) was held in Rio de Janeiro, Brazil. One of the declarations adopted by the representatives at the conference called for an end to the loss of the world's species. The declaration was signed by more than 150 of the 172 nations that attended the conference.

Scientists took an even greater step toward preserving endangered species when, in early 2001, they announced the cloning of a gaur (pronounced GOW-er). The gaur is an ox native to Southeast Asia and India. While some 30,000 still exist in the wild, their numbers are declining because of hunting and habitat loss. To clone the gaur, the scientists removed the nucleus from a cow's egg cell and replaced it with the nucleus of a gaur skin cell. They then placed the fertilized egg cell in the womb of a domestic cow, which brought the gaur to term. Sadly, the baby gaur survived only two days after birth, dying of dysentery (a disease caused by an infection that is marked by severe diarrhea). While some scientists remain optimistic about the future of cloning endangered species, others believe that such cloning could hamper efforts to conserve biodiverse habitats by offering to rescue endangered species in a lab.

[*See also* **Biodiversity; Environmental ethics; Rain forest**]

Endocrine system

The endocrine system is the human body's network of glands that produce more than 100 hormones to maintain and regulate basic bodily functions. Hormones are chemical substances carried in the bloodstream to tissues and organs, stimulating them to perform some action. The glands of the endocrine system include the pituitary, pineal, thyroid, parathyroids, thymus, pancreas, adrenals, and ovaries or testes.

The endocrine system oversees many critical life processes. These involve growth, reproduction, immunity (the body's ability to resist disease), and homeostasis (the body's ability to maintain a balance of internal functions). The branch of medicine that studies endocrine glands and the hormones they secrete is called endocrinology.

Hormonal levels in the blood

Most endocrine hormones are maintained at certain levels in the plasma, the colorless, liquid portion of the blood in which blood cells and other substances are suspended. Receptor cells at set locations throughout the body monitor hormonal levels. If the level is too high or too low,

Words to Know

Carbohydrate: A compound consisting of carbon, hydrogen, and oxygen found in plants and used as a food by humans and other animals.

Hormones: Chemical substances secreted by endocrine glands that are carried in the bloodstream to tissues and organs, stimulating them to maintain and regulate basic bodily functions.

Metabolism: Sum of all the physiological processes by which an organism maintains life.

Plasma: Colorless, liquid portion of the blood in which blood cells and other substances are suspended.

the gland responsible for its production is notified and acts to correct the situation. Most hormones have this type of regulatory control. However, a few hormones operate on a system whereby high levels of the particular hormone activate the release of another hormone. The end result is usually that the second hormone will eventually decrease the production of the initial hormone.

The pituitary

The pituitary gland has long been called the master gland because it regulates many other endocrine glands. It secretes multiple hormones that, in turn, trigger the release of other hormones from other endocrine sites. The pituitary is located at the base of the brain behind the nose and is separated into two distinct lobes, the anterior pituitary (AP) and the posterior pituitary (PP). The entire pituitary hangs by a thin piece of tissue, called the pituitary stalk, beneath the hypothalamus (the region of the brain controlling temperature, hunger, and thirst).

The pituitary secretes at least five hormones that directly control the activities of other endocrine glands. These are thyrotropic hormone (affecting the thyroid gland), adrenocorticotropic hormone (affecting the adrenal cortex), and three gonadotropic hormones (affecting the reproductive glands).

The pituitary also secretes hormones that do not affect other glands, but control some bodily function. These include somatotropic or growth hormone (which controls growth in all tissues) and antidiuretic hormone (which controls the amount of water excreted by the kidneys).

The pineal

The pineal gland or body is a small cone-shaped gland believed to function as a body clock. The pineal is located deep in the rear portion of the brain. It secretes the hormone melatonin, which fluctuates on a daily basis with levels highest at night. Scientists are not quite sure of the role of melatonin. Some believe it plays a role in the development of the male and female sex glands.

The thyroid

The thyroid is a butterfly-shaped gland that wraps around the front and sides of the trachea (windpipe). The thyroid is divided into two lobes connected by a band of tissue called the isthmus. Thyroid hormones play several important roles in growth, development, and metabolism. (Metabolism is the sum of all the physiological processes by which an organism maintains life.) The major hormones produced by the thyroid are thyroxine and calcitonin. Thyroxine controls the metabolic rate of most cells in the body, while calcitonin maintains proper calcium levels in the body.

The parathyroids

The parathyroids are four small glands (each about the size of a pea) located behind the thyroid gland. These glands secrete parathormone, which regulates calcium (and phosphate) levels in the body. Calcium has numerous important bodily functions. It makes up 2 to 3 percent of the weight of the average adult. Roughly 99 percent of the calcium in the body is contained in the bones. Calcium also plays a pivotal role in muscle contraction.

The thymus

The thymus is located in the upper part of the chest underneath the breastbone. In infants, the thymus is quite large. It continues to grow until puberty, when it begins to shrink. The size of the thymus in most adults is very small. Like some other endocrine glands, the thymus has two lobes connected by a stalk. The thymus secretes several hormones that promote the development of the body's immune system.

The pancreas

The pancreas is a large gland situated below and behind the stomach in the lower abdomen. The pancreas secretes pancreatic juice into the duodenum (the first section of the small intestine) through the pancreatic duct. The digestive enzymes in this juice help break down carbohydrates, fats, and proteins.

Scattered among the cells that produce pancreatic juice are small groups of endocrine cells. These are called the Islets of Langerhans. They secrete two hormones, insulin and glucagon, which maintain blood glucose (sugar) levels.

Insulin is secreted in response to high glucose levels in the blood. It lowers sugar levels in the blood by increasing the uptake of glucose into the tissues. Glucagon has the opposite effect. It causes the liver to transform the glycogen (a carbohydrate) it stores into glucose, which is then released into the blood.

The adrenals

The adrenals are two glands, each sitting like a cap on top of a kidney. The adrenals are divided into two distinct regions: the cortex (outer layer) and the medulla (inner layer). The cortex makes up about 80 percent of each adrenal. The adrenals help the body adapt to stressful situations.

The cortex secretes about 30 steroid hormones. The most important of these are cortisol and aldosterone. Cortisol regulates the body's me-

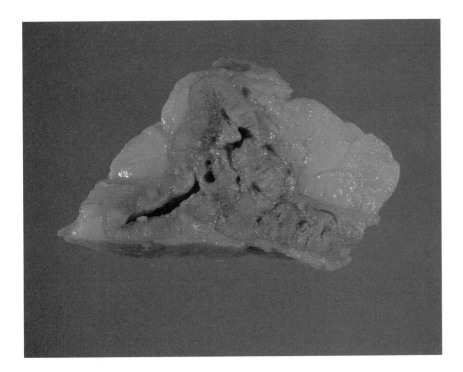

A cross-section of a human adrenal gland, showing both the outer adrenal cortex and the inner adrenal medulla. *(Reproduced by permission of Phototake.)*

tabolism of carbohydrates, proteins, and fats. Aldosterone regulates the body's water and salt balance. The cortex is extremely important to bodily processes. If it stops functioning, death occurs in just a few days.

The medulla secretes the hormones adrenaline and noradrenaline. Both of these hormones are released during dangerous or stressful situations. They increase heart rate, blood pressure, blood flow to the muscles, blood sugar levels, and other processes that prepare a body for vigorous action, such as in an emergency.

The ovaries

In females, the ovaries are located at the end of each fallopian tube and are attached to the uterus by an ovarian ligament. They produce the female reproductive hormones estrogen and progesterone. These hormones work together with the gonadotropic hormones from the pituitary to ensure fertility. They are also important for the development of sexual characteristics during puberty.

Each month after puberty, increased levels of estrogen signal the pituitary gland to secrete luteinizing hormone (LH; a gonadotropic hormone). Once LH is secreted, the ovaries release a single egg (a process called ovulation). While an egg travels down the fallopian tube, progesterone is released, which prevents another egg from beginning to mature. The egg then attaches to the lining of the uterus. If fertilization does not occur, the egg (with the lining of the uterus) is shed outside the body during the monthly process called menstruation.

During pregnancy, high levels of estrogen and progesterone prevent another egg from maturing. In addition, progesterone prevents the uterus from contracting so that the developing embryo is not disturbed, and helps to prepare breasts for lactation (the formation and secretion of milk).

At menopause, which usually occurs between the ages of 40 and 50, estrogen levels fall dramatically and the monthly cycle of ovulation and menstruation comes to an end.

The testes

The two testes are located in the scrotum, which hangs between the legs behind the penis. In addition to producing sperm, the testes produce testosterone, the principal male sex hormone. At puberty, increased levels of testosterone bring about the development of sexual characteristics (increased genital growth, facial hair, voice change). Testosterone helps sperm to mature and aids in muscular development. After about the age of 40, testosterone levels gradually decline.

Endocrine disorders

As much as 10 percent of the population will experience some endocrine disorder in their lifetime. Most endocrine disorders are caused by an increased or decreased level of particular hormones. Tumors (abnormal tissue growth) in endocrine glands are one of the major causes of hormone overproduction. Hormone underproduction is often due to defective receptor cells, which fail to notify an endocrine gland when productive of its particular hormone is too low. Injury or disease can also result in low hormone levels.

The overproduction of the growth hormone can cause giantism (unusually large stature). Underproduction of the same hormone can lead to the opposite condition, dwarfism. A similar disorder, cretinism, occurs when the thyroid does not produce enough calcitonin, which is necessary for bone growth. Addison's disease is a rare condition caused by insufficient hormone production by the adrenal cortex. It is characterized by extreme weakness, low blood pressure, and darkening of the skin and mucous membranes. Low insulin production by the Islets of Langerhans can result in diabetes mellitus, a condition marked by excessive thirst, urination, and fatigue. If left untreated, diabetes can cause death.

[*See also* **Diabetes mellitus; Hormone**]

Energy

Energy is the capacity to do work. In science, the term work has a very special meaning. It means that an object has been moved through a distance. Thus, pushing a brick across the top of a table is an example of doing work. By applying this definition of work, then, energy can also be defined as the ability to move an object through a distance. Imagine that a bar magnet is placed next to a pile of iron filings (thin slivers of iron metal). The iron filings begin to move toward the iron bar. We say that magnetic energy pulls on the iron filings and causes them to move.

Energy can be a difficult concept to understand. Unlike matter, energy cannot be held or placed on a laboratory bench for study. We know about energy best because of the effect it has on objects around it, as in the case of the bar magnet and iron filings mentioned above.

Energy can exist in many forms, including mechanical, heat, electrical, magnetic, sound, chemical, and nuclear. Although these forms appear to be very different from each other, they often have much in common and can generally be transformed from one to another.

Words to Know

Conservation of energy: A law of physics that says that energy can be transformed from one form to another, but can be neither created nor destroyed.

Joule: The unit of measurement for energy in the metric system.

Kinetic energy: The energy possessed by a body as a result of its motion.

Mass: Measure of the total amount of matter in an object.

Potential energy: The energy possessed by a body as a result of its position.

Velocity: The rate at which the position of an object changes with time, including both the speed and the direction.

Over time, a number of different units have been used to measure energy. In the British system, for example, the fundamental unit of energy is the foot-pound. One foot-pound is the amount of energy that can move a weight of one pound a distance of one foot. In the metric system, the fundamental unit of energy is the joule (abbreviation: J), named after English scientist James Prescott Joule (1818–1889). A joule is the amount of energy that can move a weight of one newton a distance of one meter.

Potential and kinetic energy

Objects possess energy for one of two reasons: because of their position or because of their motion. The first type of energy is defined as potential energy; the second type of energy is defined as kinetic energy. Think of a baseball sitting on a railing at the top of the Empire State Building. That ball has potential energy because of its ability to fall off the railing and come crashing down onto the street. The potential energy of the baseball—as well as that of any other object—is dependent on two factors: its mass and its height above the ground. The baseball has a relatively small mass, but in this example it still has a large potential energy because of its distance above the ground.

The second type of energy, kinetic energy, is a result of an object's motion. The amount of kinetic energy possessed by an object is a function of two variables, its mass and velocity. The formula for kinetic energy is $E = \frac{1}{2}mv^2$, where m is the mass of the object and v is its velocity. This formula shows that an object can have a lot of kinetic energy for two reasons: it can either be very heavy (large m) or it can be moving very fast (large v).

Imagine that the baseball mentioned previously falls off the Empire State Building. The ball can do a great deal of damage because it has a great deal of kinetic energy. The kinetic energy comes from the very high speed with which the ball is traveling by the time it hits the ground. The baseball may not weigh very much, but its high speed still gives it a great deal of kinetic energy.

Conservation of energy

In science, the term conservation means that the amount of some property is not altered during a chemical or physical change. At one time, physicists believed in the law of conservation of energy. That law states that the amount of energy present at the end of any physical or chemical change is exactly the same as the amount present at the beginning of the change. The form in which the energy appears may be different, but the total amount is constant. Another way to state the law of conservation of energy is that energy is neither created nor destroyed in a chemical or physical change.

As an example, suppose that you turn on an electric heater. A certain amount of electrical energy travels into the heater and is converted to heat. If you measure the amount of electricity entering the heater and the amount of heat given off, the amounts will be the same.

The law of conservation of energy is valid for the vast majority of situations that we encounter in our everyday lives. In the early 1900s, however, German-born American physicist Albert Einstein (1879–1955) made a fascinating discovery. Under certain circumstances, Einstein said, energy can be transformed into matter, and matter can be transformed into energy. Those circumstances are seldom encountered in daily life. When they are, a modified form of the law of conservation of energy applies. That modified form is known as the law of conservation of energy and matter. It says that the *total* amount of matter *and* energy is always conserved in any kind of change.

Forms of energy

We know of the existence of energy because of the various forms in which it occurs. When an explosion occurs, air is heated up to very high

Energy Efficiency

Energy can be converted from one form to another, but the process is often very wasteful. An incandescent lightbulb is an example. When a lightbulb is turned on, electrical current flows into the wire filament in the bulb. The filament begins to glow, giving off light. That's what the bulb is designed to do. But most of the electrical energy entering the bulb is used to heat the wire first. That electrical energy is "wasted" since it is lost as heat; the lightbulb is not designed to be a source of heat.

The amount of useful energy obtained from some machine or some process compared to the amount of energy provided to the machine or process is called the energy efficiency of the machine or process. For example, a typical incandescent lightbulb converts about 90 percent of the electrical energy it receives to heat and 10 percent to light. Therefore, the energy efficiency of the lightbulb is said to be 10 percent.

Energy efficiency has come to have a new meaning in recent decades. The term also refers to any method by which the amount of useful energy can be increased in any machine or process. For example, some automobiles can travel 40 miles by burning a single gallon of gasoline, while others can travel only 20 miles per gallon. The energy efficiency achieved by the first car is twice that achieved by the second car.

Until the middle of the twentieth century, most developed nations did not worry very much about energy efficiency. Coal, oil, and natural gas—the fuels from which we get most of our energy—were cheap. It didn't make much difference to Americans and other people around the world if a lot of energy was wasted. We just dug up more coal or found more oil and gas to make more energy.

By the third quarter of the twentieth century, though, that attitude was much less common as people realized that natural resources won't last forever. Architects, automobile and airplane designers, plant managers, and the average home owner were all looking for ways to use energy more efficiently.

temperatures. The hot air expands quickly, knocking down objects in its path. Heat is a form of energy also known as thermal energy. Temperature is a measure of the amount of heat energy contained in an object.

Other forms of energy include electrical energy, magnetism, sound, chemical, and nuclear energy. Although these forms of energy appear to be very different from each other, they are all closely related: one form of energy can be changed into another, different form of energy.

An example of this principle is an electric power generating plant. In such a plant, coal or oil may be burned to boil water. Chemical energy stored in the coal or oil is converted to heat energy in steam. The steam can then be used to operate a turbine, a large fan mounted on a central rod. The steam strikes the fan and causes the rod to turn. Heat energy from the steam is converted to the kinetic energy of the rotating fan. Finally, the turbine runs an electric generator. In the generator, the kinetic energy of the rotating turbine is converted into electrical energy.

[*See also* **Conservation laws; Electricity; Heat; Magnetism**]

Engineering

Engineering is the art of applying science, mathematics, and creativity to solve technological problems. The accomplishments of engineering can be seen in nearly every aspect of our daily lives, from transportation to communications to entertainment to health care. Engineering follows a three-step process: analyzing a problem, designing a solution for that problem, and transforming that design solution into physical reality.

Analyzing a problem

Defining the problem is the first and most critical step of the problem analysis. To best find a solution, the problem must be well understood and the guidelines or design considerations for the project must be clear. For example, in the creation of a new automobile, the engineers must know if they should design for fuel economy or for brute power. Many questions like this arise in every engineering project, and they must all be answered at the very beginning of the project.

When these issues are resolved, the problem must be thoroughly researched. This involves searching technical journals and closely examining solutions of similar engineering problems. The purpose of this step is twofold. First, it allows the engineer to make use of a tremendous body of work done by other engineers. Second, it ensures the engineer that the problem has not already been solved.

Designing a solution

Once the problem is well understood, the process of designing a solution begins. It typically starts with brainstorming, a technique by which members of the engineering team suggest a number of possible general approaches for the problem. Normally, one of the approaches is then selected as the primary candidate for further development. Occasionally, however, the team may elect to pursue multiple solutions to the problem. The members then compare the refined designs of these solutions, choosing the best one to pursue to completion.

Once a general design or technology is selected, the work is subdivided and various team members assume specific responsibilities. In the case of the automobile, for example, mechanical engineers in the group would tackle such problems as the design of the transmission and suspension systems. Electrical engineers, on the other hand, would focus on the ignition system and the various displays and electronic gauges. In any case, each of these engineers must design one aspect that operates in harmony with every other aspect of the general design.

Engineer in Geneva, Switzerland, using computer-aided design (CAD) software to design a pipe junction. (Reproduced by permission of Photo Researchers, Inc.)

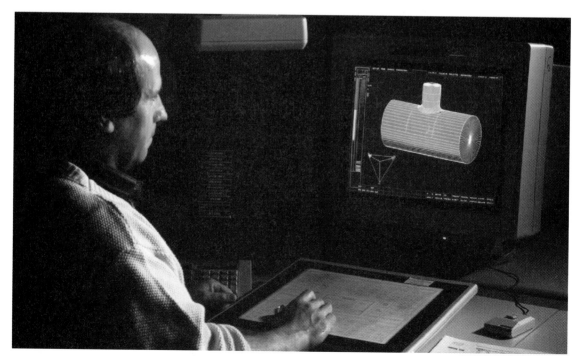

Bringing it to life

Once the design is complete, a prototype or preliminary working model is generally built. The primary function of the prototype is to demonstrate and test the operation of the device.

In the prototype stage, the device undergoes extensive testing to reveal any bugs or problems with the design. Especially with complex systems, it is often difficult to predict (on paper) where problems with the design may occur. If one aspect of the system happens to fail too quickly or does not function at all, it is closely analyzed and that subsystem is redesigned and retested (both on its own and within the complete system.) This process is repeated until the entire system satisfies the design requirements.

Once the prototype is in complete working order and the engineers are satisfied with its operation, the device goes into the production stage. Here, details such as appearance, ease of use, availability of materials, and safety are studied and generally result in additional final design changes.

Environmental ethics

Environmental ethics is a branch of philosophy that considers the moral relations between human beings and their natural environment. As a field of study, it assumes that humans have certain responsibilities to the natural world, and it seeks to help people and their leaders become aware of them and to act responsibly when they do things that impact the natural world.

The need for ethics

Most people recognize that some agreed-upon guidelines or general rules should exist between individuals when they interact with one another because if they did not, nothing in our lives would be predictable or safe. In other words, people need to know that besides actual laws, there are some basic, common ethics or principles of what is right and what is wrong that everyone agrees upon and usually follows or lives by. Ethics is sometimes called moral philosophy because it is concerned with what is morally good and bad or what is right and wrong. As a specialized part of ethics, environmental ethics is concerned with the morality (right and wrong) of human actions as they affect the environment or the natural world we live in.

Words to Know

Anthropomorphic: Described or thought of as having a human form or human attributes.

Deep ecology: Philosophical belief system that holds that all forms of life—plant, animal, human—have an intrinsic right to exist in the natural environment and that humans have a direct responsibility to maintain the environment for all life forms.

Ethics: Branch of philosophy that deals with the general nature of morals and specific moral choices.

Shallow ecology: Philosophical belief system that holds that humans have a responsibility to protect the environment so it can support human life both in the present and in the future.

Global environmental problems

As a branch of philosophy, environmental ethics is a fairly recent development, having become a body of organized knowledge only in the last decades of the twentieth century. It came about as a necessary response to a growing number of very obvious threats to the physical condition of the world in which we live. The list of some of these global environmental problems is a long and familiar one, and many of them came about because of the massive increase in the growth of the human population worldwide. As populations continue to soar, the various problems caused by too many people naturally increase in both their number and seriousness. It is predicted that the 2000 world population of six billion people will rise by another one billion people within ten years. To the many problems this causes, such as increased pollution of the air, water, and soil, is also added the depletion of these and other important natural resources.

Today, as we face such problems as the greenhouse effect, the destruction of the ozone layer, and the presence of toxic and nuclear wastes, we can easily recognize some of their negative effects. Among these are the growing disappearance of wilderness areas, a steady loss of biodiversity (the variety of species in an area) among living things, and even the actual extinction of some species. It is safe to say that at the beginning of the twenty-first century, one of the greatest challenges facing human beings is how to stop the continued harm to Earth.

Origins of environmental ethics

Many people associate the beginnings of today's environmental ethics with the first Earth Day held on April 22, 1970, in the United States. On that day (and every April since), organizers around the country rallied and demonstrated to make people and political leaders aware of the importance of caring for and preserving the environment. That first Earth Day launched the beginning of an environmental awareness in the United States and later around the world. It made many people realize that some sense of environmental responsibility should be developed and applied to our daily lives.

Most movements do not just suddenly happen out of nowhere; they are usually preceded by many other influential events. In the environmental movement, perhaps the earliest of these was the 1949 publication of a book by American naturalist Aldo Leopold (1887–1948). Leopold had fallen in love with nature as a youngster and eventually joined the newly established U.S. Forest Service in 1909. As a game management expert, he came to appreciate and understand how deeply humans affected the natural world. A year after he died, his landmark work, *A Sand County Almanac,* was published. It contained not only his strong defense of the environment but his argument that what was needed was

People continue actively campaigning for better treatment and preservation of the environment. *(Reproduced by permission of Greenpeace Photos.)*

a new philosophy about man and nature, or what would come to be called an environmental ethic. This idea was carried on by others when, two decades later, the first Earth Day was held.

Important questions

The importance of that first Earth Day was that it not only raised the environmental consciousness or awareness of many people, but it got them to start asking important questions. Once people became aware that they had some sort of a responsibility toward the natural world, it then became a matter of trying to figure out how far that responsibility extends. This naturally led to many questions, such as, does Earth exist entirely for humanity? What are the rights of nonhuman species and do we have any obligations to them? Do we have a duty to be concerned with future generations? These and many other important questions are what environmental ethics is all about. While answering them may be difficult,

An environmental display in Washington, D.C. *(Reproduced by permission of Greenpeace Photos.)*

and people may not always agree, it is significant that they are being asked and discussed.

Schools of thought

Answers to these questions are shaped by what theory or school of thought of environmental ethics an individual believes in. One of these theories says that our responsibility to the natural environment is only an indirect one and is based on our responsibilities to other people. This school of thought is definitely human-centered or anthropomorphic (pronounced an-throw-poe-MOR-fick). While it argues that we have some sort of responsibility to the environment, it says that this responsibility is not a direct one and that the focus is on how the condition of the environment affects people, both in present and in future generations. In other words, we have a duty to make sure that Earth stays in good enough shape so that human life is supported. Some call this school of thought or philosophy "shallow ecology."

A somewhat different school of thought is described as nonanthropomorphic, which means that all forms of life have an intrinsic (essential or basic) right to exist in the natural environment. This point of view gives what is called "moral standing" to animals and plants, and argues that they, like humans, are to be considered "morally significant persons." This philosophy is called "deep ecology." It states that humans have a direct responsibility toward maintaining the environment for all forms of life.

There are many versions of these two schools of thought—ranging from the argument that what is right or wrong environmentally should be judged only by how it affects people, to one that says the environment itself has direct rights. Few agree on how far our responsibility extends. Furthermore, the real disagreements are found when actual policies have to be decided upon that will guide how we act. Despite these and other disagreements, the fact that some sort of appreciation for nature has been fostered in many of us, and that we realize that nature must be appreciated and considered for its own sake and treated with respect, marks the beginning of a real ethics of the environment. For a very long time, human beings have never even been aware that they had any sort of responsibility toward the natural world and all its members. However, the development of some sort of environmental ethic that makes us consider if our environmental actions are right or wrong marks the beginning of future progress for a better world.

[*See also* **Ecology; Endangered species**]

Enzyme

An enzyme is a biological catalyst. A catalyst is a chemical compound that speeds up the rate of some chemical reaction. When that chemical reaction occurs in a living organism, the catalyst is known as an enzyme.

Catalyzed and uncatalyzed reactions

Figure 1 shows how an enzyme (or any other catalyst) affects the rate of a chemical reaction. Consider the reaction in which a complex carbohydrate, such as starch, is broken down in the body to produce the simpler sugars known as sucrose. We can express this reaction by the following chemical equation:

$$starch \rightarrow sucrose$$

The compound present at the beginning of the reaction (starch) is known as the reactant. The compound that is formed as a result of the reaction (sucrose) is known as the product.

In most instances, energy has to be supplied to the reactant or reactants in order for a reaction to occur. For example, if you heat a suspension of starch in water, the starch begins to break down to form sucrose.

Figure 1. Energy changes that take place with a catalyst. *(Reproduced by permission of The Gale Group.)*

The line labeled "Uncatalyzed reaction" in Figure 1 represents changes in energy that take place in the reaction without a catalyst. Notice that the amount of energy needed to make the reaction happen increases from its beginning point to a maximum point, and then drops to a minimum point. The graph shows that an amount of energy equal to the value E_a has to be added to make the reaction happen.

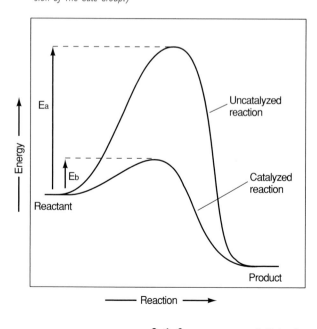

The second line in Figure 1 shows energy changes that take place with a catalyst. Energy still has to be added to the reactant to get the reaction started, but the amount of energy is much less. In Figure 1, that amount of energy is indicated by the symbol E_b. Notice that E_b is much less than E_a. The difference in those two values is the savings in energy provided by using a catalyst in the reaction.

▼ Words to Know

Amino acid: An organic compound that contains two special groups of atoms known as the amino group and the carboxylic acid group.

Catalyst: Any chemical compound that speeds up the rate of a chemical reaction.

Chemical reaction: Any change in which at least one new substance is formed.

Lock-and-key model: One of the ways in which enzymes bring about chemical reactions.

Product: A compound that is formed as the result of a chemical reaction.

Protein: A complex chemical compound that consists of many amino acids attached to each other which are essential to the structure and functioning of all living cells.

Reactant: A compound present at the beginning of a chemical reaction.

Substrate: The substance on which an enzyme operates in a chemical reaction.

Enzymes in biological reactions

Living organisms could not survive without enzymes. During each second in the life of a plant or animal, thousands of different chemical reactions are taking place. Every one of those reactions requires the input of energy, as shown in Figure 1. Every one of those reactions *could* be made to occur by adding heat, electricity, or some other form of energy—but *not* within a living organism. Imagine what would happen if the only way we had of digesting starch was to heat it to boiling inside our stomach!

Every one of those thousands of chemical reactions taking place inside plants and animals, then, is made possible by some specific enzyme. The presence of the enzyme means that the reaction can occur at some reasonable temperature, such as the temperature of a human body or the cells of a plant.

Structure of enzymes

All enzymes are proteins. Proteins are complex organic compounds that consist of simpler compounds attached to each other. The simpler compounds of which proteins are made are amino acids. An amino acid gets its name from the fact that it contains two special groups of atoms, an amino (—NH$_2$) group and a carboxylic acid (—COOH) group.

Amino acids are of particular importance because they can react with each other to form long chains. If you mix two amino acids with each other under the proper circumstances, the amino group on one amino acid will react with the carboxylic acid group on the second amino acid. If you add a third amino acid to the mixture, its amino or carboxylic acid group will combine with the product formed from the first two amino acids, and so on.

A protein, then, is a very long chain of amino acids strung together somewhat like a long piece of woolen thread.

Except that proteins are really more complex than that. The long protein does not remain in a neat threadlike shape for long. As soon as it is formed, it begins to twist and turn on itself until it looks more like a tangled mass of wool. It looks something like a skein of woolen thread would look if the family cat had a chance to play with it.

A protein molecule, then, has a complicated three-dimensional shape, with nooks and crannies and projections all over its surfaces. You could make your own model of a protein molecule by taking a Slinky™ toy and turning and twisting the coil into an irregular sphere.

Figure 2. Lock-and-key model of interaction. *(Reproduced by permission of The Gale Group.)*

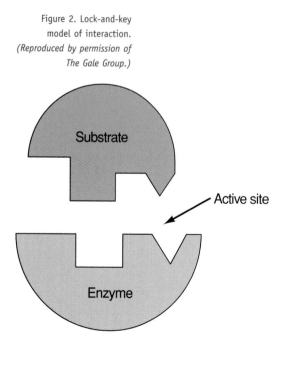

Enzyme function

Enzymes can act as catalysts because of their three-dimensional shapes. Figure 2 shows one way that enzymes act as catalysts. The lower half of the drawing in Figure 2 represents the three-dimensional structure of an enzyme molecule. Notice the two gaps—one with a rectangular shape and one with a triangular shape—in the upper face of the molecule.

A molecule with this shape has the ability to combine with other molecules that have a complementary shape. In Figure 2, a second molecule of this kind, labeled "Substrate," is shown. The term substrate is used for molecules that can be broken apart by catalysts.

Notice that the shape of the substrate molecule in Figure 2 perfectly matches the shape of the enzyme molecule. The two molecules can fit together exactly, like a key fitting into a lock.

Here is how we think many kinds of enzyme-catalyzed reactions take place: a substrate molecule, such as starch, is ready to be broken apart in a living body. The energy needed to break apart the substrate is quite large, larger than is available in the body. The substrate remains in its complete form.

An enzyme with the correct molecular shape arrives on the scene and attaches itself to the substrate molecule, as in Figure 2. Chemical bonds form between the substrate and enzyme molecules. These bonds cause bonds *within* the substrate molecule to become weaker. The bonds may actually break, causing the substrate molecule to fall apart into two parts.

After a brief period of time, the bonds between the substrate and the enzyme molecules break. The two pieces move away from each other. By this time, however, the substrate molecule itself has also broken apart. The enzyme has made possible the breakdown of the substrate without the addition of a lot of energy. The products of the reaction are now free to move elsewhere in the organism, while the enzyme is ready to find another substrate molecule of the same kind and repeat the process.

[*See also* **Catalyst; Reaction, chemical**]

Equation, chemical

A chemical equation is a shorthand method for representing the changes that take place during a chemical reaction. In describing the formation of water from its elements, a chemist could say, for example, that "two molecules of hydrogen gas combine with one molecule of oxygen to form two molecules of water." Or she could write the following chemical equation that contains the same information in a much more compact form:

$$2 \; H_2 + O_2 \rightarrow 2 \; H_2O$$

At the minimum, a chemical equation contains the chemical symbols and formulas for the elements and compounds involved in the reaction and the $+$ and $\rightarrow$ signs that indicate reactants and products. The term reactants refers to the substances present at the beginning of the reaction, and the term products refers to the substances formed in the reaction.

In the example above, the reactants are represented by the symbols H for hydrogen and O for oxygen. The product is represented by the formula H_2O for water. The $+$ sign indicates that hydrogen (H) has combined

Words to Know

Balancing an equation: The process of selecting coefficients for symbols and formulas in a chemical equation to make sure that the law of conservation of matter is not violated.

Chemical reaction: Any chemical change in which one new substance is formed.

Chemical symbol: A letter or pair of letters that represent a specific quantity of a chemical element.

Coefficient: A number selected for use in balancing a chemical equation. Coefficients are placed in front of the chemical symbols and formulas in an equation.

Products: The substances formed in a chemical reaction.

Reactants: The substances present at the beginning of a chemical reaction.

with oxygen (O) in the reaction. The $\rightarrow$ indicates that the two have reacted with each other to form water.

Balancing chemical equations

One of the fundamental laws of chemistry is the law of conservation of matter. That law says that matter can be neither created nor destroyed in an ordinary chemical reaction. In terms of the above reaction, the law means that there must be the same number of hydrogen atoms and oxygen atoms at the beginning of the reaction and at the end of the reaction.

The coefficients in the chemical equation assure that this condition is true. The coefficients are the numbers in front of the chemical symbols or formulas: $2 H_2$ and $2 H_2O$. One of the skills that beginning chemistry students need to learn is how to select the correct coefficients in order to make sure the equation obeys the law of conservation of matter. Choosing those coefficients is called balancing the chemical equation.

Additional symbols; additional information

Most chemical equations contain other symbols (in addition to chemical symbols) that provide further information about the reaction. The subscript 2 in the symbols for hydrogen and oxygen (H_2 and O_2), for example, tells that each molecule of hydrogen and oxygen consists of two atoms of the element.

Other symbols are often used to indicate the physical state of the substances in the reaction. The same reaction for the formation of water can also be represented as:

$$2 \text{ H}_2 \text{ (g)} + \text{O}_2 \text{ (g)} \rightarrow 2 \text{ H}_2\text{O (l)}$$

The symbols g and l tell us that hydrogen and oxygen are gases and water is a liquid. Other symbols used for this purpose include (s) for solids and (aq) for substances dissolved in water (the *aq*ueous condition). Upward and downward pointing arrows (↑ and ↓) can also be used to indicate the formation of gases and precipitates (solids), respectively, during a chemical reaction.

Finally, symbols can also be used to indicate the gain or loss of heat in a chemical reaction. Nearly all reactions are accompanied by such changes, and they can be represented by means of the symbol ΔH. In the case of the reaction above, for example, the complete reactions could be written as:

$$2 \text{ H}_2 \text{ (g)} + \text{O}_2 \text{ (g)} \rightarrow 2 \text{ H}_2\text{O (l)}$$

$$\Delta H = -571.6 \text{ kJ}$$

In this case, the added information, $\Delta H = -571.6$ kJ tells us that 571.6 kilojoules of heat energy were given off during the formation of water from its elements. (A joule is the metric unit of measurement for energy. One kilojoule is 1,000 joules.)

Applications

The use of chemical equations is absolutely essential in dealing with any discussion of chemical reactions. It would be completely unreasonable for chemists to describe chemical reactions in English sentences, as indicated in the first paragraph of this entry. Thus, all reports of chemical research, books and articles on chemical topics, and any other written commentaries on chemistry all include chemical equations.

[*See also* **Reaction, chemical**]

Equilibrium, chemical

Chemical equilibrium (plural equilibria) is a dynamic condition (meaning it is marked by continuous change) in which the rate at which two

Words to Know

Concentration: The amount of a substance present in a given volume, such as the number of molecules in a liter.

Dynamic condition: A condition in which components are constantly changing.

Precipitate: A solid formed during a chemical reaction.

opposing chemical changes is the same. As an example, consider the re-action in which ammonia gas (NH_3) is made from the elements nitrogen (N_2) and hydrogen (H_2). That reaction can be represented by the following chemical equation:

$$N_2 + 3\ H_2 \rightleftarrows 2\ NH_3$$

The double arrow ($\rightleftarrows$) in this equation means that two reactions are taking place at the same time. In one reaction, nitrogen and hydrogen combine to form ammonia:

$$N_2 + 3\ H_2 \rightarrow 2\ NH_3$$

In the second reaction, ammonia breaks down to form nitrogen and hydrogen. This reaction is just the reverse of the first reaction:

$$2\ NH_3 \rightarrow N_2 + 3\ H_2$$

The term chemical equilibrium refers to the condition in which both of the above two reactions are taking place at the same time.

Explanation

It is easy to show why many kinds of chemical reactions must reach a point of chemical equilibrium. In the above example, suppose that the reaction begins when nitrogen gas and hydrogen gas are mixed with each other. At that moment in time, reaction number (1) takes place, but reaction number (2) is impossible. No ammonia exists at the beginning of the reaction, so equation (2) cannot occur.

As time goes on, the rate of reaction (1) continues to be high. A lot of nitrogen and hydrogen are available to keep the reaction going. But now reaction (2) can begin to occur. As ammonia is formed, some of it can begin to break down to form the original gases—nitrogen and hydrogen. At this point, we can say that the rate of reaction (1) is greater than the rate of reaction (2).

Over time, as nitrogen and hydrogen are used up to form ammonia, the rate of reaction (1) slows down. At the same time, the amount of ammonia gets larger and the rate of reaction (2) becomes greater. Eventually, the two rates will be equal to each other: the rate of reaction number (1) will equal the rate of reaction number (2). The system has reached a state of chemical equilibrium.

What happens if the rate of reaction (1) continues to increase beyond equilibrium? That statement means that more and more hydrogen and nitrogen are used up until they are both gone. In other words, the reaction has gone to completion. That result can occur, but it usually does not take place in chemical reactions.

Consider what happens if the rate of reaction (2) becomes greater than the rate of reaction (1). That means that ammonia breaks down faster than it is being produced. At some point, all the ammonia will be gone, and only nitrogen and hydrogen will be left. So it becomes obvious that in many chemical reactions, a point of equilibrium *must* be reached.

Upsetting equilibria

The conditions under which a chemical equilibrium exists can change, thereby changing the equilibrium itself. In general, equilibria are sensitive to three factors: temperature, pressure, and concentration. Consider once again the reaction between nitrogen and hydrogen to form ammonia:

$$N_2 + 3 H_2 \rightleftarrows 2 NH_3$$

What happens to this equilibrium if the temperature is increased? An increase in temperature increases the rate at which molecules move. The faster molecules move, the more likely they are to react with each other. In the above example, increasing the temperature increases the likelihood that nitrogen and ammonia molecules will react with each other and the rate of reaction number (1) will increase. The rate of reaction (2) will not change. Eventually a new equilibrium will be established reflecting this change of reaction rates.

Changing the pressure on a reaction involving gases produces a similar effect. Increasing the pressure brings molecules more closely together and increases the chances of their reacting with each other.

Finally, changing the concentration (number of molecules present) of substances in the reaction can change the equilibrium. Suppose that a lot more hydrogen is added to the previous reaction. With more hydrogen molecules present, the rate of the forward reaction will increase. Again, a new equilibrium will be reached that reflects this changed rate of reaction.

Reactions that go to completion

Most chemical reactions can be described by the previous explanation. Some cannot. Various factors can force a reaction *not* to reach equilibrium; instead, the reaction is said to go to completion. The phrase go to completion means that the forward direction—such as reaction (1) above—continues until all reactants are used up. The product is prevented from breaking down—as in reaction (2) above—to form the original reactants.

One condition that leads to a completed reaction is the formation of a gas that escapes from the reaction. When zinc metal (Zn) is added to hydrochloric acid (HCl), for example, hydrogen gas (H_2) is formed. The hydrogen gas bubbles away out of the reaction. Since it is no longer present, the reverse reaction cannot occur:

$$Zn + 2\,HCl \rightarrow ZnCl_2 + H_2 \uparrow$$

(The upward-pointing arrow in the equation means that hydrogen escapes as a gas.)

Another condition that leads to a completed reaction is the formation of a precipitate in a reaction. A precipitate is a solid that forms during a chemical reaction. When silver nitrate ($AgNO_3$) is added to hydrochloric acid (HCl), silver chloride (AgCl) is formed. Silver chloride is insoluble and settles out of the reaction as a precipitate. Since the silver chloride is no longer present in the reaction itself, the reverse reaction ($AgCl + HNO_3 \rightarrow AgNO_3 + HCl$) cannot occur:

$$AgNO_3 + HCl \rightarrow AgCl \downarrow + HNO_3$$

(The downward-pointing arrow means that silver chloride forms as a precipitate.)

Erosion

Erosion is the general term for the processes that wear down Earth's surfaces, exposing the rocks below. The natural forces responsible for this endless sculpting include running water, near-shore waves, ice, wind, and gravity. The material produced by erosion is called sediment or sedimentary particles. Covering most of Earth's surface is a thin layer of sediment known as regolith, which is produced by the erosion of bedrock, or the solid rock surface underlying Earth's surface.

Natural sources of erosion

Running water.   Everywhere on the planet, running water continuously reshapes the land by carrying soil and debris steadily downslope. As the sediment and other eroded materials are carried along the bottoms of streams and rivers, they scour away the bedrock underneath, eventually carving deep gorges or openings. A classic example of the erosive power of running water over a great period of time is the Grand Canyon of the Colorado River.

Rain falling on dry land also can result in erosion. When raindrops strike bare ground that is not protected by vegetation, they loosen particles of soil, spattering them in all directions. During heavy rains on sloped surfaces, the dislodged soil is carried off in a flow of water.

Severe soil erosion brought about by animals overgrazing and vegetation being cleared in Kenya. *(Reproduced by permission of Photo Researchers, Inc.)*

Near-shore waves. Along seacoasts, the constant movement of tides and the pounding of waves alter the shoreline. The strong force of waves, especially during storms, erodes beaches and cliffs. Breaking waves often contain small pebbles and stones that scrape away at seacoast rocks, rubbing and grinding them into pieces. Waves can also trap air in small cracks and crevices in the rocks against which they crash. Small explosions in the rock result when air pressure builds up, sending loose chunks of rock toppling down.

Ice. Ice, in the form of huge glaciers, can plow through rock, soil, and vegetation. As the ice moves along, it scoops up great chunks of bedrock from the slopes, creating deep valleys. In turn, the rocks and soil already carried along the bottom of the glacier wear away the bedrock that is not loosened. Along many seacoasts, especially in Norway, glaciers gouged out fjords—long, narrow inlets whose bottoms can reach depths thousands of feet below sea level.

Wind. Wind erosion is referred to as eolian erosion, after Aeolus, the Greek god of wind. Erosion due to wind is more pronounced in dry regions and over land that lacks vegetation. The wind easily picks up particles of soil, sand, and dust and carries them away. Wind cannot carry as large of particles as flowing water, and it cannot carry fine particles more than a few feet or a meter above ground level. However, windblown grains of sand, when carried along at high speeds, effectively act as cutting tools. In desert regions, the bases of rocks and cliffs are often dramatically sandblasted away, resulting in mushroom-shaped rocks with large caps and slender stems.

Gravity. Gravity exerts a force on all matter, earth materials included. Gravity, acting alone, moves sediment down slopes. Gravity also causes water and ice to flow down slopes, transporting sediment with them. When bare soil on steep slopes becomes waterlogged and fluid, the downward pull of gravity results in a landslide. Sometimes landslides are simple lobes of soil slumped down a hillside; other times they can be an avalanche of rocks and debris hurtling downslope.

Human contributions to erosion

Soil loss results naturally from erosion. A balance exists on Earth between the erosion of land and its rejuvenation by natural forces. However, human activities have overwhelmed this balance in many parts of the world. The removal of vegetation, poor farming practices, strip mining, logging, construction, landscaping, and other activities all increase erosion. In general, any land use or activity that disturbs the natural vegetation or that changes the slope or surface materials of an area will increase the chances of erosion.

The Dust Bowl that took place in the prairie states of America in the 1930s is an example of an ecological disaster resulting from erosion. In the years leading up to the Dust Bowl, farmers planted wheat on lands that were formerly used for livestock grazing. After several growing seasons, the livestock were returned and allowed to graze. Their hooves pulverized the unprotected soil, which strong winds then carried aloft in huge dust clouds. Crops and land were destroyed by the dust storms, and many families were forced to abandon their farms.

[*See also* **Soil**]

Europe

Europe is the world's sixth largest continent. Together with its adjacent islands, it occupies an area of about 4,000,000 square miles (10,360,000 square kilometers), roughly 8 percent of the world's land area. Geographically, Europe can be seen as a peninsula of the single great continent called Eurasia (Europe and Asia combined). However, because Europe has such a distinctive history and culture, it is considered a separate continent.

The boundaries of the European continent are recognized as the Ural Mountains and the Ural River in the east; the Caspian Sea and the Caucasus Mountains in the southeast; and the Black Sea and the Bosporus and Dardenelle Straits in the south. The Mediterranean Sea and the Strait of Gibraltar separate Europe from the African continent, while the Atlantic Ocean borders it in the west and the Arctic Ocean borders it in the north. Numerous islands around the continental landmass are considered to be a part of Europe. More than 40 independent counties lie within the boundaries of the European continent.

The highest point on the continent is Mount Elbrus in the Caucasus Mountains, which rises 18,481 feet (5,633 meters) above sea level. The lowest point occurs at the surface of the Caspian Sea, 92 feet (28 meters) below sea level.

Chief rivers and lakes

Europe's longest river is the Volga, which runs for almost 2,300 miles (3,700 kilometers) in central and western Russia before emptying

Words to Know

Bedrock: Solid rock lying beneath the soil on the surface of Earth.

Bog: Area of wet, spongy ground consisting of decayed plant matter.

Fjord: Long, narrow, steep-sided inlet of the sea.

Glacier: Large mass of ice slowly moving over a mountain or through a valley.

Moor: Broad stretch of open land, often with boggy areas.

Moraine: Mass of boulders, stones, and other rock debris carried along and deposited by a glacier.

into the Caspian Sea. It drains an area of about 533,000 square miles (1,380,470 square kilometers). Europe's second longest river, the Danube, runs through the heart of the continent. About 1,770 miles (2,850 kilometers) long, it drains an area of roughly 320,000 square miles (828,800 square kilometers). A third prominent river is the Rhine, which winds through west-central Europe for 820 miles (1,320 kilometers) before emptying into the North Sea. Other chief European rivers include the Elbe in central Europe; the Dnieper and Don in Russia; the Garonne, Loire, and Rhône in France; the Tagus in Spain; and the Oder and Vistula in Poland.

The Caspian Sea, with an area of 143,550 square miles (371,795 square kilometers), is the largest inland body of water in the world. The largest lake within the boundaries of Europe proper is Russia's Lake Ladoga, which covers approximately 7,000 square miles (18,100 square kilometers). Other large European lakes include Geneva and Zurich in Switzerland; Constance on the border of Switzerland, Germany, and Austria; Balaton in Hungary; Como, Garda, and Maggiore in Italy; and Vättern and Vänern in Sweden.

Major physical regions

Europe may be divided geographically into four physical regions: the Northwestern Uplands, the Central Plain, the Central Uplands, and the Alpine mountain chain.

Northwestern Uplands. Uplands—high plateaus, rugged mountains, and deep valleys—stretch along Europe's northwest coast from western

France through the United Kingdom to the Scandinavian peninsula. Farming in this area is often difficult because of the rocky soil, and the climate is often rainy. Moors and bogs (areas of wet spongy ground) dominate in the northern sections.

Europe. *(Reproduced by permission of The Gale Group.)*

During the last Ice Age, which ended about 11,000 years ago, glacial ice covered much of the far northern areas. When the ice retreated, it left deep valleys along the shores into which ocean water flowed. These narrow arms of the sea—called fjords—reach far inland and are bordered by steep mountains.

Central Plain. The most densely settled part of Europe, with its largest cities and manufacturing sites, is the Central Plain. Starting at the Atlantic coast of France, it spreads out in a V-shape, growing wider as it extends west. At the Ural Mountains, it stretches from the Arctic Ocean to the Black Sea. Except for being perfectly flat in the Netherlands, the plain features occasional hills and isolated ridges. Much of the plain holds fertile agricultural soil.

Around the Baltic Sea, Ice Age glaciers left mounds of boulders, stones, and other rock debris they had carried along. These remaining hills, called terminal moraines, mark the leading edge of these glaciers.

Glaciers subject earth materials beneath them to the most intense kind of scraping and scouring. An alpine glacier has the power to tear bedrock (solid rock beneath soil) apart and move the shattered pieces miles away. These are the forces that shaped the sharp mountain peaks and U-shaped mountain valleys of modern Europe. Many European mountain ranges bear obvious scars from alpine glaciation, and the flat areas of the continent show the features of a formerly glaciated plain.

Central Uplands. Between the Central Plain and the Alpine mountains lies a band of uplands. It stretches from Spain's Atlantic coast through France and Germany to Poland. Important mountainous and wooded plateaus in this band include the Meseta (in Spain), the Massif Central (in France), the Ardennes (across Belgium, Luxembourg, and France), the Black Forest (in Germany), and the Bohemian Forest (along the northern Czech-German border).

Alpine mountain chain. Southern Europe from Spain to the southern part of western Russia is dominated by the Alpine mountain chain. Beginning at the western edge, the mountains forming this chain are the Sierra Nevada range in Spain, the Pyrenees between Spain and France, the Alps in south-central Europe, and the Apennines in Italy.

The Sierra Nevada range in southern Spain runs parallel to the Mediterranean Sea for about 60 miles (100 kilometers). The highest peak in the range is Mulhacén, which rises to a height of 11,411 feet (3,478 meters).

The Pyrenees form an effective barrier between the Iberian Peninsula (on which Portugal and Spain lie) and the rest of Europe. They extend 270 miles (435 kilometers) in an almost straight line from the Bay of Biscay on the west to the Gulf of Lions on the east. The highest peak in the Pyrenees is Pico de Aneto, 11,168 feet (3,404 meters) above sea level.

The Alps are Europe's great mountain system. They stretch in an arc for almost 660 miles (1,060 kilometers) from the Mediterranean coast between France and Italy into Switzerland and along the northern boundary of Italy, through southwest Austria, before ending in Slovenia. The Alps, composed of more than 15 principal mountain ranges (all of which have offshoot ranges), cover an estimated 80,000 square miles (207,200 square kilometers). They form a barrier between southern Europe and western and central Europe. The highest peak in the Alps is Mont Blanc, 15,771 feet (4,807 meters) in height. Many peaks in the Alps rise above the snowline, 8,000 to 10,000 feet (2,440 to 3,050 meters), and thus are permanently snowcapped.

The Apennines run the entire length of the Italian peninsula. They extend about 840 miles (1,350 kilometers) from the Ligurian Alps (which they resemble geologically) in northwest Italy south to the Strait of Messina. The highest peak in the Apennines is Monte Corno, which stands 9,560 feet (2,914 meters) above sea level. Most rivers in Italy find their source in the Apennines. The central and southern portions of the

The Matterhorn in Switzerland, at 14,690 feet (4,480 meters), was carved by alpine glaciers. *(Reproduced by permission of JLM Visuals.)*

mountain system are marked by crater lakes and volcanoes. Two of those volcanoes—Vesuvius and Etna—are still active. It was Vesuvius that erupted on August 24, A.D. 79, burying the cities of Pompeii and Herculaneum.

Boundary mountains

The Caucasus Mountains, extending for about 750 miles (1,210 kilometers), act as a divide between Europe and the Middle East. The mountain system is volcanic in origin, and many of its peaks rise above 15,000 feet (4,600 kilometers). Included in this group is Mount Elbrus, Europe's highest mountain. Lying northeast of the Caucasus are the Ural Mountains, the far eastern boundary of Europe. Unlike the Caucasus, the Urals do not form an almost impassable wall. They are low and covered with forests. The Urals, extending about 1,500 miles (2,400 kilometers) from the Arctic tundra to the deserts near the Caspian Sea, average only 3,000 to 4,000 feet (900 to 1,200 meters) in height. The highest peak in the range is Mount Narodnaya, which rises 6,214 feet (1,894 meters) above sea level.

Geological forces in present-day Europe

Europe continues to change today. From the Atlantic coast of the Iberian Peninsula to the Caucasus, Europe's southern border is geologically active. It will remain so effectively forever. Africa, Arabia, and the Iranian Plateau all continue to move northward, which will insure continued mountain-building in southern Europe.

Geologists are concerned about volcanic hazards, particularly under the Bay of Naples and in the Caucasus. Smaller earthquakes, floods, and other natural disasters happen almost every year. In historic times, entire European cities have been devastated or destroyed by volcanos, earthquakes, and seismic sea waves. These larger-scale natural disasters can and will continue to happen in Europe on an unpredictable schedule.

Eutrophication

Eutrophication (pronounced you-tro-fi-KAY-shun) is a natural process that occurs in an aging lake or pond as that body of water gradually builds up its concentration of plant nutrients. Cultural or artificial eutrophication occurs when human activity introduces increased amounts of these nutri-

Words to Know

Algae: Single-celled or multicellular plants or plantlike organisms that contain chlorophyll, thus making their own food by photosynthesis. Algae grow mainly in water.

Nitrate: A salt or ester of nitric acid, which is a transparent corrosive liquid composed of nitrogen, hydrogen, and oxygen.

Phosphate: A salt or ester of a phosphoric acid, which is any of three acids that are formed when the oxide of phosphorus reacts with water.

ents, which speed up plant growth and eventually choke the lake of all of its animal life.

In nature, eutrophication is a common phenomenon in freshwater ecosystems and is really a part of the normal aging process of many lakes and ponds. Some never experience it because of a lack of warmth and light, but many do. Over time, these bodies of freshwater change in terms of how productive or fertile they are. While this is different for each lake or pond, those that are naturally fed rich nutrients from a stream or river or some other natural source are described as "eutrophic," meaning they are nutrient-rich and therefore abundant in plant and animal life. Eutrophication is not necessarily harmful or bad, and the word itself is often translated from the Greek as meaning "well nourished" or "good food." However, eutrophication can be speeded up artificially, and then the lake and its inhabitants eventually suffer as the input of nutrients increases far beyond what the natural capacity of the lake should be.

Too much of a good thing

Natural eutrophication is usually a fairly slow and gradual process, occurring over a period of many centuries. It occurs naturally when for some reason, production and consumption within the lake do not cancel each other out and the lake slowly becomes overfertilized. While not rare in nature, it does not happen frequently or quickly. However, artificial or human-caused eutrophication has become so common that the word eutrophication by itself has come to mean a very harmful increase and acceleration of nutrients. It is as if something receives too much fertilizer or has too much of what is a good thing.

Humans increase the rate of eutrophication

Human activities almost always result in the creation of waste, and many of these waste products often contain nitrates and phosphates. Nitrates are a compound of nitrogen, and most are produced by bacteria. Phosphates are phosphorous compounds. Both nitrates and phosphates are absorbed by plants and are needed for growth. However, the human use of detergents and chemical fertilizers has greatly increased the amount of nitrates and phosphates that are washed into our lakes and ponds. When this occurs in a sufficient quantity, they act like fertilizer for plants and algae and speed up their rate of growth.

Algae are a group of plantlike organisms that live in water and can make their own food through photosynthesis (using sunlight to make food from simple chemicals). When additional phosphates are added to a body of water, the plants begin to grow explosively and algae takes off or "blooms." In the process, the plants and algae consume greater amounts of oxygen in the water, robbing fish and other species of necessary oxygen.

All algae eventually die, and when they do, oxygen is required by bacteria in order for them to decompose or break down the dead algae. A cycle then begins in which more bacteria decompose more dead algae,

An eutrophic lake. *(Reproduced by permission of The Gale Group.)*

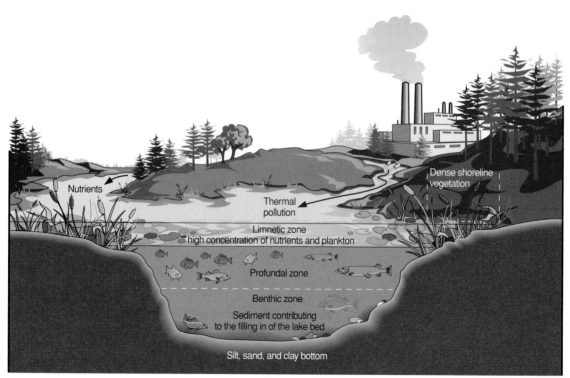

Nutrients

Dense shoreline vegetation

Thermal pollution

Limnetic zone
high concentration of nutrients and plankton

Profundal zone

Benthic zone

Sediment contributing to the filling in of the lake bed

Silt, sand, and clay bottom

consuming even more oxygen in the process. The bacteria then release more phosphates back into the water, which feed more algae. As levels of oxygen in the body of water become lower, species such as fish and mollusks literally suffocate to death.

Eventually, the lake or pond begins to fill in and starts to be choked with plant growth. As the plants die and turn to sediment that sinks, the lake bottom starts to rise. The waters grow shallower and finally the body of water is filled completely and disappears. This also can happen to wetlands, which are already shallow. Eventually, there are shrubs growing where a body of water used to be.

In the 1960s and 1970s, Lake Erie was the most publicized example of eutrophication. Called a "dead lake," the smallest and shallowest of the five Great Lakes was swamped for decades with nutrients from heavily developed agricultural and urban lands. As a result, plant and algae growth choked out most other species living in the lake, and left the beaches unusable due to the smell of decaying algae that washed up on the shores. New pollution controls for sewage treatment plants and agricultural methods by the United States and Canada led to drastic reductions in the amount of nutrients entering the lake. Forty years later, while still not totally free of pollutants and nutrients, Lake Erie is again a biologically thriving lake.

[*See also* **Lake**]

Evaporation

Evaporation is the name given to the process in which a liquid is converted to the gaseous state. Everyone is familiar with the process of evaporation. Suppose that you spill a teaspoon of water on the kitchen table. If you come back a few hours later, the water will have disappeared. It has changed from liquid water into water vapor, or evaporated.

Molecular explanation

Evaporation occurs because all molecules of all substances are constantly in motion. Consider the molecules that make up a teaspoon of water, for example. Those molecules are constantly in motion, flying back and forth within the water, sometimes colliding with each other. When collisions occur, some molecules gain energy from other molecules.

Those changes make little difference for molecules deep within the water. But for molecules at the surface of the water, the situation is different.

Molecules at the surface that pick up energy from other molecules begin to travel faster. Eventually, they may be able to travel fast enough to escape from the surface of the water or to evaporate from the water.

This process continues as long as water molecules remain. Molecules that were once inside the water eventually work their way to the surface. When they pick up enough energy by colliding with other water molecules, they too escape. Eventually, no water molecules remain. The liquid has completely evaporated.

The remaining liquid

This description explains an interesting fact about an evaporating liquid: its temperature decreases as evaporation occurs. Remember that surface molecules escape from the liquid as they pick up energy from other molecules. The molecules left behind, therefore, have less energy than they had before the collisions. Since they have less energy, they also have a lower temperature.

The human body uses this principle to remain cool. On a warm day, we perspire (sweat). Sweat evaporates from the skin, taking body heat with it. As a result, the body is cooled.

Commercial applications

Evaporation is an important commercial process by which liquids are removed from solids. In many instances, a product is formed as the result of a chemical reaction that takes place in water. One way to obtain the final product is to simply allow the water to evaporate leaving the solid product behind.

[*See also* **Matter, states of**]

Evolution

The term evolution in general refers to the process of change. For example, one can describe the way in which a section of land evolves over time. Geologic evolution comes about as the result of forces such as earthquakes, volcanoes, land movements, rain, snow, wind, and other factors. In biology, the term evolution refers to changes that take place in organisms over long periods of time. For example, one can study the changes that take place in a population of fruit flies over many generations. The characteristics of that population after 100 generations is likely to be quite different from the characteristics of the first generation of flies.

Scientists and laypeople often refer to the theory of evolution. The term "theory" in this phrase does not refer to a scientific guess, as the term is sometimes used. Instead, the term refers in this case to a large collection of well-established laws and facts about the ways organisms change over time. The theory of evolution is not in any sense an idea whose truth needs to be tested. Instead, it is one of the most fundamental and most important general concepts in all of the biological sciences.

Historical background

The English naturalist Charles Darwin (1809–1882) is generally regarded as the father of modern evolutionary theory. However, evolutionary thought can be traced to much earlier periods. In the mid-eighteenth century, for example, the French mathematician Pierre-Louis Maupertuis (1698–1759; last name pronounced moe-per-TWEE) and the French encyclopedist Denis Diderot (1713–1784; name pronounced da-NEE dee-duh-ROE) proposed evolutionary theories that contained ideas that reappeared in Darwin's own theory a century later.

The French naturalist Jean-Baptiste Lamarck (1744–1829) was the first to clearly explain the theory that species could change over time into new species. In his 1809 book *Philosophie zoologique,* he argued that living things progress inevitably toward greater perfection and complexity. The driving force behind that change, he said, was the natural environment. According to Lamarck's theory, changes in the environment altered the needs of living creatures. These creatures, in turn, responded by using certain organs or body parts more or less. As the body parts were either used or disused, they would change in size or shape. That change would then be inherited by the creatures' offspring, Lamarck said. Such changes could then be regarded as "acquired characters." According to this notion of the inheritance of acquired characteristics, also known as Lamarckism, giraffes would have "acquired" their long necks from stretching to reach leaves not available to other animals. Members of each succeeding generation would have stretched their necks to attain leaves at ever higher levels, leading to the modern giraffe. Although this theory was later discredited

Charles Darwin. *(Reproduced by permission of Archive Photos, Inc.)*

Words to Know

DNA (deoxyribonucleic acid): A large, complex chemical compound that makes up the core of a chromosome and whose segments consist of genes.

Fitness: The ability of an organism to survive in an environment as measured by the average number of offspring produced by individuals with a certain set of genes, relative to that of individuals with a different set of genes.

Gene: A section of a DNA molecule that carries instructions for the formation, functioning, and transmission of specific traits from one generation to another.

Mutation: A change in the physical structure of an organism's DNA (deoxyribonucleic acid), resulting in a genetic change that can be inherited.

Natural selection: Also referred to as "survival of the fittest," the process by which some organisms are better able to survive and reproduce in some present environment.

and abandoned, Lamarck remains the first scientist to acknowledge the adaptability of organisms.

Darwin and his contemporary, Alfred Russell Wallace (1823–1913), are credited with independently providing the first logical theory for a mechanism to explain evolutionary change. Darwin and Wallace called that theory natural selection. However, Wallace did not develop his ideas as fully as did Darwin. As a result, it is Darwin who is generally given credit for having founded the modern theory of evolution. He outlined the fundamental ideas of that theory in his 1859 book *The Origin of Species by Means of Natural Selection* and his later works. One major difference between the two men was that Wallace did not believe that natural selection could have produced the human brain. He thought that human intellect could only have been created by a higher power (a god), a concept that Darwin rejected.

In *The Origin of Species,* Darwin concluded that some individuals in a species are better equipped to find food, survive disease, and escape predators than others. He reasoned that these individuals are more likely to survive, mate, and produce offspring. Individuals that are not as well-adapted to their environment are less likely to survive, mate, and produce offspring. As a result, each generation of a population will consist of individuals that are better and better adapted to their environment. The overall characteristics of the population will change to reflect this better adaptation.

The major problem with Darwin's theory—which he acknowledged—was that he didn't know the mechanism by which successful adaptations could be passed from one generation to the next. The solution to that problem lay in the research done by the Austrian monk and botanist Gregor Mendel (1822–1884). Mendel discovered that hereditary characteristics are transmitted from generation to generation in discrete units that he called "factors" and that we now call genes. Darwin's theory can be restated to say that individuals who are better adapted to their environment are more likely to pass their genes to the next generation than are other members of a population.

Evidence for evolution

Support for the theory of evolution comes from a number of sources. One of these sources is the science of embryology, the study of early forms of an organism. Darwin reasoned that organisms that have passed through a period of evolution will retain some reminders of that history within their bodies. As its turns out, virtually all living creatures possess vestigial features. A vestigial feature is a structure that once served some function in an ancestor and remains in an organism at some stage of its development. But the structure no longer serves any function in that organism.

As an example, the embryos of all vertebrates (animals with backbones) look remarkably alike at an early stage. They all contain, for example, a tail-like structure that may or may not be lost as the individual develops. Also, fetal whales, still in their mothers' wombs, produce teeth like all vertebrates. However, those teeth are later reabsorbed in preparation for a life of filtering plankton from their ocean habitat. Snakes, whose vertebrate ancestors ceased walking on four legs millions of years ago, still possess vestigial hind limbs with reduced hip and thigh bones.

In some cases, the same structures may be adapted for new uses. The cat's paw, the dolphin's flipper, the bat's wing, and a human hand all have a similar structure. They all contain counterparts of the same five bones forming the digits or fingers (in humans). There is no known environmental or functional reason why there should be five digits. In theory, there could just as easily be four or seven. The point is that the ancestor to all tetrapods (vertebrates with four legs) had five digits. Thus, all living tetrapods have that number, although in a modified form.

Another important source of evidence about evolution comes from the fossil record. In general, one would expect, if evolutionary theory is correct, that the older a fossil is the simpler and more primitive it is. Such, in fact, is the case. Fossil invertebrates (animals that lack backbones), plants, and animals appear in the rocky layers of Earth's crust in the same order that their anatomical complexity suggests they should: with the more primitive organisms in the older layers, beneath the increasingly complex organisms in the more recent deposits. No one has ever found a flowering plant or a mammal in deposits from 400 million years ago, for instance, because those organisms did not appear on Earth until much later.

In some cases, evolution can actually be observed. Organisms that reproduce rapidly can be exposed to environmental factors that would affect the make-up of the population. In one famous experiment, Joshua Lederberg (1925–) and Esther Lederberg (1922–) exposed bacterial colonies to an antibiotic. In the first stages of the experiment, most bacteria in the colony were killed off by the antibiotic; only a very few survived. As the colony reproduced, however, that pattern began to change. More and more individuals in the population were resistant to the antibiotic. Eventually, the antibiotic was no longer successful in killing off the new strain of bacteria that had evolved.

Finally, evidence for evolution can be found in the most fundamental part of living organisms: the structure of their DNA molecules. DNA (deoxyribonucleic acid) is the molecule in all living cells that controls the functions of those cells. When one studies the DNA of animals that appear to be related to each other on a superficial level, such as humans and chimpanzees, very close similarities in the DNA of these animals can also be observed.

Evolutionary mechanisms

One of the fundamental questions in evolutionary thought is *how* changes take place within a species. How does it happen that the organisms that make up a population today are different in important ways from the organisms that made up a similar population a thousand or a million years ago?

For biologists, that question can be rephrased in terms of changes in gene frequencies. Suppose one could make a list of all the genes in a population of muskrats in a particular geographical region. Since all the individuals in that population are muskrats, they will share a great many genes in common with each other. However, all muskrats in the population will not have identical genes. There will be some variability among those genes.

Origin of Life

So, how did it all begin? Any discussion of evolution eventually leads to the most basic question of all: how did life begin on Earth?

Humans have wondered about that question for centuries. One of the oldest beliefs is that organisms are created by the process of spontaneous generation. According to this theory, organisms arise out of nonliving matter almost magically—from garbage, refuse, muddy water, and other places where dirt collects. In the 1860s, French chemist Louis Pasteur (1822–1895) showed that living organisms only come from other living organisms. So the question remained, where did the first organisms come from?

The most popular theory today is that the first living organisms probably grew out of the warm "chemical soup" that existed on Earth's surface three to four billion years ago. That soup consisted of compounds of nitrogen, oxygen, carbon, and hydrogen. With energy provided by sunlight, lightning, and the heat of volcanoes, those compounds apparently came together to form amino acids. Those amino acids, in turn, reacted with each other to form proteins, the building blocks of all forms of life. In 1953, American chemist Stanley Miller (1930–) showed in a laboratory experiment how such reactions might take place. Since that time, more and more experiments have strengthened the "chemical soup" theory of the origin of life.

Still, other theories remain. For example, some scientists believe that the seeds from which life on Earth began arrived on our planet millions of years ago from outer space, brought by meteors that fell to the planet's surface. Recent discoveries by astronomers of the presence of these "life-giving" chemicals (complex carbon molecules and water) in comets, in the dust and gas of distant stars, and in the emptiness of outer space lend some support to this theory.

Natural selection. An important factor in the evolution of a species is that, as a whole, a species tends to overproduce. That is, under most circumstances, more muskrats (or any other organism) are born each year than can possibly survive. Environmental factors such as food, water, and living space limit the number of individuals that will survive in any one year.

For all living organisms, then, life can be seen as a struggle. A constant battle goes on among the individuals to determine which individuals survive and which will die. In determining the outcome of that battle, it should be obvious that those individuals best adapted to an environment will survive. For example, in a cold environment, individuals that are somewhat better able to live in cold temperatures are more likely to live than those that are adapted to a somewhat warmer environment.

More to the point, individuals that are adapted to an environment are more likely to live *and to reproduce.* Those individuals are more likely to survive, reproduce, and pass their genes on to the next generation. Individuals that are less well-adapted are less likely to reproduce and pass on their generations. Over a long period of time, the individuals that make up a population are better and better adapted to the environment in which they live.

This fact of life has been summarized in one of the most famous expressions in all of biology, the "survival of the fittest." The phrase simply means that individuals that "fit" the needs, demands, and opportunities of the environment are most likely to have offspring that will also "fit in" with the environment.

This process is described as natural selection. The term natural selection refers to the tendency of organisms that are better adapted to an environment to survive, reproduce, and pass on their genes to the next generation.

The effects of natural selection can be seen when an environment changes. As an environment changes, the characteristics needed to survive within it also change. Evolution continues, but the direction it takes may alter.

For example, suppose that global climate changes occur. Suppose that the annual average temperature in northern Canada begins to drop. Over a one-million year period, the region becomes much colder. In such a case, organisms that are better adapted to cold climates will survive, reproduce, and pass on their "cold weather" genes to their offspring. The individuals that make up a population will differ from the individuals in a population one million years earlier because the population has adapted to new environmental conditions. Natural conditions have "selected" those individuals (along with their genes) best adapted to the new environment.

Mutation. An important factor in evolution is mutation. Mutation is the process by which changes occur in an organism's genes that are transmitted to the organism's offspring. Mutations are often regarded as undesirable events because they often lead to genetic disorders that result in the death of individuals. But mutations also can be positive events.

For example, consider a group of disease-causing bacteria that are exposed to an antibiotic. The vast majority of those bacteria will be killed by the antibiotic. The use of antibiotics to cure certain diseases is an example of this fact. But suppose that a mutation has occurred in a small fraction of the bacteria—in even a single bacterium—treated with the antibiotic. And assume that that mutation provides the bacteria with an immunity (tolerance) to the antibiotic. In such a case, the vast majority of bacteria *lacking* the mutant gene will die off. The few bacteria that *have* the mutant gene will be able to survive, reproduce, and pass on their immunity to the antibiotic to their offspring.

In fact, this kind of evolution takes place all the time in the real world. Any antibiotic that has ever been discovered or invented eventually loses its effectiveness in treating disease. The reason is that bacteria with mutant genes become resistant to the antibiotic, reproduce, and eventually become the dominant forms of the bacteria.

The same kind of change occurs in every kind of organism. A mutant gene may provide a tree with the ability to grow taller, giving it an advantage over other trees lacking the mutant gene. A tiger may attain a mutant gene that makes it more aggressive, stronger, or able to out-hunt its brothers and sisters. A mutant gene in the human brain may provide a person with more intelligence, better perception, or some other trait that gives him or her a slight advantage over his or her peers. In each case, the mutant gene changes the course of evolution and gives one individual a survival advantage over other individuals in the same population.

[*See also* **Adaptation; Genetics; Geologic time; Mendelian laws of heredity; Migration; Mutation; Nucleic acid**]

Excretory system

The excretory system is a system of organs that removes waste products from the body. When cells in the body break down proteins (large molecules that are essential to the structure and functioning of all living cells), they produce wastes such as urea (a chemical compound of carbon, hydrogen, nitrogen, and oxygen). When cells break down carbohydrates (compounds consisting of carbon, hydrogen, and oxygen and used as a food), they produce water and carbon dioxide as waste products. If these useless waste products are allowed to accumulate in the body, they would become dangerous to the body's health. The kidneys, considered the main excretory organs in humans, eliminate water, urea, and other waste products from the body in the form of urine.

Words to Know

Antidiuretic hormone: Chemical secreted by the pituitary gland that regulates the amount of water excreted by the kidneys.

Hemodialysis: Process of separating wastes from the blood by passage through a semipermeable membrane.

Nephron: Filtering unit of the kidney.

Urea: Chemical compound of carbon, hydrogen, nitrogen, and oxygen produced as waste by cells that break down protein.

Ureter: Tube that carries urine from a kidney to the urinary bladder.

Urethra: Duct leading from the urinary bladder to outside the body through which urine is eliminated.

Other systems and organs in the body also play a part in excretion. The respiratory system eliminates water vapor and carbon dioxide through exhalation (the process of breathing out). The digestive system removes feces, the solid undigested wastes of digestion, by a process called defecation or elimination. The skin also acts as an organ of excretion by removing water and small amounts of urea and salts (as sweat).

Urinary system

The kidneys are bean-shaped organs located at the small of the back near the spinal column. The left kidney sits slightly higher than the right one. The size of an adult kidney is approximately 4 inches (10 centimeters) long and 2 inches (5 centimeters) wide. To maintain human life, it is necessary for at least one of the kidneys to function properly.

Blood carries waste products to the kidneys via the renal artery. Inside each kidney, blood is transported to 1.2 million filtering units called nephrons (pronounced NEFF-rons). The cells in nephrons take in the liquid portion of the blood and filter out impurities (urea, mineral salts, and other toxins). Necessary substances such as certain salts, water, glucose (sugar), and other nutrients are returned to the blood stream via the renal vein.

The waste-containing fluid that remains in the nephrons is called urine. Urine is 95 percent water, in which the waste products are dissolved.

A pair of tubes called ureters carry urine from the kidneys to the urinary bladder. Each ureter is about 16 to 18 inches (40 to 45 centimeters) long. The bladder is a hollow muscular sac located in the pelvis that is collapsed when empty, but pear-shaped and distended when full. The bladder in an adult can hold more than 2 cups (0.6 liters) of urine. The bladder empties urine into the urethra, a duct leading to outside the body. In males, the urethra is about 8 inches (20 centimeters) long. In females, it is less than 2 inches (5 centimeters) long. A sphincter muscle around the urethra at the base of the bladder controls the flow of urine between the two.

The volume of urine excreted is controlled by the antidiuretic hormone (ADH), which is released by the pituitary gland (a small gland lying at the base of the skull). If an individual perspires a lot or fails to drink enough water, special nerve cells in the hypothalamus (a region of the brain controlling body temperature, hunger, and thirst) detect the low water concentration in the blood. They then signal the pituitary gland to release ADH into the blood, where it travels to the kidneys. With ADH present, the kidneys reabsorb more water from the urine and return it to the blood. The volume of urine is thus reduced. On the other hand, if an individual takes in too much water, production of ADH decreases. The kidneys do not reabsorb as much water, and the volume of urine is increased. Alcohol inhibits ADH production and therefore increases the output of urine.

Urinary disorders

Disorders of the urinary tract (kidneys, ureters, bladder, and urethra) include urinary tract infections (UTI). An example is cystitis, a disease in which bacteria infect the urinary bladder, causing inflammation. Most UTIs are treated with antibiotics. Sometimes kidney stones, solid salt crystals, form in the urinary tract. Kidney stones can obstruct the urinary passages and cause severe pain and bleeding. If they do not pass out of the body naturally, a physician may remove them surgically or disintegrate them using shock waves.

Chronic renal failure is the permanent loss of kidney function. Hemodialysis and kidney transplant are two medical treatments for this condition. In hemodialysis, an artificial kidney device cleans the blood of wastes. During the procedure, blood is taken out of an artery in the patient's arm and passed through a tubing that is semipermeable (allows certain materials to pass through its sides). The tubing is immersed in a solution. As the blood passes through the tubing, wastes pass out of the tubing and into the surrounding solution. The cleansed blood then returns to the body. In a kidney transplant, a surgeon replaces a diseased kidney with a closely matched donor kidney. Although about 23,000 people in the United States wait for donor kidneys each year, fewer than 8,000 receive kidney transplants.

[*See also* **Digestive system; Integumentary system; Respiratory system; Transplant, surgical**]

Expansion, thermal

Thermal expansion is the change in size of an object as its temperature changes. Normally, as the temperature increases, the size of an object also increases. Conversely, most objects shrink as the temperature drops. On a hot summer day, electrical power lines sag between power poles. The sag occurs because the wires grow longer as the temperature increases. Long bridges often have interlocking metal fingers along the joints where sections of the bridge are joined to each other. The metal fingers allow the bridge sections to expand and contract with changes in the temperature.

A relatively small number of substances contract when they are heated and expand when they are cooled. Water is the most common example. As water is cooled from room temperature to its freezing point, it contracts, like most other substances. However, just four degrees Celsius above its freezing point, it begins to expand. At its freezing point a gram of ice takes up more space than does a gram of liquid water. This change explains the fact that ice floats on top of water.

Factors affecting thermal expansion

Imagine that a long, thin metal wire is heated. The wire expands. The amount by which it expands depends on three factors: its original length, the temperature change, and the thermal (heat) properties of the metal itself.

Some substances simply expand more easily than others. If you heat wires of aluminum, iron, and tungsten metals—all the wires being the same size and heated to the same temperature—each wire will expand by a different amount. The ease with which a substance expands is given by its coefficient of expansion. For comparison, the coefficients of expansion for aluminum, iron, and tungsten are 23×10^{-6}, 12×10^{-6}, and 5×10^{-6} per degree Celsius, respectively.

The values given in the previous sentence actually refer to the coefficients of linear expansion. They measure how much a substance expands in only one direction. But suppose the above experiment were done with blocks of aluminum, iron, and tungsten rather than wires. In that case, the expansion would occur in all three directions: length, width, and depth. The measure of expansion in all three directions is called the coefficient of volume expansion.

Length and temperature.   Suppose this discussion is limited to a single kind of material, say an iron wire. The amount by which that wire expands when heated depends on only two factors: its original length and the temperature to which it is heated. An iron bar that is 16 feet (5 meters) long will expand more than a bar that is 3 feet (1 meter) long. And a 16-foot (5-meter) bar will expand more if heated by 68°F (20°C) than a 16-foot (5-meter) bar that is heated by 50°F (10°C).

Applications

Engineers and architects must always take into consideration the fact that objects usually expand when they are heated. As a result, they have to design buildings, bridges, power lines, and other structures to compensate for expansion and contraction.

Thermal expansion also is used in the construction of certain appliances and devices in homes and industry. One example is the bimetallic strip. A bimetallic strip consists of two pieces of metal welded to each other. The two metals are chosen to have different coefficients of expansion. When the bimetallic strip is heated, it bends one way or the other as one metal expands faster than the other.

One use of bimetallic strips is in thermostats used to control room temperatures. As a room warms up or cools down, the bimetallic strip in the thermostat bends one way or the other. If it bends far enough, it comes into contact with a button that turns a furnace on or off.

Explosives

Explosives are materials that produce violent chemical or nuclear reactions. These reactions generate large amounts of heat and gas in a fraction of a second. Shock waves produced by rapidly expanded gases are responsible for much of the destruction seen following an explosion.

Probably the oldest known explosive is black gunpowder, a mixture of charcoal (carbon), sulfur, and saltpeter (potassium nitrate). When these three chemicals are ignited, a chemical reaction takes place very quickly.

Words to Know

Chemical explosive: A compound or mixture that releases chemical energy violently and rapidly, creating heat and a shock wave generated by a release of gases.

Dynamite: An explosive made by soaking an inert (inactive or stable), absorbent substance with a mixture of (1) nitroglycerin or ammonium nitrate, (2) a combustible substance (a substance with the ability to burn), such as wood pulp, and (3) an antacid.

Gunpowder: An explosive mixture of charcoal, potassium nitrate, and sulfur often used to propel bullets from guns and shells from cannons.

Nitroglycerine: An explosive liquid used to make dynamite. Also used as a medicine to dilate blood vessels.

Nuclear explosive: A device that obtains its explosive force from the release of nuclear energy.

TNT: Trinitrotoluene, a high explosive.

The products of that reaction are carbon dioxide, carbon monoxide, sulfur dioxide, and nitric oxide (all gases) as well as potassium carbonate and potassium sulfide (two solids). The four gases formed in the reaction are heated to very high temperatures and expand very rapidly. They form shock waves that have the ability to knock down trees, buildings, people, and other objects in their way. The shock wave also carries with it very hot gases that can burn objects and initiate fires. The combination of shock wave and high temperature is characteristic of most kinds of explosives.

History

Gunpowder was first invented in China no later than about A.D. 850. For hundreds of years, it was used mainly to create fireworks. The Chinese did not use gunpowder as a weapon of war; it was the Europeans who first adapted explosives for use in weapons. By the fourteenth century, Europeans were widely using the explosive as a military device to project stones, spearlike projectiles, and metal balls from cannons and guns.

For the next 500 years, gunpowder was used almost exclusively for pyrotechnic (fireworks) displays and in warfare. Then, in 1856, Italian chemist Ascanio Sobrero (1812–1888) invented the first modern explosive, nitroglycerin. Sobrero's discovery was, unfortunately for many early users, too unstable to be used safely. Nitroglycerin readily explodes if bumped or shocked.

In 1859, Swedish inventor Alfred Nobel (1833–1896) began to look for a way to package nitroglycerin safely. His solution was to mix nitroglycerin with an inert (inactive) absorbent material called *kieselguhr.* He called his invention dynamite.

Virtually overnight, Nobel's invention revolutionized the mining industry. Dynamite was five times as powerful as gunpowder, relatively easy to produce, and reasonably safe to use. For the first time in history, explosives began to be used for a productive purpose: the tearing apart of land in order to gain access to valuable minerals.

Nobel became extremely wealthy as a result of his discovery. But he is said to have been worried about the terrible potential for destruction that his invention had made possible. When he died, he directed that his fortune be used to create the Nobel Foundation, the purpose of which was to bring about lasting peace and advance technology. The Nobel Prizes in various fields of science are now the highest honors that scientists can earn.

Types of explosives

Explosives can be classified into one of four large categories: primary, low, high, and nuclear explosives.

Primary explosives. Primary explosives are generally used to set off other explosives. They are very sensitive to shock, heat, and electricity and, therefore, must be handled with great care. Two common examples are mercury fulminate and lead azide. Primary explosives also are known as initiating explosives, blasting caps, detonators, or primers.

Low explosives. Low explosives are characterized by the fact that they burn only at their surface. For example, when a cylinder of black gunpowder is ignited, it begins burning at one end of the cylinder and then continues to the other end. This process takes place very rapidly, however, and is complete in just a few thousandths of a second.

This property of slowed combustion is preferred in guns and artillery because too rapid an explosion could cause the weapon itself to blow up. A slower explosive has the effects of building up pressure to force a bullet or shell smoothly out of the weapon. Fireworks also are low explosives.

High explosives. High explosives are much more powerful than primary explosives. When they are detonated, all parts of the explosive blow up within a few millionths of a second. Some also are less likely than primary explosives to explode by accident. Examples of high explosives include ANFO (ammonium nitrate-fuel oil mixture), dynamite, nitroglycerin, PETN (pentaerythritol tetranitrate), picric acid, and TNT (trinitrotoluene). They provide the explosive force delivered by hand grenades, bombs, and artillery shells.

High explosives that are set off by heat are called primary explosives. High explosives that can be set off only by a detonator are called secondary explosives. When mixed with oil or wax, high explosives become like clay. These plastic explosives can be molded into various shapes to hide them or to direct explosions. In the 1970s and 1980s, plastic explosives became a favorite weapon of terrorists (people who use violence in order to force a government into granting their demands). Plastic explosives can even be pressed flat to fit into an ordinary mailing envelope for use as a "letter bomb."

Nuclear explosives. Research during World War II (1939–45) produced an entirely new kind of explosive: nuclear explosives. Nuclear explosives produce their explosive power not by chemical reactions, as with traditional explosives, but through nuclear reactions. In some types of nuclear reactions, large atomic nuclei are split (or fissioned) into two pieces

A nuclear explosion at sea. *(Reproduced by permission of The Stock Market.)*

with the release of huge amounts of energy. In a second type of nuclear reaction, small atomic nuclei are combined (or fused) to make a single large nucleus, again with the release of large amounts of energy.

These two kinds of nuclear explosives were first used as weapons at the end of World War II. The world's first atomic bomb, dropped on Hiroshima, Japan, in 1945, for example, was a fission weapon. The world's first hydrogen bomb, tested at Bikini Atoll in the Pacific Ocean in 1952, was a fusion weapon.

Since the end of World War II, a half-dozen nations in the world have continued to develop and build both fission and fusion weapons. Efforts also have been made to find peaceful uses for nuclear explosives, as in mining operations, although these efforts have not been fully successful.

Extrasolar planet

Extrasolar planets, or exoplanets, are planets that exist outside our solar system. These planets may orbit stars other than our Sun or move independently through interstellar space.

The existence of extrasolar planets has been suspected since the time of ancient Greece. For centuries, however, extrasolar planets existed only in theory because they are extremely difficult to observe directly. Planets shine only by reflected light from the stars they orbit. Because they are so far away from Earth, the faint light they reflect is lost in the scattered light from nearby stars.

The modern search

In the twentieth century, astronomers first tried to detect extrasolar planets by viewing stars that wobble. The motion of celestial bodies is affected by their closeness to other bodies. The gravitational force of one body will "pull" another to it as they pass close to each other. The orbits of the planets in our solar system have a direct effect on the motion of the Sun as it travels through the Milky Way galaxy. Seen from another part of the galaxy, the Sun would appear to wobble as moved along its path. This method only can be used for stars nearest to the Sun because the farther away the star is, the smaller its wobble.

A more accurate method for detecting extrasolar planets is the use of a spectroscope, a device that breaks down light into its component frequencies. A change in the color of a star (meaning a change in the wavelength of light it emits) would show that the star is moving toward or away from Earth. This movement might be the result of the gravitational pull of an orbiting planet.

In late 1995 and early 1996, three planet-sized objects were discovered. The first planet, discovered by Swiss astronomers Michel Mayor and Didier Queloz of the Geneva Observatory, orbits a star in the constellation Pegasus, about forty light-years away from Earth. The next two planets were discovered by American astronomers Geoffrey Marcy and R. Paul Butler. One is in the constellation Virgo and the other is in Ursa Major. By late 2000, astronomers had found evidence of more than 40 additional planets outside of our solar system.

In 1999, astronomers announced they had discovered the first planetary system outside of our own. They detected three planets circling the star Upsilon Andromedae, some 44 light-years away. Two of the three planets are at least twice as massive as Jupiter. The innermost lies extremely close to Upsilon Andromedae—about one-eighth the distance at which Mercury circles the Sun.

In early 2001, stunned astronomers disclosed they had found two more planetary systems in the universe. Each bears little resemblance to the other or to our solar system. In one, a star like our Sun is accompanied by a massive planet and an even larger object 17 times as massive as Jupiter. Astronomers believe this large object could be a dim, failed star or an astronomical object that simply has not been seen before. In the second system, two planets of a more standard size orbit a small star. However, their orbits around the star are perplexing: the inner planet goes around twice (it has an orbital period of 30 days) for each orbit of the outer planet (it has an orbital period of 61 days). These discoveries have left astronomers wondering just what a normal planetary system is in the universe.

[*See also* **Binary star; Solar system; Star**]

Eye

The eye is the organ of sight (vision) in humans and animals. The eye works by transforming light waves into visual images. Eighty percent of all information received by the human brain comes from the eyes. These organs are almost spherical in shape and are housed in the eye (orbital) sockets in the skull.

Sight begins when light waves enter the eye through the cornea (the transparent layer at the front of the eye), pass through the pupil (the

Words to Know

Aqueous humor: Clear liquid filling the small cavities between the cornea and the iris and between the iris and the lens.

Astigmatism: Vision disorder caused by an uneven curvature in the cornea (sometimes the lens), resulting in indistinct or slightly out-of-focus images.

Cataract: A clouding of the lens of the eye.

Choroid: Delicate membrane between the sclera and the retina.

Cones: Light-sensitive nerve cells of the retina that function chiefly in bright light and are sensitive to color.

Cornea: Protective lens covering the iris.

Farsightedness: Vision disorder caused by an eyeball that is too short or a lens that is too weak; objects far away are seen easily while those up close appear blurry.

Glaucoma: Serious vision disorder caused by a buildup of aqueous humor, resulting in pressure against the retina.

Iris: Colored portion around the pupil that regulates the amount of light entering the eye.

Lacrimal gland: Tear-producing gland that lies immediately above each eyeball at the outer corner of the eye socket.

Nearsightedness: Vision disorder caused by an eyeball that is too long or a lens that is too strong; objects up close are seen easily while those far away appear blurry.

Pupil: Adjustable opening in the center of the iris through which light enters the eye.

Retina: Photosensitive lining inside the eye.

Rods: Light-sensitive nerve cells of the retina that function chiefly in dim light.

Sclera: Tough, fibrous outer covering (the "white") of the eyeball.

Vitreous humor: Clear, gel-like substance inside the large cavity in back of the lens (the center of the eyeball).

opening in the center of the colored portion of the eye, called the iris), then through a clear lens behind the iris. The lens focuses light onto the retina, which functions like the film in a camera. Nerve cells in retinas, called rods and cones, convert light energy into electrical impulses. These impulses are then carried via the optic nerve to the brain where they are interpreted as images.

The human eyeball is about 0.9 inch (2.3 centimeters) in diameter and is not perfectly round, being slightly flattened in the front and back. The eye consists of three layers: the sclera (pronounced SKLIR-a), the choroid (pronounced KOR-oid), and the retina.

Sclera

The sclera, the outer fibrous layer, encases and protects the eyeball. The visible portion of the sclera is seen as the "white" of the eye. When that portion is irritated, the small blood vessels contained in the layer enlarge, producing a "bloodshot eye." In the center of the visible portion of the sclera is the cornea, which projects slightly forward. A delicate membrane, the conjunctiva, covers the cornea and visible portion of the sclera.

Choroid

The choroid is a thin membrane lying underneath the sclera. It is composed of a dense pigment and numerous blood vessels that nourish the internal tissues of the eye. At the front end of the choroid is the ciliary body. Running like a ring around the visible portion of the eye, the ciliary body connects the choroid with the iris. The ciliary body contains muscles that are connected by ligaments to the lens behind the iris. The iris is the visible portion of the choroid. It gives the eye its color, which varies depending on the amount of pigment present in the choroid. Dense pigment makes the iris brown, while little pigment makes the iris blue. If there is no pigment the iris is pink, as in the eye of a white rabbit. In bright light, muscles in the iris constrict the pupil, reducing the amount of light entering the eye. Conversely, the pupil dilates (enlarges) in dim light, increasing the amount of light entering. Extreme fear, head injuries, and certain drugs can also dilate the pupil.

Lens

The lens is a crystal-clear, flexible body that is biconvex (curving outward on both surfaces). The entire surface of the lens is smooth and shiny, contains no blood vessels, and is encased in an elastic membrane. The lens sits behind the iris and focuses light on the retina. In addition to holding the lens in place, the muscles of the ciliary body contract and re-lax, causing the lens to either fatten or become thin. As the shape of the lens changes, so does its focus.

Retina

The retina is the innermost layer of the eye. The retina is thin, delicate, sensory tissue composed of layers of light-sensitive nerve cells. The retina begins at the ciliary body (not at the front of the eye) and encircles the entire interior portion of the eye. Rods and cones, nerve cells of the retina, convert light first to chemical energy and then electrical energy. Rods function chiefly in dim light, allowing limited night vision: it

A cutaway anatomy of the human eye. *(Reproduced by permission of The Gale Group.)*

Vertical section of the right eye, shown from the nasal side

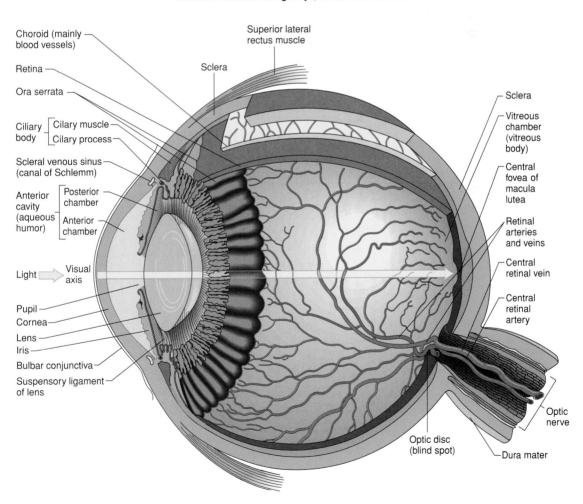

is with rods that we see the stars. Rods cannot detect color, but they are the first cells to detect movement. Cones function best in bright light and are sensitive to color. In each eye there are about 126 million rods and 6 million cones.

Fluids of the eye

Between the cornea and the iris and between the iris and the lens are two small cavities. These cavities are filled with a clear watery fluid known as aqueous humor. This fluid aids good vision by helping maintain eye shape, providing support for the internal structures, supplying nutrients to the lens and cornea, and disposing of the eyes' cellular waste.

The large cavity in back of the lens (the center of the eyeball) is filled with a clear gel-like substance called vitreous humor. Light passing through the lens on its way to the retina passes through the vitreous humor. The vitreous humor is 99 percent water and contains no cells. It helps to maintain the shape of the eye and support its internal components.

Other structures of the eye

Tears are produced by the lacrimal gland, which lies immediately above each eyeball at the outer corner of the eye socket. Tears flow through ducts from this gland to the area beneath the upper eyelid. Blinking spreads the tears across the cornea's outside surface, keeping it moist and clean. Tear fluid then either evaporates or drains from the inner corner of the eye into the nasal cavity.

Eyelashes, eyelids, and eyebrows all help to protect the eye from dust and dirt. Extending from the eye socket to the eyeball are six small muscles that contract and relax, allowing the eye to move in various directions.

Vision disorders

Farsightedness and nearsightedness are common vision disorders. They occur because of a defect in the shape of the eyeball or in the refractive power (ability to bend light rays) of the lens. In these cases, the image the eye perceives is distorted because the parallel rays of light that enter the eye do not fall perfectly on a tiny hollow (called the fovea) in the retina at the back of the eye. However, corrective eyeglasses can easily overcome these disorders.

With farsightedness, objects far away are seen easily while those up close appear blurry. The cause may be that the eyeball is too short or the lens is too weak.

With nearsightedness, objects up close are seen easily while those far away appear blurry. The cause may be that the eyeball is too long or the lens is too strong.

Astigmatism, another common vision disorder, can occur in combination with farsightedness or nearsightedness. Individuals with astigmatism see indistinct or slightly out-of-focus images. The condition is brought about by an uneven curvature in the cornea (sometimes the lens). As a result, some light rays entering the eye focus on the fovea while others focus in front or behind it. Like farsightedness and nearsightedness, astigmatism can be corrected with eyeglasses or contact lenses.

A cataract is the clouding of the lens, which alters the amount of light entering the eye. The most common cataracts are senile cataracts, a result of aging that occurs in almost all people over 65 years old. These cataracts grow slowly over months or years, cause no pain, usually affect both eyes, and gradually reduce vision. If not treated, they eventually cause blindness. Clear vision can be restored by a relatively simple surgical procedure in which the entire lens is removed and an artificial lens is implanted.

Glaucoma is a serious vision disorder caused by a buildup of aqueous humor, which is prevented for some reason from properly draining. The excessive amount of fluid causes pressure against the retina, affecting vision. Long-term diseases like diabetes or a malfunctioning thyroid gland can bring about glaucoma. If left untreated, glaucoma will result in permanent blindness. The condition can be controlled with drugs that either increase the outflow of aqueous humor or decrease its production.

[*See also* **Radial keratotomy**]

F

Fault

A fault is a crack or fracture in Earth's crust caused by the movement of landmasses, called plates, on either side of the fault line. Faults are found either at the surface (fault surface) or underground (fault plane). Most earthquakes occur along fault lines. The principle types of faults are: normal, reverse, thrust, and slip-strike.

Normal faults form when two plates are under tension and are being pulled or stretched apart. When this occurs, Earth's crust thins and one plate rises or drops against the other. More than 200 million years ago, North America and Africa were one huge landmass. Plates on either side of a massive fault line ruptured and began drifting apart. Oceanic waters, now known as the Atlantic Ocean, surged into the valley between, and two separate continents were born.

In contrast, reverse faults form from compression: two plates are being pushed into one another. The compression forces one plate up and over the other. (See photo on page 856.)

Thrust faults are low-angled reverse faults. Such faults are noteworthy because they produce great horizontal movement. Thrust faults have created most of the great mountain chains found around the world.

Strike-slip faults move horizontally along the fault line. The edge of one plate grinds against the edge of the other as it slips sideways. Most of these movements are quiet and continuous. Sometimes, however, plates shift with a sudden lurch, causing earthquakes. Such is the case with the San Andreas Fault in the western United States where the North American and Pacific plates meet. Land west of this fault is edging northwest.

[*See also* **Earthquake; Geologic map; Plate tectonics**]

The San Andreas Fault in California. See entry on page 855. *(Reproduced by permission of JLM Visuals.)*

Felines

Felines, generally known as cats, are mammals in the family Felidae of the order Carnivora. Cats are the most carnivorous of all meat-eating animals. The predatory instinct in wild cats can be seen in the domestic cats, for even well-fed domestic cats will hunt mice and birds. Members of the cat family occur naturally in all parts of the world, except Australia and Antarctica.

The cat family includes both big cats (lions, tigers, and leopards) and small cats (lynx, servals, and ocelots). Small cats purr but do not roar, whereas big cats roar but do not purr. The reason for this difference is that the tongue muscles of large cats are attached to a pliable cartilage at the base of the tongue, which allows roaring. In contrast, the tongue muscles of small cats are attached to the hyoid bone, which allows purring, but not roaring.

Most cats have 30 teeth, including large canine and carnassial teeth, and few cheek teeth. This arrangement is well suited to crushing bones and tearing, cutting, and gripping prey. Cats' jaws are limited to vertical movements, and their chewing action is aided by sharp projections on the tongue (papillae) that grip and manipulate food.

Evolution and history

Modern cats first appeared about 25 million years ago. One of the earliest members of the family was the saber-toothed tiger, which lived in Europe, Asia, Africa, and North America. This cat had long, upper canine teeth for stabbing its prey. The remains of saber-toothed tigers have been found to be as recent as 13,000 years old.

Cats were first domesticated in ancient Egypt about 5,000 years ago. The Egyptians used cats to protect grain supplies from rodents. They also worshiped cats and mummified large numbers of them along with their owners. Since that time, the domestic cat has spread throughout Europe, Asia, Africa, and the Americas. Breeding of cats into specific pedigrees did not begin, however, until the middle of the nineteenth century.

Senses

Cats have excellent binocular (involving the use of both eyes) eyesight, which allows them to judge distances. Cats cannot see in complete darkness, but need at least dim light in order to distinguish objects at night. Cats' eyes have a special reflective layer behind the retina. This layer allows light that has not been absorbed on its first pass through the retina to stimulate the retina a second time, providing good vision in poor light. It is this layer that makes cats' eyes appear to glow in the dark when a light flashes on them.

The senses of smell and taste in cats are closely connected, as they are in all mammals. Distinctive to cats is the absence of response to sweets, and cats avoid foods that taste sweet. The taste buds of cats are located along the front and side edges of their tongues. Their vomeronasal organ, also known as Jacobson's organ, is a saclike structure located in the roof of the mouth. This organ is believed to be involved in sensing chemical messages associated with sexual activity. When a male cat smells a female's urine, he may wrinkle his nose and curl back his upper lip in a gesture known as flehmening. He also will raise his head and bare his teeth.

Cats have the ability to hear high-frequency sounds that humans are unable to hear. This ability is particularly helpful when cats are stalking prey such as mice, since the cats can detect the high-frequency sounds

Words to Know

Digitigrade posture: A manner of walking on the toes, as cats and dogs do, as opposed to walking on the ball of the feet, as humans do.

Flehmening: A gesture of cats that involves curling the lips upwards, baring the teeth, wrinkling the nose, and raising the head.

Righting reflex: The ability of a cat to land on all fours after a fall.

Vomeronasal organ: A pouchlike structure on the roof of a cat's mouth whose purpose is probably related to sexual behavior in cats.

emitted by these rodents. The external ears of cats are flexible and can turn as much as 180 degrees to locate sounds precisely.

A cat's whiskers have a sensory function, helping it avoid objects in its path in the dimmest light. If a cat passes an object that touches its whiskers, it will blink, thus protecting its eyes from possible injury. Besides the long cheek whiskers, cats have thicker whiskers above their eyes. Cats use their nose to determine the temperature, as well as the smell, of food. The hairless paw pads of cats are an important source of tactile (touch) information gained from investigating objects with their paws.

Behavior

In the wild, most forest-living members of the cat family tend to be solitary hunters. Some species of cats live in pairs, while others, such as lions, live in family groups. Cats engage in daily grooming, which not only keeps their fur in good condition, but also helps them regulate their body temperature and keeps their coat waterproof.

Cats need a great deal of sleep, which is consistent with the large amounts of energy they expend during their hunting periods. They sleep on-and-off almost two-thirds of the day. Because of a slight fall in their body temperatures when they sleep, they look for warm, sunny spots for dozing.

Cats are excellent climbers, great jumpers, and have remarkable balance. Except for the cheetah, cats have retractable claws that are curved, sharp, and sheathed. The claws are particularly useful to cats when climbing trees. The bones of their feet (like those of dogs) are arranged in a digitigrade posture, meaning that only their toes make contact with the ground, which increases their speed of running. Cats have the remarkable ability—called the righting reflex—to right themselves during a fall. The righting reflex causes first a cat's head, then the rest of its body, to turn toward the ground as it falls. Thus, the cat lands on all four feet.

Cats follow a well-defined hunting sequence that begins with the sighting or smelling of prey. The hunting skills that cats display are in some aspects instinctual and in others learned. Cats begin learning how to hunt through the play they engage in when they are young. Mother cats are involved in teaching hunting skills to their young, first by bringing back dead prey, later by bringing back immobilized (injured) prey, allowing young cats to kill the prey themselves. Still later, the mother cat will take the young cat on a stalking and killing mission so that it learns how to successfully hunt. Cats that do not have the opportunity to learn to hunt from their mothers do not become good hunters.

Cats are territorial, marking their territory by spraying the boundaries with urine. Cats also scratch and rub against fixed objects to mark their territory. Within a male territorial boundary, there may be several female territories. During mating, the male seeks out or is lured to nearby females that are ready to breed. Females may vocalize loudly when they are ready to mate, thus attracting males. Frequent scenting and rubbing against trees also help the male cat know the female is ready to mate. In cats, frequent sexual contact is important to insure successful ovulation (production of egg cells), which is brought on during sexual intercourse.

The gestation (pregnancy) period in cats depends upon their body size. Domestic cats have a gestation period of about 60 days, and an average litter size of about four kittens. In the wild, gestation ranges from slightly less than 60 days for the smaller species of cats to about 115 days for large cats, such as lions. The number in the litter varies from one to seven; the body size of the cat does not seem to be the factor that determines litter size. It may have more to do with the availability of food and the survival rate in the area the cat inhabits. With the exception of lions, the care and training of the young are left to the mother. Nursing continues until the cubs or kittens are gradually weaned and learn to eat meat.

Species of big cats

There are eight species of big cats, including the lion, tiger, leopard, cheetah, jaguar, snow leopard, clouded leopard, and cougar. The onza is a possible undescribed species or subspecies from Mexico that resembles the cougar and has been seen only rarely. Sightings of the onza go back to the time of the Spanish conquest of Mexico in 1521. The first specimen of this cat was collected only in 1986 by a Mexican rancher, who shot what he thought was a puma (mountain lion).

The lion.   Lions were once distributed over much of Europe, Asia, and Africa. Today, lions are found only in sub-Saharan Africa and in the Gir Forest, a wildlife sanctuary in India. Lions prefer open grasslands to forest, but also are found in the Kalahari Desert. Adult male lions weigh between 300 and 500 pounds (135 and 225 kilograms), while the female weighs about 300 pounds (135 kilograms). Lions are a light tawny color with black markings on the abdomen, legs, ears, and mane. Lions live up to 15 years, reaching sexual maturity in their third year. Male lions have been observed to kill cubs that they have not fathered.

Lions are the most social of the cats, living in family groups called prides, consisting of four to twelve related adult females, their young, and one to six adult males. The size of the pride usually reflects the amount of available food. Where prey is abundant, lion prides tend to be larger, making them better able to protect their kills from hyenas and other scavengers. Most lion kills are made by the females. Males defend the pride's territory, which may range from 8 square miles (20 square kilometers) to more than 150 square miles (400 square kilometers).

The tiger.   The tiger is the largest member of the cat family, with males weighing from 400 to 600 pounds (180 to 275 kilograms) and females from 300 to 350 pounds (135 to 160 kilograms). Tigers range from a pale yellow to a reddish-orange color (depending on habitat), with characteristic vertical stripes. Tigers live in habitats with a dense vegetation cover, commonly forests and swamps in India, Southeast Asia, China, and Indonesia. A century ago, tigers inhabited areas as far north as Siberia, all of India and Southeast Asia, and regions along the eastern part of China. Today, all eight subspecies of tigers are endangered.

The tiger lives a solitary life and systematically protects its territory by marking its boundaries with urine, feces, glandular secretions, and scrape marks on trees. Tigers are solitary nocturnal (night-time) hunters, approaching their prey stealthily in a semicrouching position. When close enough, the tiger makes a sudden rush for the prey, attacking from the side or the rear. The prey is seized by the shoulder or neck with the tiger's front paws and jaws, while keeping its hind feet on the ground. The tiger applies a throat bite that usually suffocates its victim, which it carries into cover and consumes.

The leopard.   Male leopards weigh about 200 pounds (90 kilograms), with females weighing about half that amount. Leopards are found in sub-

Saharan Africa, India, and Southeast Asia. Some small populations of leopards are still found in Arabia and North Africa. Leopards have a distinctive coloring, black spots over a pale brown coat. Their habitats include rain forests, dry savanna grasslands, and cold mountainous areas.

Leopards feed on a variety of small prey, usually hunting at night by ambush. Leopards use trees as resting places and frequently drag their catches up into trees to eat them. The number of leopards is declining worldwide due to hunting and habitat destruction from human population pressures.

The cheetah. Cheetahs are the fastest animals on land, reaching speeds of up to 70 miles per hour (110 kilometers per hour). Over short distances, a cheetah can outrun any other animal. Cheetahs resemble leopards in that they have a black-spotted pattern over a tawny coat, but are distinguished by large black "tear" stripes under their eyes, a long, lithe body, and a relatively small head. Cheetahs are the only members of the cat family that do not have retractable claws. Cheetahs are solitary hunters, feeding on gazelles and impalas. They hunt mainly in the morning and early afternoon, when other large cats are usually sleeping, thereby enabling them to share hunting areas with other carnivores. Cheetahs are found in north and east Africa and along the eastern regions of southern Africa, as well as in selected areas of the Middle East and southern Asia. There is

A Siberian tiger. *(Reproduced by permission of Field Mark Publications.)*

a considerable trade in cheetah skins, and hunting, together with the loss of habitat, threatens their survival in the wild.

Other big cats.   Among other large cats are the jaguar, the snow leopard, and the clouded leopard. These three cats inhabit a forest wilderness, and all are solitary and nocturnal. Jaguars are found in Central and South America, while the snow leopard is found in Central Asia, and the clouded leopard in Southeast Asia. The average weight of the jaguar is about 125 pounds (55 kilograms). The snow leopard is found in the Himalayas at elevations from 9,000 feet (2,750 meters) to nearly 20,000 feet (6,000 meters). The clouded leopard and the snow leopard have a rigid hyoid bone in their throats which prevents them from roaring. The black panther is a black form of the jaguar. Its spots are visible within its black coat. The cougar, also known as the puma or mountain lion, is about the size of a leopard and ranges from western Canada to Argentina. The cougar is found in mountains, plains, deserts, and forests, and preys on deer and other medium-sized herbivores (plant eaters).

The small wild cats

The small wild cats, such as the lynx and the bobcat, are considered to be the ancestors of the domestic cat. They are native to most areas of

A Canadian lynx. (Reproduced by permission of The Stock Market.)

the world, except Australia and Antarctica. Other features small wild cats share with domestic cats include the inability to roar, retractable claws, and a hairless strip along the front of their noses. Small wild cats include the European wild cat; the African wild cat; the sand cat, of the Sahara; the African tiger cat, of tropical forests; the golden cat; and Pallas' cat, of central Asia.

Asian medium-sized cats include the African serval and the caracal or desert lynx of the Sahara. Medium-sized cats of the Americas include the ocelot of South and Central America and the jaguarundi.

The wildcat or bobcat of North America is colored to blend in with the rocky, densely vegetated background of its habitat. Bobcats rely more on hearing than on sight to catch their prey, and the tufts on their ears are thought to improve their hearing. The lynx lives in cold climates and has long legs, to make trekking through deep snow easier, and foot pads covered with fur, to protect them while walking in snow. The Canada lynx differs from the common lynx in that it is larger, has longer hair, and does not have a spotted coat.

The other 26 species of small wild cats live mainly in forests and feed on small prey, such as rodents, hares, lizards, small deer, fish, snakes, squirrels, insects, and birds. Most species have a spotted or striped coat and usually have a rounded head. Small wild cats are either solitary or form groups, depending on the abundance of the food supply. Some species, such as the ocelot, are hunted for their spotted skin and are in danger of becoming extinct.

Domestic cats

The breeding of domestic cats involves basic principles of heredity, with consideration of dominant and recessive (suppressed) traits. It was in England that cat breeding first became serious enough that so-called "purebred" cats were displayed at cat shows. In England a system of authenticating a cat's genetic lineage was also begun by issuing a pedigree certificate. Special associations were established to regulate the cat pedigrees and to sponsor the cat shows.

Cat breeds can be categorized as either long-haired breeds or short-haired breeds. Within each group, head and ear shape and size, body formation, hair color and length, eye color and shape, and special markings like stripes and color variations on the feet, tail, face, and neck distinguish the breeds from one another.

More than 100 different breeds of cats are recognized around the world, subdivided into five broad groups. One group includes Persian longhairs; another, the rest of the long-haired cats; a third, the British short-haired cats; a fourth, the American short-haired cats; and a fifth, the Oriental short-haired cats.

The Persian cat, highly prized among cat fanciers, has a round body, face, eyes, and head with a short nose and legs. Its fur is long and woolly, and its tail is fluffy and bushy. Persians vary from black to white, cream, blue, red, blue-cream, cameo, tortoiseshell, smoke, silver, tabby, calico, pewter, chocolate, and lilac. Other popular long-haired cats include the Balinese, the ragdoll, the Turkish angora, and the Maine coon cat. Among the short-haired cats, the Manx, British shorthair, American short-hair, Abyssinian, Burmese, and Siamese are popular. One breed is hairless: the sphynx, bred from a mutant kitten in 1966, does not even have whiskers.

The domestic cat is rivaled only by the dog as a household pet, and in recent years has outnumbered the dog as an urban pet. Cats are more self-sufficient than dogs in that they self-groom, need little if any training to use the litter box, and don't have to be walked. Cats are generally quiet and aloof, but will display affection to their owners. They have the reputation of being fussy eaters, but will usually adapt quickly to a particular brand of cat food.

Fermentation

In its broadest sense, fermentation refers to any process by which large organic molecules are broken down to simpler molecules as the result of the action of microorganisms (organisms so small they can be seen only with the aid of a microscope). The most familiar type of fermentation is the process by which sugars and starches are converted to alcohol by enzymes in yeasts. (Enzymes are chemicals that act as catalysts, which spark reactions.) To distinguish this reaction from other kinds of fermentation, the process is sometimes known as alcoholic or ethanolic fermentation.

History

Ethanolic fermentation was one of the first chemical reactions observed by humans. In nature, various types of food "go bad" as a result of bacterial action. Early in history, humans discovered that this kind of change could result in the formation of products that were actually enjoyable to consume. The "spoilage" (fermentation) of fruit juices, for example, resulted in the formation of primitive forms of wine.

Words to Know

Enzyme: An organic compound that speeds up the rate of chemical reactions in living organisms.

Ferment: An early term used to describe the substances we now know as enzymes.

Gasohol: A synthetic fuel consisting of a mixture of about 90 percent gasoline and 10 percent alcohol.

Vitalism: The concept that compounds found within living organisms are somehow essentially different from those found in nonliving objects.

Wastewater: Water that carries away the waste products of personal, municipal, and industrial operations.

Wild yeast: A naturally occurring yeast.

The mechanism by which fermentation occurs was the subject of extensive debate in the early 1800s. It was a key issue among those arguing over the concept of vitalism, the notion that living organisms are in some way essentially different from nonliving objects. One aspect in this debate centered on the role of so-called "ferments" in the conversion of sugars and starches to alcohol. Vitalists argued that ferments (what we now know as enzymes) are linked to a living cell. Destroy a cell, they said, and ferments can no longer cause fermentation.

A crucial experiment on this issue was carried out in 1896 by the German chemist Eduard Buchner (1860–1917). Buchner ground up a group of cells with sand until they were totally destroyed. He then extracted the liquid that remained and added it to a sugar solution. His assumption was that fermentation could no longer occur since the cells that had held the ferments were dead. Thus, they no longer carried the "life-force" needed to bring about fermentation. He was amazed to discover that the cell-free liquid did indeed cause fermentation. It was obvious that the ferments themselves, distinct from any living organism, could cause fermentation.

Theory

The chemical reaction that occurs in fermentation can be described quite easily. Starch is converted to simple sugars such as sucrose and glucose. Those sugars are then converted to alcohol (ethyl alcohol) and carbon dioxide:

$$\text{starch} \rightarrow \frac{\text{simple sugars}}{\text{(sucrose + glucose)}} \rightarrow \text{alcohol + carbon dioxide}$$

This description does not really provide an idea as to how complex the fermentation process really is. During the 1930s, two German biochemists, Gustav Embden (1874–1933) and Otto Meyerhof (1884–1951), worked out the sequence of reactions by which glucose ferments. Embden and Meyerhof found that it required a sequence of 12 reactions in order to accomplish the "simple" change from glucose to ethyl alcohol and carbon dioxide. A number of enzymes are needed to carry out this sequence of reactions, the most important of which is zymase, found in yeast cells. These enzymes are sensitive to environmental conditions in which they live. When the concentration of alcohol in a liquid reaches about 14 percent, they are inactivated. For this reason, no fermentation product (such as wine) can have an alcoholic concentration of more than about 14 percent.

Uses

The alcoholic beverages that can be produced by fermentation vary widely, depending primarily on two factors, the plant that is fermented and the enzymes used for fermentation. Human societies use, of course, the materials that are available to them. Thus, various peoples have used grapes, berries, corn, rice, wheat, honey, potatoes, barley, hops, cactus juice, cassava roots, and other plant materials for fermentation. The products of such reactions are various forms of beer, wine, or distilled liquors, which may be given specific names depending on the source from which they come. In Japan, for example, rice wine is known as *sake.* Wine prepared from honey is known as mead. Beer is the fermentation product of barley, hops, and/or malt sugar.

Early in human history, people used naturally occurring yeasts for fermentation. The products of such reactions depended on whatever enzymes might occur in those "wild" yeasts. Today, wine-makers are able to select from a variety of specially cultured (grown) yeasts that control the precise direction that fermentation will take.

Ethyl alcohol is not the only useful product of fermentation. The carbon dioxide generated during fermentation is also an important component of many baked goods. When the batter for bread is mixed, for example, a small amount of sugar and yeast are added. During the rising period, sugar is fermented by enzymes in the yeast, with the formation of carbon dioxide gas. The carbon dioxide gives the batter bulkiness and texture that would be lacking without the fermentation process.

Fermentation has a number of commercial applications beyond those described thus far. Many occur in the food preparation and processing industry. A variety of bacteria are used in the production of olives, cucumber pickles, and sauerkraut from raw olives, cucumbers, and cabbage, respectively. The selection of exactly the right bacteria and the right conditions (for example, acidity and salt concentration) is an art in producing food products with exactly the desired flavors. An interesting line of research in the food sciences is aimed at the production of edible food products by the fermentation of petroleum.

In some cases, antibiotics and other drugs can be prepared by fermentation if no other commercially efficient method is available. For example, the important drug cortisone can be prepared by the fermentation of a plant steroid known as diosgenin. The enzymes used in the reaction are provided by the mold *Rhizopus nigricans.*

One of the most successful commercial applications of fermentation has been the production of ethyl alcohol for use in gasohol. Gasohol is a mixture of about 90 percent gasoline and 10 percent alcohol. The alcohol needed for this product can be obtained from the fermentation of agricultural and municipal wastes. The use of gasohol provides a promising method for using renewable resources (plant material) to extend the availability of a nonrenewable resource (gasoline).

Another application of the fermentation process is in the treatment of wastewater. In the activated sludge process, aerobic bacteria (bacteria that can live without oxygen) are used to ferment organic material in wastewater. Solid wastes are converted to carbon dioxide, water, and mineral salts.

[*See also* **Alcohol; Bacteria; Brewing; Carbon dioxide; Enzyme; Yeast**]

Fertilization

Fertilization is the process by which the nucleus of a sperm (a male reproductive cell) fuses (combines) with the nucleus of an egg (a female reproductive cell; also called an ovum). Fertilization occurs somewhat differently in plants and animals. In flowering plants, two sperm cells are involved in the process of fertilization. The first sperm cell combines with an egg cell, while the second sperm cell combines with two nuclei present in the ovule (the structure that eventually becomes the seed). The structure formed in the second fertilization eventually forms a storage site for nutrients needed by the fertilized egg cell.

A fertilized egg cell is known as a zygote. Once formed, the zygote undergoes continuous cell division that eventually produces a new multicellular organism.

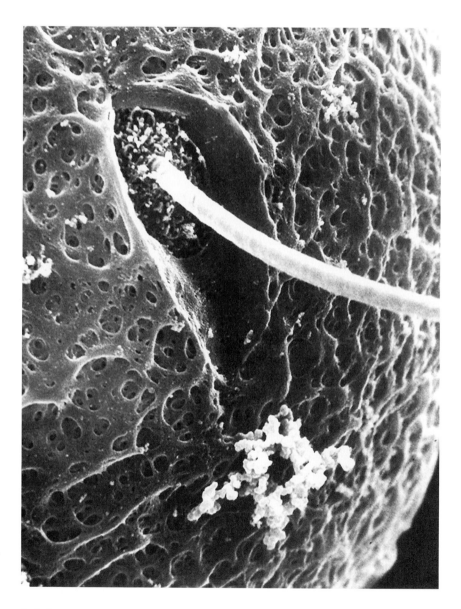

Sperm penetrating a hamster egg cell. *(Reproduced by permission of Photo Researchers, Inc.)*

Fertilization in humans

In humans, fertilization occurs in the fallopian tubes of the female reproductive tract. It takes place within hours following sexual intercourse. Approximately 300 million sperm are released into a female's vagina during intercourse. However, only one of these sperm can actually fertilize the single female egg cell (also called an ovum). The successful sperm cell must enter the uterus and swim up the fallopian tube to meet the egg cell. There it passes through the thick coating surrounding the egg. This coating is known as the zona pellucida.

The head of the sperm cell contains enzymes (certain types of chemicals) that break through the zona pellucida and make it possible for the sperm to penetrate into the egg. Once the head of the sperm is inside the egg, the tail of the sperm falls off. The outside of the egg then thickens to prevent another sperm from entering.

In humans, a number of variables affect whether or not fertilization occurs following intercourse. One factor is a woman's ovulatory cycle. The ovulatory cycle is the series of events that bring about the ripening of an egg and its release from the ovaries. Human eggs can be fertilized for only a few days after ovulation, which usually occurs only once every 28 days.

Fertilization in other species

Nearly all forms of terrestrial (land) animals use some form of internal fertilization similar to that in humans. External fertilization, however, is more common among aquatic animals. It is simple enough for aquatic animals simply to dump their sperm and eggs into the water and let currents mix the two kinds of cells with each other.

Reproduction of the sea urchin is a typical example of external fertilization among aquatic animals. A male sea urchin releases several billion sperm into the water. These sperm then swim towards eggs released in the same area. Fertilization occurs within seconds when sperm come into contact and fuse with eggs.

External fertilization in animals

Although it does not occur naturally in animals very often, external fertilization is also a possibility. In the case of humans, for example, some form of external fertilization may be necessary when a male and female wish to have a child but one or the other is biologically incapable of contributing to the normal process of internal fertilization.

An example is the process known as in vitro fertilization. The expression in vitro means "in glass," that is, in a glass test tube or petri dish.

The term is used in contrast to in vivo fertilization, where in vivo means "in a living organism."

During in vitro fertilization, eggs are removed surgically from a female's reproductive tract. Those eggs then can be fertilized by sperm that has been taken from a male and then stored in a test tube or petri dish. After the fertilized eggs have divided twice, they are reintroduced into the female's body. If all goes well, the embryo and fetus develop, eventually resulting in a normal birth.

In vitro fertilization has been performed successfully on a variety of domestic animals since the 1950s. In 1978, the first human birth following in vitro fertilization occurred in England. Since that time, the procedure has become a routine treatment for infertile couples who wish to have children.

[*See also* **Reproduction; Reproductive system**]

Fiber optics

Optical fiber is a very thin strand of glass or plastic capable of transmitting light from one point to another. Since the late 1950s, optical fibers have emerged as revolutionary tools in the fields of medicine and telecommunications. These fibers can transmit light pulses containing data up to 13,000 miles (20,900 kilometers), and do so without significant distortion. The fibers also permit the "piping" of light into the body, allowing doctors to see and diagnose conditions without the use of surgery. Optical fibers operate by continuously reflecting light (and images) down the length of the glass core.

Production of optical fibers

Optical fibers are manufactured in a multistep process: the inner wall of a silica glass tube is coated with 100 or more successive thin layers of purer glass. The tube is then heated to 3,632°F (2,000°C) and stretched into a strand of thin, flexible fiber. The result is a clad fiber, approximately 0.0005 inch (0.0013 centimeter) in diameter. By comparison, a human hair measures 0.002 inch (0.005 centimeter).

The use of fiber optics

Optical fibers were first used in medicine in the late 1950s when fiber optic bundles were added to endoscopes (optical instruments used to examine the inside of hollow organs or tubes in the body). The new endoscope, called a fiberscope, consisted of two bundles of fibers. One bundle carried light down to the area to be studied, while the other carried a color image of the area back to the physician. Because of its small size and flexibility, the fiberscope can view many areas inside the body, such as veins, arteries, the digestive system, and the heart.

The field of telecommunications first used optical fibers in 1966. Today a telephone conversation can be carried over optical fibers by a method called digital transmission. In this method, sound waves are converted into electrical signals, each of which is then assigned a digital code of 1 or 0. The light carries the digitally encoded information by emitting a series of pulses: a 1 would be represented by a light pulse, while a 0 would be represented by the absence of a pulse. At the receiving end, the process is reversed: light pulses are converted back into electronic data, which are then converted back into sound waves.

By using digital transmission, telecommunications systems carry more information farther over a smaller cable system than its copper wire predecessor. A typical copper bundle measuring 3 inches (7.6 centimeters) in diameter can be replaced by a 0.25-inch (0.64-centimeter) wide optical fiber carrying the same amount of data. This improvement be-

A bundle of optical fibers. (Reproduced by permission of Photo Researchers, Inc.)

comes important where telephone cables must be placed underground in limited space.

The tiny size of optical fibers also brings about a significant reduction in the weight of a particular system. Replacing copper aircraft instrument wiring can save up to 1,000 pounds (454 kilograms), allowing for more economical fuel consumption. Optical fibers are also immune to electromagnetic interference, making them roughly 100 times more accurate than copper. They typically allow only 1 error in 100 million bits of data transmitted.

Optical fibers and television

Optical fibers have proven to be an ideal method of transmitting high-definition television (HDTV) signals. Because its transmission contains twice as much information as those of conventional television, HDTV features much greater clarity and definition in its picture. However, standard television technology cannot transmit so much information at once. Using optical fibers, the HDTV signal can be transmitted as a digital light-pulse, providing a near-flawless image. HDTV reproduction is far superior to broadcast transmission, just as music from a digital compact disc is superior to that broadcast over FM radio.

Filtration

Filtration is the process by which solid materials are removed from a fluid mixture, either a gas or liquid mixture. Anyone who has ever prepared foods in a kitchen has probably seen one of the simplest forms of filtration. After cooking pasta, for example, the contents of the pot may be poured through a colander or sieve. (A colander looks like a big pot with holes in it.) The pasta is captured in the colander, and the wastewater runs through holes and is usually thrown away.

Beginning science students often use filtration, too. The solid material (precipitate) formed in a chemical reaction can be separated from the liquid part of a mixture by passing the mixture through a filter paper. The filter paper traps solid particles in the mixture, while a clear solution passes through the filter, down the funnel, and into a receiving container.

Filtration is carried out for one of two general purposes: in order to capture the solid material suspended in the fluid or in order to clarify the

Words to Know

Cake filter: A type of filter on which solid materials removed from a suspension collect in a quantity that can be physically removed.

Clarification: The process by which unwanted solid materials are removed from a suspension in order to produce a very clear liquid.

Diatomaceous earth: A finely divided rocklike material obtained from the decay of tiny marine organisms known as diatoms.

Fluid: A gas or liquid.

Precipitate: A solid material that is formed by some physical or chemical process within a fluid.

Suspension: A temporary mixture of a solid in a gas or liquid from which the solid will eventually settle out.

fluid in which the solid is suspended. The general principle is the same in either case, although the specific filtration system employed may differ depending on which of these objectives is intended.

In the world outside of chemistry laboratories, a very great variety of filtration systems are available. These systems can be categorized according to the fluids on which they operate (gaseous or liquid) and the driving force that moves fluids through them (gravity, vacuum, or pressure). They also can be subdivided depending on the type of material used as a filter.

Liquid filtration

Liquid filtration occurs when a suspension of a solid in a liquid passes through a filter. That process takes place when the liquid is pulled through the filter by gravitational force (as in the laboratory example mentioned above) or is forced through the filter by some pressure applied to the mixture. In some filtration systems, a vacuum is maintained in the receiving container. Then normal atmospheric pressure has a greater effect in forcing the mixture through the filter.

One of the most familiar gravity filters in the industrial world is that used for the purification of water. A water filtration system generally makes use of a thick layer of granular materials, such as sand, gravel, and charcoal. Such a filter may be many feet thick and is known, therefore, as a deep-bed filter. When impure water passes through such a filter, suspended solids are removed, allowing relatively pure water to be collected at the bottom of the filter. In commercial water purification plants, the deep-bed filter may be modified to remove other impurities. For example, dissolved gases that add unpleasant odors and taste to the water may be removed if activated carbon (finely divided charcoal) is included in the filter. The gases responsible for offensive odor and taste are absorbed on particles of charcoal, leaving behind fluid that is nearly odorless and tasteless.

The filtration of smaller volumes of solution than those normally encountered in a water filtration plant is often accomplished by means of positive pressure systems. A positive pressure system is one in which the fluid to be filtered is forced through a filtering medium by an external pressure. A number of variations on this concept are commercially available. For example, in one type of apparatus, the fluid to be filtered is introduced under pressure at one end of a horizontal tank and then forced through a series of vertical plates covered with thin filtering cloths. As the fluid passes through these filters, solids are removed and collect on the surface of the cloths. The material that builds up on the filters is known as a cake, and the filters themselves are sometimes called cake filters.

In another type of pressure filter a series of filter plates is arranged one above the other in a cylindrical tank. Liquid is pumped into the tank under pressure, which forces it downward through the filters. Again, solids suspended in the liquid collect on the filters while the clear liquid passes out of the tank through a drain pipe in the center of the unit.

A variety of vacuum filters also have been designed. In a vacuum filter, the liquid to be separated is poured onto a filtering medium and a vacuum is created below the medium. Atmospheric pressure above the filter then forces the liquid through the medium with suspended solids collecting on the filter and the clear liquid passing through.

Probably the most common variation of the vacuum filter is the continuous rotary vacuum filter. In this device, a drum with a perforated surface rotates on a horizontal axis. A cloth covering the drum acts as the filter. The lower part of the drum is submerged in the liquid to be separated and a vacuum is maintained within the drum. As the drum rotates, it passes through the liquid; atmospheric pressure then forces liquid into its interior. Solids suspended in the liquid are removed by the filter and collect as a cake on the outside of the drum. Because the cake can constantly be removed by a stream of water, the drum can continue to rotate and filter the suspension in the pan below it.

Clarifying filters

The filters described thus far are used most commonly to collect a solid material suspended in a liquid. Clarifying filters, on the other hand, are designed to collect a liquid that is as free from solid impurities as possible. The most important feature of a clarifying filter, then, is the filter itself. It must be constructed in such a way as to remove the very smallest particles suspended in the liquid. A number of systems have been developed to achieve this objective. Some rely on the use of wires or fibers spaced very closely together. Others make use of finely powdered materials, such as diatomaceous earth.

Gas filtration

Examples of gas filtration are common in everyday life. For example, every time a vacuum cleaner runs, it passes a stream of dust-filled air through a filtering bag inside the machine. Solid particles are trapped within the bag, while clean air passes out through the machine.

The removal of solid particles from air and other gases is a common problem in society. Today, air conditioning and heating systems not only change the temperature of a room, but also remove dust, pollen, and other particles that may cause respiratory problems for humans.

The cleansing of waste gases is also a significant problem for many industrial operations. Gases discharged from coal- and oil-burning power plants, for example, usually contain solid particles that cause air pollution and acid rain. One way to remove these particles is to pass them through a filtering system that physically collects the particles leaving a clean (or cleaner) effluent gas.

[*See also* **Hydrologic cycle; Waste management**]

Fish

Ocean saltwater covers more than three-quarters of Earth's surface; lakes, rivers, streams, ponds, canals, swamps, marshes, and other forms of freshwater cover vast expanses of the planet's surface as well. One of the most successful groups of animals that have evolved to fill all these habitats are fish.

There are two types of fish: a small group with skeletons made of cartilage (a bonelike elastic tissue less rigid than true bone) and an enormous group with skeletons made of bone (like that found in humans).

Cartilaginous fish include the sharks, skates, rays, and dogfish. The remainder—more than 25,000 species (more than all other species of vertebrates combined)—are known as bony fish.

All fish are cold-blooded, meaning they do not have a constant body temperature but take on the temperature of the surrounding water. The majority of fish species have bodies that are streamlined; their bodies are covered with tiny, smooth scales that offer no resistance to a fish's movement through water. The scales themselves are covered with a slimy coating that further reduces friction. Additionally, a fish's external appendages (fins) have been reduced to produce minimal resistance to the water as they propel the fish through it. Fins fall into two categories: vertical fins, which occur individually, and paired fins. Examples of the vertical fins are a dorsal fin that runs down the middle of a fish's back and the anal fin that runs along its underside. Examples of paired fins are those that appear on either side of a fish's upper body, below and behind its eyes.

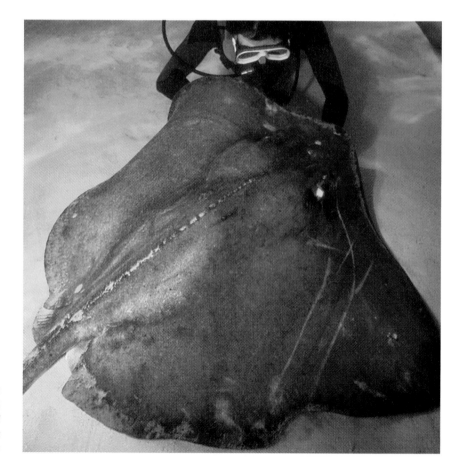

A diver swimming with a stingray in the Grand Cayman Islands. *(Reproduced by permission of The Stock Market.)*

The form, size, and number of fins varies considerably according to an individual species' habitat and requirements. In fast-swimming species, such as the tuna or mackerel, the dorsal and anal fins have thin, sharp shapes that reduce friction. In puffer or porcupine fish, by contrast, the fins are greatly reduced—for use in short paddling movements. Other species, such as eels, have lost almost all traces of external fins and swim instead by rhythmic movements of their muscular bodies.

Another important adaptation made by fish is their swim bladder. The swim bladder is a chamber filled with air that allows a fish to remain at the same level in water while expending very little energy.

Fish breathe through structures known as gills. When a fish takes in water through its mouth, the flaps that cover its gills are closed. When the fish closes its mouth, the flaps open and water is expelled through the gills. In this process, oxygen dissolved in the water is absorbed into the fish's bloodstream.

Bony fish are either carnivorous (meat-eating), herbivorous (plant-eating), or both. And fish are, of course, one of the world's most popular foods. In island nations and countries with long coastlines, fish are a major part of the diet. They are also a healthful food since they are high in protein and low in fat content.

Cartilaginous fish

The cartilaginous fish—whose skeletons are made of cartilage—include both sharks and rays. An intriguing characteristic of sharks is the presence of tiny primitive teeth on their skin. These denticles are similar in some ways to human teeth, although much smaller in size. Thus the texture of a shark's skin is similar to that of fine sandpaper. Human swimmers can be badly cut by coming into contact with the skin of a shark. The skin of a ray, on the other hand, is entirely smooth except for the back or upper tail surface, where denticles have developed into large, strong spines.

The jaw teeth of both sharks and rays are, in fact, modified denticles. These teeth are lost when they become worn and are replaced by rows of new teeth from the space behind them. In some species of sharks, the jaw looks like an assembly line, with new teeth filling spaces immediately.

Like bony fish, both sharks and rays breathe through gills. They also have an opening called a spiracle on both sides of the head behind the eye. The spiracle allows water to flow through the gills without taking in large amounts of mud and sand. This adaptation is especially useful for rays, which often bury in the sand, and for sharks, which often rest on the ocean bottom. Unlike the bony fish, sharks and rays do not possess a swim bladder.

Cartilaginous fish are predatory: they feed on other animals, from zooplankton to shellfish to whales. And they themselves are sought after by humans as a food source. Shark meat, once marketed under the pseudonyms of flake and steakfish, is now popular worldwide. Shark fins have long been popular in Asia. Rays are considered delicacies in Great Britain and France, and thornback rays and flapper skates are often sold as sea trout.

[*See also* **Coelacanth**]

Flower

A flower is the reproductive part of a plant that produces seeds. Plants that produce flowers and fruit are called angiosperms. There are more than 300,000 species of angiosperms, and their flowers and fruits vary significantly. Flowers and fruits are among the most useful features for identifying plant species.

Study of flowers throughout history

Many modern cultures consider flowers attractive, and scholars have been fascinated with flowers for thousands of years. Dioscorides, a first-century Greek physician, wrote the most influential early book on plants, *De materia medica*. This was the first text about the medicinal uses of plants, and it contained many diagrams of plants and their flowers. The book helped other physicians identify the species of plant to prescribe to their patients for a particular ailment. *De materia medica* remained an important reference on botany (the study of plants) for more than 1,500 years.

In the mid-1700s, Swedish botanist Carolus Linnaeus revolutionized the field of botany. He classified plant species according to the morphology (form and structure) of their flowers and fruits. Modern botanists continue to rely upon his classification system.

Up until the late 1700s, people believed that flowers with beautiful colors and sweet smells were created by God to please humans. However, German botanist Christian Konrad Sprengel disputed this view. He held that the characteristics of flowers (shape, color, smell) are related to their method of reproduction. Sprengel published his theory of flowers in 1793 in *The Secret of Nature Revealed*. Although not widely accepted in his own time, Sprengel's views were soon considered scientifically correct.

▼ Words to Know

Angiosperm: Plant that produces flowers and seeds.

Anther: Top part of the stamen that produces pollen.

Filament: Stalk of the stamen that bears the anther.

Corolla: Layers of petals in a flower.

Morphology: Branch of biology dealing with the form and structure of living organisms.

Ovary: Base part of the pistil that bears ovules and develops into a fruit.

Ovule: Structure within the ovary that develops into a seed after fertilization.

Petal: Whorl of a flower just inside the sepals that is often colored.

Pistil: Female reproductive organ of flowers that is composed of the stigma, style, and ovary.

Pollen: Powdery grains that contain the male reproductive cells of angiosperms.

Pollination: Transfer of pollen from the male reproductive organs to the female reproductive organs of a plant.

Sepal: External whorl of a flower that is typically leaflike and green.

Stamen: Male reproductive organ of flowers that is composed of the anther and filament.

Stigma: Top part of the pistil upon which pollen lands and germinates.

Style: Stalk of the pistil that connects the stigma to the ovary.

Parts of the flower

There are considerable differences among the many species of flowers. Flowers can develop on different places on a plant. Terminal flowers, like a tulip, are single flowers that bloom at the apex or end of an upright stalk. Other flowers arise in an inflorescence, a branched cluster of individual flowers. Begonias are an example of this type. Those flowers that grow at the base of a leaf where it attaches to the stem of the plant are called axillary flowers. Snapdragons are an example of axillary flowers.

There are four concentric whorls (rings) of organs in a complete flower. From the center to the outside, they are the pistil, stamens, petals, and sepals. Fundamentally, these four parts are modified leaves.

The pistil, a long stalk arising in the center, is the female reproductive organ of a flower. It is composed of the stigma, style, and ovary. The stigma is the sticky knob at the outer end of the stalk. The style is the portion of the stalk connecting the stigma to the ovary. The ovary is the round base that contains one or more undeveloped seeds called ovules. In each ovule is an egg waiting to be fertilized by a sperm.

Stamens, the male reproductive organs, also arise from the center of the flower and encircle the pistil. The stamens are composed of a stalk, called a filament, topped by an anther. The anther produces many microscopic pollen grains. The male sex cell, a sperm, develops within each pollen grain.

Petals, the often-brightly colored portion surrounding the pistil and stamens, are a flower's showpiece. They attract the attention of passing insects, birds, and people. The layers of petals in a flower comprise the corolla.

Sepals lie below the petals and are usually green and leaflike in appearance. Sepals form a temporary, protective cover over an unopened flower. When the petals of a flower are ready to unfurl, the sepals fold back.

In some species, one or more of the four whorls of floral organs is missing, and the flower is referred to as an incomplete flower. A bisexual flower is one with both stamens and a pistil, whereas a unisexual flower is one that has either stamens or a pistil, but not both. All complete flowers are bisexual since they have all four floral whorls. All unisexual flowers are incomplete since they lack either stamens or a pistil.

Pollination

In angiosperms, pollination is the transfer of pollen from an anther to a stigma. Pollen grains land on the sticky stigma, where they begin to germinate or grow. A pollen tube then forms down the style, sperm is delivered to the ovules, and fertilization takes place.

If the transfer of pollen occurs between an anther and the stigma of the same plant, it is known as self-pollination. Complete flowers are able to self-pollinate. When the transfer of pollen occurs between an anther and the stigma of different plants, it is known as cross-pollination. Of the two methods, cross-pollination produces stronger and healthier off-spring since it mixes up the genetic make-up of plants. Cross-pollination can be brought about by wind, rain, mammals, birds, and insects.

Pollination by wind. Many angiosperms are pollinated by wind. Wind-pollinated flowers, such as those of corn and all grasses, tend to have a simple structure lacking petals. The anthers dangle on long filaments, allowing the light pollen grains to be easily caught by the wind. The stigma are freely exposed to catch the airborne pollen. Large amounts of pollen are usually wasted because they do not reach female reproductive organs. For this reason, most wind-pollinated plants are found in temperate regions, where members of the same species often grow close together.

Pollination by animals. In general, pollination by insects and other animals is more efficient than pollination by wind. Many times flowers

A bumblebee pollinating a flower. *(Reproduced by permission of Field Mark Publications.)*

offer "rewards" to attract these animals—sugary nectar, oil, solid food, a place to sleep, or even the pollen itself. Generally, plants use color and fragrances to lure their pollen-transporting agents.

The flowers of many species of plants are marked with special pigments that absorb ultraviolet light (light whose wavelengths are shorter than visible light). These pigments are invisible to humans and most animals. But the eyes of bees are sensitive enough to detect the patterns created by the pigments and so the bees are drawn to them.

Having been attracted to a flower, an insect or other small animal probes inside for its reward. In doing so, it brushes against the anthers and picks up dust pollen on its body. When the animal moves on to the next flower, it brushes past the stigma, depositing pollen. Many flowers are designed precisely to match the body forms of the animals participating in this pollen transfer. In this way, contact with both the anthers and the stigma is ensured. A few orchids use a combination of smell, color, and shape to mimic the female of certain species of bees and wasps. The male bees and wasps then try to mate with the flower. In the process, they either pick up or transfer pollen to that flower.

Fluid dynamics

Fluid dynamics is the study of the flow of liquids and gases, usually in and around solid surfaces. For example, fluid dynamics can be used to analyze the flow of air over an airplane wing or over the surface of an automobile. It also can be used in the design of ships to increase the speed with which they travel through water.

Scientists use both experiments and mathematical models and calculations to understand fluid dynamics. A wind tunnel is an enclosed space in which air can be made to flow over a surface, such as the model of an airplane. Smoke is added to the air stream so that the flow of air can be observed and photographed.

The data collected from wind tunnel studies and other experiments are often very complex. Scientists today use models of fluid behavior and powerful computers to analyze and interpret those data.

The field of fluid dynamics is often subdivided into aerodynamics and hydrodynamics. Aerodynamics is the study of the way air flows around airplanes and automobiles with the aim of increasing the efficiency of motion. Hydrodynamics deals with the flow of water in various situations such as in pipes, around ships, and underground. Apart from the

▼ Words to Know

Boundary layer: The layer of fluid that sticks to a solid surface and through which the speed of the fluid decreases.

Compressibility: The property that allows a fluid to be compressed into a smaller volume.

Laminar: A mode of flow in which the fluid moves in layers along continuous, well-defined lines known as streamlines.

Turbulent: An irregular, disorderly mode of flow.

Viscosity: The internal friction within a fluid that makes it resist flow.

more familiar cases, the principles of fluid dynamics can be used to understand an almost unimaginable variety of phenomena such as the flow of blood in blood vessels, the flight of geese in V-formation, and the behavior of underwater plants and animals.

Factors that influence flow

Flow patterns in a fluid (gas or liquid) depend on three factors: the characteristics of the fluid, the speed of flow, and the shape of the solid surface. Three characteristics of the fluid are of special importance: viscosity, density, and compressibility. Viscosity is the amount of internal friction or resistance to flow. Water, for instance, is less viscous than honey, which explains why water flows more easily than does honey.

All gases are compressible, whereas liquids are practically incompressible; that is, they cannot be squeezed into smaller volumes. Flow patterns in compressible fluids are more complicated and difficult to study than those in incompressible ones. Fortunately for automobile designers, at speeds less than about 220 miles (350 kilometers) per hour, air can be treated as incompressible for all practical purposes. Also, for incompressible fluids, the effects of temperature changes can be neglected.

Laminar and turbulent flow

Flow patterns can be characterized as laminar or turbulent. The term laminar refers to streamlined flow in which a fluid glides along in layers that do not mix. The flow takes place in smooth continuous lines called

Mach Number

The Mach number is a measurement used in fluid dynamics that compares the velocity of an object traveling through a fluid to the speed of sound in that fluid. For example, the speed of sound in air at sea level at a temperature of 59°F (15°C) is about 760 miles per hour (340 meters per second). Imagine an airplane flying just above the ocean at a speed of 380 miles per hour (170 meters per second). In that case, the Mach number of the airplane would be 380 miles per hour divided by 760 miles per hour (380 mph ÷ 760 mph) or 0.5.

The Mach number is named after Austrian physicist and philosopher Ernst Mach (1838–1916), who pioneered the study of supersonic (faster than sound) travel. The Mach number is especially important in the field of fluid dynamics because fluids flow around an object in quite different ways. For example, when an airplane flies at a speed greater than the speed of sound, sound waves are not able to "get out of the way" of the airplane. Shock waves are produced, resulting in the sonic booms heard when an airplane exceeds the speed of sound.

Aircraft designers have to take differences in fluid behavior at different Mach numbers into account when designing planes that take off and climb to altitude at speeds in the subsonic (less than the speed of sound) region, then pass through the transonic (about equal to the speed of sound) region, and cruise at speeds in the supersonic region.

streamlines. You can observe this effect when you open a water faucet just a little so that the flow is clear and regular. If you continue turning the faucet, the flow gradually becomes cloudy and irregular. This condition is known as turbulent flow.

Fluid flow concepts

Bernoulli's principle. Swiss mathematician Daniel Bernoulli (1700–1782) was the first person to study fluid flow mathematically. For his research, Bernoulli imagined a completely nonviscous and incompressible or "ideal" fluid. In this way, he did not have to worry about all the many complications that are present in real examples of fluid flow. The mathematical equations Bernoulli worked out represent only ideal situations, then, but they are useful in many real-life situations.

A simple way to understand Bernoulli's result is to picture water flowing through a horizontal pipe with a diameter of 4 inches (10 centimeters). Then imagine a constricted section in the middle of the pipe with a diameter of only 2 inches (5 centimeters). Bernoulli's principle says that water flowing through the pipe has to speed up in the constricted portion of the pipe. If water flowed at the same rate in the constricted portion of the pipe, less water would get through. The second half of the pipe would not be full.

What Bernoulli showed was that water in the constricted section of the pipe (through which liquid moves more quickly) experiences less water pressure. Suppose the water pressure in the wide part of the pipe is 20 newtons per square meter. Then the pressure in the constricted part of the pipe might be only 15 newtons per square meter. More generally, Bernoulli's principle says that the pressure exerted by a fluid decreases as the velocity of that fluid increases.

Bernoulli's principle is easy to demonstrate. Hold both ends of a piece of paper in your two hands and blow over the upper surface of the paper. The paper appears to rise, as if by magic. The "magic" is that air passing over the surface of the paper causes reduced pressure from above on the paper. Normal atmospheric pressure below the paper pushes it upward. This simple demonstration also illustrates the principle on which airplanes fly. Air flying over the wings of the airplane produces a lifting effect from below on the wings.

Boundary layer effects. Bernoulli's principle works very well in many cases. But assuming that fluids have no viscosity, as Bernoulli did, does introduce some errors in real life. The reason for these errors is that even in fluids with very low viscosity, the fluid right next to the solid boundary sticks to the surface. This effect is known as the no-slip condition. Thus, however fast or easily the fluid away from the boundary may be moving, the fluid near the boundary has to slow down gradually and come to a complete stop exactly at the boundary. This effect is what causes drag on automobiles and airplanes in spite of the low viscosity of air.

The treatment of such flows was considerably simplified by the boundary layer concept introduced by German physicist Ludwig Prandtl (1875–1953) in 1904. According to Prandtl, a fluid slows down only in a thin layer next to the surface. This boundary layer starts forming at the beginning of the flow and slowly increases in thickness. It is laminar in the beginning but becomes turbulent after some period of time. Since the effect of viscosity is confined to the boundary layer, the fluid away from the boundary may be treated as ideal.

Shape and drag. Moving automobiles and airplanes experience a resistance or drag due to the viscous force of air sticking to their surface. Another source of resistance is pressure drag, which is due to a phenomenon known as flow separation. This happens when there is an abrupt change in the shape of the moving object, and the fluid is unable to make a sudden change in flow direction and stay with the boundary. In this case, the boundary layer gets detached from the body, and a region of low pressure turbulence or wake is formed below it, creating a drag on the vehicle (due to the higher pressure in the front). That is why aerodynamically designed cars are shaped so that the boundary layer remains attached to the body longer, creating a smaller wake and, therefore, less drag. There are many examples in nature of shape modification for drag control. The sea anemone, for instance, with its many tentacles, continuously adjusts its form to the ocean currents in order to avoid being swept away while gathering food.

Fluorescent light

Fluorescent light is the most common type of electrical light used in the United States. It is estimated that there are 1.5 billion fluorescent lamps in use nationwide, mostly in commercial settings such offices, factories, stores, and schools. Fluorescent lighting is popular due to its high efficiency: it produces four to six times more light than an incandescent lamp consuming the same electrical power.

Luminescence is the term used to describe the process in which light is produced by a means other than heating (incandescence refers to the production of light from heat). Fluorescence is luminescence in which light of a visible color is emitted from a substance that is stimulated or excited by light or other forms of electromagnetic radiation (radiation that has properties of both an electric and magnetic wave and that travels through a vacuum with the speed of light) or by certain other means. Once the stimulation stops, however, the light emitted by the stimulated substance lasts no more than about 10 nanoseconds (10 billionths of a second).

Humans observed fluorescence in certain rocks and other substances for hundreds of years before fully understanding its nature. In 1852, English mathematician and physicist George Gabriel Stokes (1819–1903) finally named and explained the phenomena (he named it after fluorite, a strongly fluorescent mineral). Stokes discovered that fluorescence can be induced or brought about in certain substances by stimulating them with ultraviolet light (ultraviolet radiation is electromagnetic radiation of a

Words to Know

Electrode: A material that will conduct an electrical current, usually a metal, used to carry electrons into or out of an electrochemical cell.

Electromagnetic radiation: Radiation (a form of energy) that has properties of both an electric and magnetic wave and that travels through a vacuum with the speed of light.

Fluorescence: Luminescence (glowing) that stops within 10 nanoseconds after an energy source has been removed.

Incandesacence: Glowing due to heat.

Phosphor: A material that absorbs energy over some period of time, then gives off light for a longer period.

Ultraviolet radiation: Electromagnetic radiation (energy) of a wavelength just shorter than the violet (shortest wavelength) end of the visible light spectrum and thus with higher energy than visible light.

wavelength just shorter than the violet end of the visible light spectrum and thus with higher energy than visible light). From his discovery, he formulated Stoke's law, which states that in fluorescence, the wavelength of the emitted or fluorescent light is always longer than that of the stimulating radiation.

Construction and operation

Even though Stokes uncovered the science behind fluorescence, fluorescent lamps were not commercially produced until 1938. Since then, improvements have been made in all aspects of the lamp, but the basic principle has remained the same.

A fluorescent lamp is formed from a sealed, hollow glass tube that is straight, although other shapes also can be used. The tube contains a low-pressure mixture of argon gas and mercury vapor. Electrodes are located at either end of the tube, which has a coating of an inorganic phosphor on its inside surface (a phosphor is a material that absorbs energy over some period of time, then gives off light for a longer period). When activated, the electrodes discharge a stream of electrons that flow between them through the gas mixture. The electrons interact with the mercury vapor atoms floating in the gas mixture, exciting them. As the mercury atoms return to an unexcited state, they release photons of ultraviolet light. These ultraviolet photons then collide with the phosphor on the inside surface of the tube, and the phosphor emits visible photons—it fluoresces to create light. When the lamp is turned off, the phosphor stops fluorescing. The color of the emitted light is determined by the chemical compounds used in the phosphor. Most compounds produce what is perceived as white light.

Lifetime

A fluorescent lamp produces less heat than an incandescent one. Thus, it runs cooler for the same effective light output. Fluorescent bulbs also last much longer: 10,000 to 20,000 hours versus 1,000 hours for a typical incandescent bulb. The lifetime of a fluorescent lamp is limited primarily by the phosphor and by the electron-emitting material on the electrodes. Over time, frequent on-off cycles begin to erode both. The induction lamp, a commercial version of which was introduced by the General Electric Company in 1994, contains no electrodes, and the discharge current is induced by a radio-frequency discharge. Since there is no erosion problem, the induction lamp has the capability of lasting for up to 60,000 hours, many times longer than standard fluorescent lamps.

[*See also* **Incandescent light**]

A woman examining a small mercury fluorescent lightbulb. *(Reproduced by permission of Field Mark Publications.)*

Fluoridation

Fluoridation is the process of adding the chemical fluoride to a substance (often drinking water) to reduce tooth decay. In the human body, fluoride acts to prevent tooth decay by strengthening tooth enamel and inhibiting the growth of plaque-forming bacteria. Fluoridation was first introduced into the United States in the 1940s in an attempt to study its effect on the reduction of tooth decay. Since then many cities have added fluoride to their water supply systems.

Early fluoridation studies

In 1901, Frederick McKay (1874–1959), a dentist in Colorado Springs, Colorado, noticed that many of his patients had brown stains, called mottled enamel, on their teeth. After studying the cause of this staining for three decades, McKay concluded that it was due to high concentrations of fluoride in the patients' drinking water. McKay also observed that although unsightly, the stained teeth of his patients seemed to be more resistant to decay. After experimentation, he found that the ideal level of fluoride in water should be one part fluoride per million parts of water (or one ppm). That was enough to stop decay but too little to cause mottling.

The U.S. Public Health Service (USPHS) grew interested in fluoride and, following safety tests on animals, conducted field tests. In 1945, the public water systems of Newburgh, New York, and Grand Rapids, Michigan, became the first ever to be artificially fluoridated with sodium fluoride.

Results of these tests seemed to show that fluoridation reduced dental cavities by as much as two-thirds. Based on those results, the USPHS recommended in 1950 the fluoridation of all public water systems in the United States. Later that year, the American Dental Association added its endorsement, and the American Medical Association followed suit in 1951.

To fluoridate or not to fluoridate

Even though almost the entire dental, medical, and public health establishment favored fluoridation, the recommendation was immediately controversial, and has remained so. Opponents objected to fluoridation because of possible health risks (fluoride is toxic, or poisonous, in large amounts). They also objected to being deprived of the choice whether to consume a chemical. Despite the opposition, nearly 60 percent of people in the United States now drink fluoridated water. Fluoridation also is practiced in about 30 other countries.

Words to Know

Fluoride: A form of the element fluorine that is soluble in water. It is often added to drinking water to reduce tooth decay.

Parts per million (ppm): A way to express low concentrations of a substance in water. For example, 1 ppm of fluoride means 1 gram of fluoride is dissolved in 1 million grams of water.

Fluoridation today

Over the years, other ways of applying fluoride have been developed. In 1956, Procter & Gamble added fluoride to one of its brands of toothpaste, Crest. Four years later, the Council on Dental Therapeutics of the ADA gave Crest its seal of approval as "an effective decay-preventive dentifrice." The ADA now estimates that brushing with fluoride-containing toothpaste reduces tooth decay by as much as 20 to 30 percent.

By the 1990s, the initial claims that fluoridation in drinking water produced two-thirds less tooth decay had been modified to about 20 to 25 percent reduction. Researchers now believe that the overall reduction of tooth decay levels in the twentieth century has been brought about by the addition of fluoride to many items, including food, salt, toothpaste, and mouth rinses. Education and better dental hygiene also have played a part. In 1993, the National Research Council published a report stating the maximum recommended level of four ppm for fluoride in drinking water was appropriate. Since then, the scientific debate of the health benefits of fluoridation versus its possible health risks has continued. Both sides agree that further research into this area is needed.

[*See also* **Poisons and toxins**]

Food preservation

Food preservation refers to any one of a number of techniques used to prevent food from spoiling. All foods begin to spoil as soon as they are harvested or slaughtered. Some spoiling is caused by such microorganisms as bacteria and mold. Other spoilage results from chemical changes within the food itself due to natural processes such as enzyme action or oxidation.

Ancient methods

Ages-old food preservation techniques include drying, smoking, cooling, freezing, fermenting, salting, pickling, and canning.

Drying and smoking. One of the most ancient methods of food preservation is sun- or air-drying. Drying works because it removes much of the food's water. Without adequate water, microorganisms cannot multiply and chemical activities greatly slow down. Dried meat was one of the earliest staple foods of hunters and nomads (people who constantly moved about). Once fire was discovered, prehistoric cave dwellers heat-dried meat and fish, which probably led to the development of smoking as another way to preserve these foods. The Phoenicians of the Middle East air-dried fish. Ancient Egyptians stockpiled dried grains. Native North Americans produced a nutritious food called pemmican by grinding together dried meat, dried fruit, and fat.

Cooling and freezing. Early northern societies quickly learned that coolness as well as freezing helped preserve foods. Microbe growth and chemical changes slow down at low temperatures and completely stop when water is frozen. Pre-Columbian natives in Peru and Bolivia freeze-dried potatoes, while the early Japanese and Koreans freeze-dried their fish. Water evaporating through earthenware jars was used as a coolant in 2500 B.C. by Egyptians and East Indians. Ancient Chinese, Greeks, and Romans stored ice and mountain snow in cellars or icehouses to keep food cool.

Fermenting. Fermentation was particularly useful for people in southern climates, where cooling and freezing were not practical. When a food ferments, it produces acids that prevent the growth of organisms that cause spoilage. Grapes, rice, and barley were fermented into wine and beer by early people. Fermentation also was used to produce cheese and yogurt from milk.

Salting and pickling. Salting, which also inhibits bacteria growth, was a preferred method of preserving fish as early as 3500 B.C. in the Mediterranean world, and also was practiced in ancient China.

Substances besides salt were found to slow food spoilage. The Chinese began using spices as preservatives around 2700 B.C. Ancient Egyptians used mustard seeds to keep fruit juice from spoiling. Jars of fruit

Words to Know

Additive: A chemical compound that is added to foods to give them some desirable quality, such as preventing them from spoiling.

Antioxidant: A chemical compound that has the ability to prevent the oxidation of substances with which it is associated.

Dehydration: The removal of water from a material.

Fermentation: A chemical reaction in which sugars are converted to organic acids.

Irradiation: The process by which some substance, such as a food, is exposed to some form of radiation, such as gamma rays or X rays.

Oxidation: A chemical reaction in which oxygen reacts with some other substance.

preserved with honey have been found in the ruins of Pompeii, Italy. Melted fat—as Native North Americans discovered with pemmican—preserved meat by sealing out air. Pickling—preserving foods in an acid substance like vinegar—also was used during ancient times.

Early canning. By the Middle Ages (400–1450), all of these ancient methods of preserving foods were widely practiced throughout Europe and Asia, often in combination. Salted fish became the staple food of poor people during this time—particularly salted herring, introduced in 1283 by Willem Beukelszoon of Holland. As the modern era approached, the Dutch navy in the mid-1700s developed a way of preserving beef in iron cans by packing it in hot fat and then sealing the cans. By the late 1700s, the Dutch also were preserving cooked, smoked salmon by packing it with butter or olive oil in sealed cans.

Modern methods

Modern methods of food preservation include canning, mechanical refrigeration and freezing, the addition of chemicals, and irradiation.

With the Industrial Revolution (1760–1870), populations became concentrated in ever-growing cities and towns. Thus other methods were needed to preserve food reliably for transportation over long distances and for longer shelf life.

The crucial development was the invention of sophisticated canning techniques during the 1790s by the Frenchman Nicolas François Appert (1750–1841), who operated the world's first commercial cannery in 1804. Appert's method, which first used bottles, was greatly improved by the 1810 invention of the tin can in England. Used at first for Arctic expeditions and by the military, canned foods came into widespread use among the general population by the mid-1800s.

Packaged frozen foods. The 1851 invention of a commercial ice-making machine by American John Gorrie (1803–1855) led to the development of large-scale commercial refrigeration of foods for shipping and storage. Clarence Birdseye (1886–1956) introduced tasty quick-frozen foods in 1925. Shortages of canned goods after World War II (1939–45) helped boost the popularity of frozen foods.

Dehydrated foods. Modern methods of drying foods began in France in 1795 with a hot-air vegetable dehydrator. Dried eggs were widely sold in the United States after 1895, but dried food was not produced in volume in the United States until it was used by soldiers during World War I (1914–18). World War II led to the development of dried skim milk, potato flakes, instant coffee, and soup mixes. After the war, freeze-drying was applied to items such as coffee and orange juice, and the technique continues to be applied to other foodstuffs today.

Chemicals, sterile packages, and irradiation. Chemicals are now commonly added to food to prevent spoilage. They include benzoic acid, sorbic acid, and sulfur dioxide. Antioxidants such as BHA (butylated hydroxyanisole) and ascorbic acid (vitamin C) prevent compounds in food from combining with oxygen to produce inedible changes. The use of chemical additives has not been without controversy. The spread of often unnecessary and sometimes harmful chemical additives to food during the late 1800s led to governmental regulation in both England and the United States.

Aseptic packaging is a relatively new way to keep food from spoiling. A food product is sterilized and then sealed in a sterilized container. Aseptic packages, including plastic, aluminum foil, and paper, are lighter and cheaper than the traditional metal and glass containers used for canning. Aseptically processed foods are also sterilized much more quickly, so their flavor is better. Aseptic packaging became commercially available in 1981. However, controversy has developed about the amount of disposable containers produced by this method.

Food irradiation uses low doses of radiation to kill microorganisms in food and to extend the amount of time in which food can be sold and eaten safely. Strawberries that are treated with irradiation can last for up to two weeks, compared to less than a week for untreated berries. The process, which remains controversial, is a relative newcomer among food-preserving techniques. The U.S. government first approved its use on fresh fruits and vegetables in 1986 and for poultry in 1990.

Food web and food chain

The terms food chain and food web both refer to groups of organisms that are dependent on each other for food. A food chain is a single series of organisms in which each plant or animal depends on the organism above or below it. As an example, a food chain might consist of garden plants, such as lettuce and carrots, fed upon by rabbits which, in turn, are fed upon by owls which, in turn, are fed upon by hawks.

A food chain is largely a theoretical idea and probably seldom, if ever, exists in the real world. It is a useful concept, however, as it helps ecologists understand how specific plants and animals are dependent upon one another.

The feeding relationships of organisms in the real world is almost always more complex than suggested by a food chain. For that reason, the term food web is more accurate than is food chain. A food web differs from a food chain in that it includes all the organisms whose feeding habits are related in some way or another to those of other organisms. In the example above, small animals other than rabbits feed on lettuce and carrots and, in turn, those animals are fed upon by a variety of larger animals.

Structure of food webs

Food webs are organized into three main categories, depending on the kinds of organisms they contain. These three categories are known as trophic levels. The three primary trophic levels are those that consist of (1) producers, (2) consumers, and (3) decomposers. Producers are organisms that can make their own organic compounds or food using energy and simple inorganic compounds. Producers are sometimes called autotrophs, meaning "self-feeders." For example, green plants are autotrophs because they manufacture the compounds they need through photosynthesis.

The next trophic level above the producers consists of consumers. Consumers are organisms that cannot make their own foods and so have to eat other organisms to obtain the nutrients they use. The consumer trophic level can be subdivided depending on the kind of organisms included. Immediately above the producers are the herbivores, organisms

▼ Words to Know

Biomagnification: The increasing concentration of compounds at higher trophic levels.

Food chain: A sequence of organisms directly dependent on one another for food.

Food web: An interconnection of many food chains.

Photosynthesis: The conversion of solar energy into chemical energy that is stored in the tissues of primary producers (for example, green plants).

Primary consumer: An organism that eats primary producers.

Primary producer: An organism that makes its own food.

Trophic level: A feeding level in a food web.

that eat plants only. Some common examples of the herbivores include squirrels, rabbits, mice, deer, cows, horses, sheep, and seed-eating birds. The herbivores are sometimes called first-order consumers or primary consumers because they occupy the first level above the producer trophic level.

Above the primary consumers, the food web fans out to include two other kinds of consumers. The carnivores are animals that eat other animals, and the omnivores are animals that eat both plants and animals. Within the food web, carnivores and omnivores can be on any higher trophic levels. Some are secondary consumers or second-order consumers, meaning that they eat primary consumers. Snakes that eat mice (primary consumers) are secondary consumers. Other higher-level consumers are tertiary consumers or third-order consumers, and eat further up on the food web or perhaps on many levels. Examples of third-order consumers are mountain lions and hawks, both of whom eat second-order consumers such as snakes and owls.

The third trophic level consists of decomposers or detritivores (pronounced de-TRY-tuh-vorz). Organisms in this trophic level survive by eating dead organisms. Some decomposers, such as earthworms, feed directly on dead plants and animals. These organisms convert dead organisms to simpler substances that are then digested even further by other decomposers, such as bacteria and fungi.

Unlike organisms in the consumer/producer part of the food web, decomposers are extremely efficient feeders. They can rework the remains of dead organisms, progressively extracting more and more energy. Eventually the waste materials are broken down into simple inorganic chemicals such as water, carbon dioxide, and simple nutrients. The nutrients may then be reused by the primary producers in the lowest part of the food web. The decomposer food web is very active inside of compost piles where kitchen wastes are converted into a soil conditioner. Decomposers are active in all natural ecosystems.

Ecological pyramids

Food webs are, of course, collections of organisms. However, they also can be thought of as accumulations of energy. Think, for example, of the energy changes involved in the food chain described at the beginning of this essay. Lettuce and carrots, like other green plants, have the ability to capture solar energy from sunlight and convert it into the stored chemical energy of starches and other chemical compounds. When rabbits eat lettuce and carrots, they take in that stored energy. At the next level, owls that eat rabbits take in the energy stored in the bodies of their prey.

No organism ever collects 100 percent of the energy stored in the plant or animal it eats, however. In fact, studies have shown that only about 10

An ecological or energy pyramid. The lowest level consists of producers, the next higher level of first-order consumers, the next higer level of second-order consumers, and so on. Note that the total number of organisms found in any one level decreases as one goes up the pyramid. *(Reproduced by permission of The Gale Group.)*

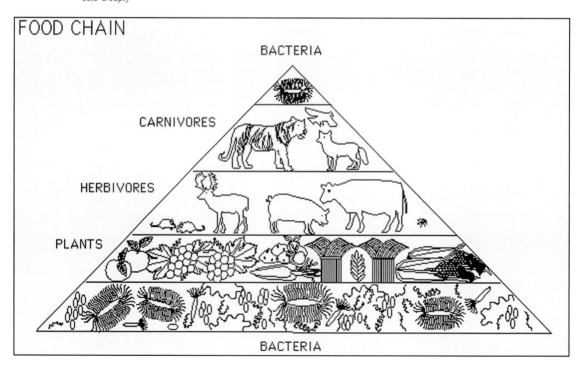

FOOD CHAIN

BACTERIA

CARNIVORES

HERBIVORES

PLANTS

BACTERIA

percent of the energy stored in an organism gets transferred from one trophic level to the next: the rabbit gets only 10 percent of the energy stored in a carrot, the owl 10 percent of the energy stored in the rabbit, and so on.

One way to illustrate this fact is by means of an ecological pyramid or energy pyramid. The lowest level of an ecological pyramid consists of producers, the next higher level of first-order consumers, the next higher level of second-order consumers, and so on.

An ecological pyramid makes clear two important facts about food webs. First, as pointed out previously, the total amount of energy at any one level decreases as one goes up the pyramid. That is, the producer level contains the greatest amount of energy, the first-order-consumer level the next largest amount, the second-order-consumer level the next largest amount, and so on. Second, the total number of organisms found in any one level also decreases in going up the pyramid. An ecosystem that contains 10,000 lettuce plants may be able to support no more than 100 rabbits, 10 owls, and 1 hawk, as an example.

Biomagnification

One interesting phenomenon associated with food webs is bio-magnification. The term biomagnification refers to the accumulation of

Manatees have an enormous capacity to eat aquatic plants. *(Reproduced by permission of the U.S. Fish and Wildlife Service.)*

certain substances as one moves up the food web. Biomagnification has become an important issue in ecology because of the presence in the environment of certain human-made substances that can have harmful effects on animals.

For example, suppose that a farmer sprays his or her fields with a pesticide designed to control insects that destroy his or her crops. A small amount of that pesticide will be washed off into rivers, streams, and lakes near the field. The pesticide will be ingested by fish living in those bodies of water. Those fish, in turn, may be eaten by larger fish, by birds, by bears, by humans, and by higher-level carnivores.

At each stage of the food web, however, the amount of pesticide stored in an organism's body increases. A single bass, for example, might eat a dozen perch in a month. A single hawk or bear or human might eat a dozen bass in a month. The amount of pesticide stored in one perch gets multiplied many times over in the body of other animals that feed on perch. In one study of a food web in Lake Ontario, scientists found a concentration of pesticide 630 times greater in herring gulls than in primary consumers, such as zooplankton found in the lake.

Biomagnification has serious consequences for all species. It is particularly dangerous for predator species at the top of long food webs. Those predators are at risk because the degree of biomagnification is high by the time it reaches their trophic level. Also, top predators usually consume large quantities of meat, which has lots of fatty tissue and contaminants. Polar bears, humans, eagles, and dolphins are examples of top predators, and all of these organisms are vulnerable to the effects of biomagnification.

[*See also* **DDT (dichlorodiphenyltrichloroethane); Energy**]

Forensic science

Forensic science is the application of science to matters of law. A basic principle of forensic science is that a criminal always brings something to the scene of a crime that he or she leaves behind. The "something" left behind is the evidence that detectives and criminalists (people who make use of science to solve crimes) look for. It might be fingerprints, footprints, teeth marks, blood, semen, hair, fibers, broken glass, a knife or gun, or a bullet. It also might be something less tangible such as the nature of the wounds or bruises left on a victim's body, which might indicate the nature of the weapon or the method of assault. Careful analysis of evidence left at the scene of a crime often can be used in establishing the guilt or innocence of someone on trial.

Fingerprints

Although fingerprints have been used by crime investigators for more than a century, they remain one of the most sought after pieces of evidence. All human beings are born with a characteristic set of ridges on their fingertips. The ridges, which are rich in sweat pores, form a pattern that remains fixed for life. Even if the skin is removed, the same pattern will be evident when the skin regenerates. Some of the typical patterns found in fingerprints are arches, loops, and whorls.

Oils from sweat glands collect on these ridges. When we touch something, a small amount of the oils and other materials on our fingers are left on the surface of the object we touched. The pattern left by these substances, which collect along the ridges on our fingers, make up the fingerprints that police look for at the scene of a crime. Fingerprints collected as evidence can be compared with fingerprints on file or taken from a suspect. The Federal Bureau of Investigation (FBI) maintains a fingerprint library with patterns taken from more than 10 percent of the entire United States population.

Fingerprints being recorded onto an electronic tracking system. *(Reproduced by permission of Phototake.)*

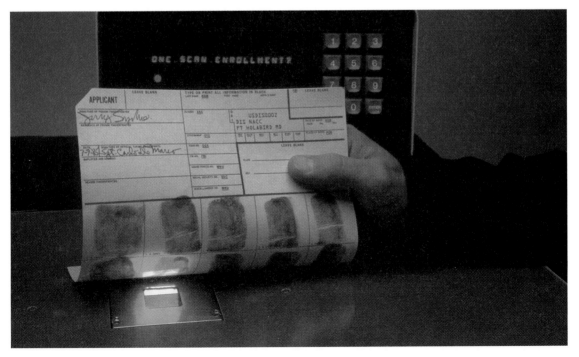

Fingerprints are not the only incriminating patterns that a criminal may leave behind. Lip prints are frequently found on glasses. Footprints and the soil left on the print may match those found in a search of an accused person's premises. Tire tracks, bite marks, toe prints, and prints left by bare feet also may provide useful evidence. In cases where identifying a victim is difficult because of tissue decomposition or death caused by explosions or extremely forceful collisions, a victim's teeth may be used for comparison with dental records.

Genetic fingerprinting

The nuclei within our cells contain coiled, threadlike bodies called chromosomes. Chromosomes are made of deoxyribonucleic acid (DNA). DNA carries the "blueprint" (genes) that directs the growth, maintenance, and activities that go on within our bodies.

Although certain large strands of DNA are the same in all of us, no two people have exactly the same DNA (except for identical twins). It is these unique strands of DNA that are used by forensic scientists to establish a characteristic pattern—the so-called genetic fingerprint. Because different people have different DNA, the prints obtained from different people will vary considerably; however, two samples from the same person will be identical. If there is a match between DNA extracted from semen found on the body of a rape victim and the DNA obtained from a rape suspect's blood, the match is very convincing evidence and may well lead to a conviction or possibly a confession.

Other evidence used in forensic science

Long before DNA was recognized as the "ink" in the blueprints of life, blood samples were collected and analyzed in crime labs. The evidence available through blood typing is not as convincing as genetic fingerprinting, but it can readily prove innocence or increase the probability of a defendant being guilty. All humans belong to one of four blood groups: A, B, AB, or O. If a person accused of a homicide has type AB blood and it matches the type found at the crime scene, the evidence for guilt is more convincing than if a match were found for type O blood.

Bullets and the remains of tools can be used as incriminating evidence. When a bullet is fired, it moves along a spiral groove in the gun barrel. It is this groove that makes the bullet spin so that it will follow a straight path much like that of a spiraling football. The markings on a bullet made by the groove are unique to each gun. Similarly, tool marks, which are often left by burglars who pry open doors or windows, can serve as useful evidence if comparisons can be made with tools associated with a person accused of the crime. Particularly incriminating are jigsaw matches—pieces of a tool left behind that can be shown to match pieces missing from a tool in the possession of the accused.

Autopsies

An autopsy can often establish the cause and approximate time of death. Cuts, scrapes, punctures, and rope marks may help to establish the cause of death. A drowning victim will have soggy lungs, water in the stomach, and blood diluted with water in the left side of the heart. A person who was not breathing when he or she entered the water will have undiluted blood in the heart. Bodies examined shortly after the time of death may have stiff jaws and limbs. Such stiffness, or rigor mortis, is evident about ten hours after death, but disappears after about a day when the tissues begin to decay at normal temperatures. Each case is different, of course, and a skillful coroner can often discover evidence that the killer never suspected he or she had left behind.

[*See also* **Nucleic acid**]

Forestry

Forestry is usually defined as the science of the harvesting, planting, and tending of trees, primarily in managed forested landscapes. In the first 250 years after Europeans came to North America, little or no effort was made to protect the continent's forest resources. Most people thought they could harvest trees without limit almost anywhere. The vastness of the North American continent gave the impression that an unlimited supply of timber was available.

By the late nineteenth century, however, some individuals saw the foolishness of this philosophy. Vast forest areas in the eastern and midwestern United States had been totally cleared of trees. Similar efforts to cut down and use trees as rapidly as possible were occurring at the nation's last frontier, the Far West. At this point, a movement was initiated to think more carefully about the nation's forest resources. People began to develop plans either to preserve or conserve those resources. Preservation meant protecting forests entirely from human use, while conservation meant using forest resources wisely to ensure that they would be available for future generations. Out of this movement grew the modern science of forestry in the United States.

▼ Words to Know

Clear-cutting: A forest harvesting system that involves the cutting of all trees of economic value in a given area at the same time.

Conservation: The act of using natural resources in a way that ensures that they will be available to future generations.

Forest harvesting: Methods used to cut and remove trees from the forest.

Game animal: An animal that is hunted for food or recreational purposes.

Herbicide: Any chemical that kills plants.

Natural regeneration: A method of growth in which foresters rely largely on natural processes for trees to regrow in an area.

Prescribed burn: The controlled burning of vegetation in an area to achieve some effect.

Preservation: The act of protecting a natural resource from any human use.

Regeneration: The process by which the trees in a forest ecosystem are restored over time.

Selection-tree system: A forest management system in which some of the larger individual trees of a desired species in an area are harvested every ten or more years.

Shelter-wood cutting: A forest management technique in which certain large trees are left behind in an area that is otherwise cut.

Silviculture: The branch of forestry that is concerned with the cultivation of trees.

Strip-cutting: A forest management system in which long and narrow clear-cuts are made, with alternating uncut strips of forest left between.

Forestry and agriculture

In many respects, forestry is similar to agricultural science, and foresters are comparable to farmers. Forestry and agriculture both deal with the harvesting and management of ecological systems. Both fields also look for ways to make the best possible use of land to produce valuable products. However, some important differences between the two fields exist. In the first place, agriculture deals with a greater variety of species and products, while forestry deals essentially with one species: trees. In addition, farmers deal with a wider range of harvesting and management systems, most of which are much more intensive than in forestry. Finally, agriculture involves relatively short harvesting rotations, with most crops being planted and harvested once a year. Still, the goals of forestry and agriculture are very much alike: harvesting and managing crops to produce ongoing yields of organic products that are required by society.

Another shared feature of forestry and agriculture is that both substantially deteriorate the original ecosystems of the area. For example, populations of many native species of plants and animals may be reduced, threatened, or even eliminated. The soil is often eroded, the environment may become contaminated with pesticides and fertilizers, and the beauty of the landscape may be degraded. One of the most important challenges to both forestry and agriculture is to achieve their primary goals of maintaining harvests while keeping the environmental damage within acceptable limits.

Goals of forest management

Forests are important for a number of reasons. They are used to provide a vast array of products that include lumber, plywood, pulp and paper, and other wood products. Many fish (particularly salmon) and fur-bearing animal species (marten, fisher, and beaver) that live in forested lands are valuable commodities. Forests are home to species of game animals such as deer, rabbits, and quails that are hunted for food and for recreational purposes. But the great majority of the species of forested landscapes are nongame animals which, though not economically important, are nonetheless valuable.

Forests also provide people with recreation: bird watching and other wildlife observation, hiking, and cross-country skiing. And many people enjoy forests simply for their great beauty. Forests also play a vital role in the ecology of the planet. In addition to preventing erosion and helping to maintain the water cycle, these stands of trees provide atmospheric oxygen.

Highly publicized, intense debates rage as to the best possible uses of forest resources. For instance, in North America there are concerns about the negative effects of forestry on endangered species, such as the spotted owl and red-cockaded woodpecker, and on endangered ecosystems, such as old-growth forests. In a few cases, these concerns have been addressed by declaring large tracts of natural forests to be off limits to commercial harvesting of timber. In general, however, logging industry interests are seen as having a higher value to society.

Harvesting and management

There are a number of methods used to cut and remove trees from the forests. Forest harvesting methods vary greatly in their intensity. Clear-cutting is the most intensive system, involving the harvest of all trees of economic value at the same time. The areas of clear-cuts can vary greatly, from cuts smaller than a hectare in size to enormous harvests thousands of hectares in area.

Strip-cutting is a system in which long and narrow clear-cuts are made, with alternating uncut strips of forest left between. One advantage of strip-cutting is seeds from uncut trees fall into the harvested strips, and new trees soon begin to grow there.

Shelter-wood cutting is a technique in which certain large trees are left behind in an area that is otherwise cut. The large trees produce seeds from which the next generation of trees will be born. In addition, the large trees will be even larger at the time of the next cutting in the area.

The least intensive method of harvesting is the selection-tree system. In this system, some of the larger individual trees of a desired species are harvested every ten or more years. The forest overall, however, is always left essentially intact.

Regeneration. Forest management involves decisions not only as to how trees are to be harvested, but how the forest is to be regenerated. Ideally, one might hope that a new tree grows in an area for every older tree that was taken out. One method for dealing with this problem is natural regeneration. Natural regeneration refers to the practice of simply allowing a forested area to grow back on its own, once trees have been harvested. Natural regeneration can be aided by humans in a number of ways, such as leaving younger trees in place while only larger trees are harvested and preparing the ground to increase the rate of germination for tree seeds.

Natural regeneration is an ecologically responsible way to promote the regrowth of a forest area. But the process often takes a great deal of time and, therefore, may not be economically desirable.

More managed forms of regeneration are also possible. For example, young seedlings of valuable tree species may be planted and grown in greenhouses before being transplanted to the forest. This technique assures that high-quality trees of just the right species will grow in a particular area.

Once an acceptable population of trees has been planted in an area, intensive tending may be needed to protect these trees from forest fires, attack by pests, and intrusion of undesirable species. This form of management is very time-consuming, and is more likely used on tree farms.

One of the more widely used methods of forest management is known as a prescribed burn. A prescribed burn is the controlled burning of vegetation to achieve some effect. Most commonly, fires are intentionally set to reduce the amount of logging debris present after clear-

A scientist calculating the age of a tree. *(Reproduced by permission of The Stock Market.)*

cutting. This practice is generally undertaken to make the site more accessible to tree planters.

Sometimes prescribed burns are also useful in developing better seedbeds for planting tree seedlings. Prescribed burns also can be used to encourage natural regeneration by particular types of trees that are economically valuable, such as certain species of pines. When using fire for this purposes, it is important to plan for the survival of an adequate number of mature seed trees. If this is not accomplished, the burned site would have to be planted with seedlings grown in a greenhouse.

Silviculture

Silviculture is a special field of forest management that involves the development of activities designed to establish, tend, protect, and harvest crops of trees, especially for use as timber. The term silviculture was invented to compare its activities with those of agriculture. Whereas agriculture deals with a great variety of different crops, silviculture (*silvi* means "trees") deals with trees only.

As with forestry systems in general, silviculture can use techniques ranging from entirely natural to highly intensive. An example of an intensive system used in North America might involve the following series

Foresters use precipitation collection sites such as this one to better manage forest resources. *(Reproduced by permission of the U.S. Forest Service.)*

of activities: (1) whole-tree clear-cut harvesting of the natural forest, followed by (2) breaking up of the surface of the site to prepare it for planting, then (3) an evenly spaced planting of young seedlings of a very specific type of a single species (usually a conifer), with (4) one or more applications of herbicides to free seedlings from the harmful effects of competition with weeds, and (5) one or more thinnings of the maturing plantation, to optimize spacing and growth rates of the residual trees. Finally, the stand is (6) harvested by another whole-tree clear-cut, followed by (7) establishment, tending, and harvesting of the next stand using the same silvicultural system.

In contrast, a more natural silvicultural system might involve periodic selection and harvesting of a mixed-species forest, perhaps every decade or two, and with reliance on natural regeneration to ensure renewal of the economic resource.

Because silvicultural systems can differ so much in their intensity, they also vary in their environmental impacts. As is the case with agriculture, the use of intensive systems generally results in substantially larger yields of the desired economic commodity, in this case, trees. However, intensive systems have much greater environmental impacts associated with their activities.

[*See also* **Forests**]

Forests

A forest is an ecosystem or ecological community whose most important organisms are trees. Forests occur any place where the climate provides a sufficiently long growing season, adequate air and soil temperature, and suitable amount of moisture. Forests can be classified into broad types on the basis of their geographic position and dominant types of trees. Regional and local variations of all of these types can be found as well.

Types of forests

The designation of forest types varies from country to country throughout the world. One of the most widely used systems is the one proposed by the United Nations Educational, Scientific and Cultural Organization (UNESCO). This scheme lists 24 forest types, divided into two broad categories. One category includes forests with a canopy of at least 16 feet (5 meters) high and interlocking tree crowns. (The canopy is the forest's "covering," or the highest level of tree branches in the forest.)

Words to Know

Biodiversity: The wide range of organisms—plants and animals—that exist within any given geographical region.

Boreal: Located in a northern region.

Canopy: The "covering" of a forest consisting of the highest level of tree branches in the forest.

Conifer: Plants whose seeds are stored in cones and that retain their leaves all year around.

Deciduous: Plants that lose their leaves at some season of the year, and then grow them back at another season.

Deforestation: The loss of forests as they are cut down to produce timber or to make land available for agriculture.

Ecosystem: An ecological community, including plants, animals, and microorganisms, considered together with their environment.

Old-growth forest: A mature forest, dominated by long-lived species but also including younger trees, with a complex physical structure that has multiple layers in the canopy, large trees, and many large dead standing trees and dead logs.

Temperate: Mild or moderate.

Tropical: Characteristic of a region or climate that is frost free with temperatures high enough to support—with adequate precipitation—plant growth year round.

The second category consists of open woodlands with a relatively sparse, shorter canopy. Some example of the UNESCO categories with their general characteristics are described below.

Tropical rain forests.   Tropical rain forests grow in regions of high rainfall and constant, warm temperatures. Because of these favorable conditions, tropical rain forests are extraordinarily biodiverse: these areas contain a wide variety of tree species and the largest concentration of plants, animals, insects, and microorganisms on the planet.

Tropical and subtropical evergreen forests.   Tropical and subtropical evergreen forests also contain a great diversity of biological species, but they are found in regions with a relatively limited rainfall. Some tree species are deciduous, meaning they lose their leaves at one point or another during the year. Still, enough species retain their leaves at any one time that the forest never becomes completely bare.

Mangrove forests.   Mangrove forests are found in muddy coastal regions in the tropics and subtropics. Compared to the rain forests, mangrove forests have relatively few plant species. Those that do thrive are able to withstand exposure to salt.

Temperate deciduous forests.   The trees in a temperate deciduous forest lose their leaves sometime during the year, only to grow them back again later. This type of forest occurs in regions that have moderately cold winters with a fair amount of rainfall.

Temperate winter-rain evergreen broadleaf forests.   Temperate winter-rain evergreen broadleaf forests are not very common because the climatic conditions on which they depend are somewhat unusual. These types of forests thrive in areas with a definite wet season followed by a very dry summer, such as those in coastal regions of southern California.

Cold-deciduous forests.   Cold-deciduous forests grow in regions with very cold winters. Typical tree species include aspen, birch, and larch.

A forest of tall deciduous trees. *(Reproduced by permission of The Stock Market.)*

Forests as habitats

Although trees are the largest, most productive organisms in forests, the forest ecosystem contains a great many other species of plants, along with numerous animals and microorganisms. Most of the species found in forests cannot live anywhere else. Often that need is very specific. For example, a bird species may require a particular type of tree species, tree age, and other conditions found only in a certain type of forest.

An old-growth Douglas-fir forest in the Pacific Northwest. *(Reproduced by permission of Photo Researchers, Inc.)*

Old-growth Forests

Which is more important: a lumberman's job or the survival of the northern spotted owl? That question highlights one of the most dramatic ecological debates going on in the United States today. The debate centers on old-growth forests, which are ecosystems dominated by large, old trees, usually representing many species. The physical structure of old-growth forests is very complex, and includes multiple layers and gaps of foliage within the canopy, great variations of tree sizes, and many large, standing dead trees and dead logs lying on the forest floor.

Old-growth forests provide a habitat with very special ecological characteristics. These features are not present or as well developed in forests that are younger than old-growth forests. Some wildlife species require these specific qualities of old-growth habitats. As a result, they need extensive areas of old-growth forest as all or a major part of their range.

Some well-known, North American examples of species considered to be dependent on old-growth forests are birds such as the northern spotted owl, marbled murrelet, and red-cockaded woodpecker, and mammals such as marten and fisher. Some species of plants also may require or be much more abundant in old-growth forests than in younger, mature forests. Examples include Pacific yew and various species of lichens occurring in old-growth Douglas-fir forests of western North America.

The controversy over jobs versus owls arises because old-growth forests contain many very old, very large trees of highly desirable species. Lumber companies can realize very large economic profits from the cutting and removal of old-growth trees.

The destruction of old-growth forests presents two problems. In the first place, the loss of such forests destroys the habitats of many animals, such as the spotted owl and the marbled murrelet. Additionally, such forests are unlikely to be replaced. They develop over hundreds or thousands of years when left entirely untouched. In an age when humans are eager to harvest as much mature wood as possible, the chances of new old-growth forests developing are relatively small.

For example, Kirtland's warbler is a bird that nests only in stands of jack pine of a particular age and density in northern Michigan. This species does not breed in any other type of forest, including younger or older stands of jack pine. As jack pine forests have been cut down, the Kirtland's warbler has lost its natural habitat and is today listed as endangered. Similarly, the endangered spotted owl lives only in certain types of old-growth conifer forests in western North America. These same old-growth forests also sustain other species that cannot exist in younger stands, for example, certain species of lichens, mosses, and liverworts.

The previous examples are somewhat unusual. More commonly, animal species can survive in a more diverse habitat. In eastern North America, for example, white-tailed deer do well in a mixture of habitats, including relatively young stands that have abundant and nutritious food, along with mature forests, with some conifer-dominated areas that have shallower snow depths in winter.

More generally, forests provide the essential habitat for most of Earth's species of plants, animals, and microorganisms. This is especially true of tropical rain forests. Recent reductions of forest area are a critical environmental problem because they endanger or threaten animal and plant species and have an impact on climates around the world. The problem is especially difficult to deal with since most destruction of tropical rain forests has been performed in order to convert forest land to agricultural use.

Forests as a natural resource

Forests are extremely important because they provide a number of essential natural resources for human societies. The challenge is to find ways to harvest these resources while ensuring that they will continue to exist and be productive for generations in the future.

Wood is by far the most important product harvested from forests. That wood is commonly manufactured into paper, lumber, plywood, and other products. Moreover, in most of the forested regions of the less-developed world, firewood is the most important source of energy used for cooking and heating. Potentially, all of these forest products can be harvested without much danger to the ecosystem. Unfortunately, in most cases forests have been overharvested, resulting in the permanent loss of forest resources and widespread ecological damage.

Many other plant products also may be collected from forests. Some examples include fruits, nuts, mushrooms, and latex for manufacturing rubber. In addition, many species of animals are hunted in forests, for recreation or for food. Forests provide additional goods and services that are important to both human welfare and to the environment, including control of erosion and water flows and cleansing of air and water.

Deforestation

The term deforestation refers to the loss of forests as they are cut down to produce timber or to make land available for agriculture. In some cases, deforestation is a temporary condition as new trees grow back to replace those that are lost to the timber industry. In other cases, deforestation is a permanent condition, in which forests are lost forever.

The most common single cause of deforestation is human activities. Forest fires and attacks by insects also produce deforestation, although those produced by nature are generally only temporary conditions.

Some dramatic examples of deforestation are known from history. For example, forests mentioned in the Bible were long ago cut down to produce wood for human needs. Places such as the Forest of Hamath, the Wood of Ziph, and the Forest of Bethel are now deserts. Vast regions of the eastern and midwestern United States once covered by forests have become farmland or urban areas.

By some estimates, about 12 percent of Earth's forests have been destroyed since the beginning of human history. A large fraction of that loss has taken place in temperate and arctic regions. In recent decades, however, that pattern has changed. The forest cover in Western Europe and North America, for example, has become stable or has actually

Deforestation in the jungle in Brazil. *(Reproduced by permission of Photo Researchers, Inc.)*

increased. By contrast, the rates of deforestation in Latin America, Africa and Asia have increased at an alarming rate in recent decades.

This deforestation is driven by the rapid growth in size of the human population of these regions. As these populations grow, so do the needs to create more agricultural land to provide additional food and to harvest forests as fuel. In addition, large areas of tropical forest have been converted to agricultural use in order to grow crops for markets in wealthier countries, often at the environmental expense of local peoples.

The great threat of deforestation is, of course, the loss of a valuable renewable natural resource. In addition to the loss of economically important products, such as lumber, pulp for the manufacture of paper, and fuel wood to produce energy, essential animal habitats are destroyed. This habitat loss results in the decline of populations of both game animals and the great diversity of animals not hunted for sport or food. In addition, important ecological services that help maintain clean air and water and the control of erosion disappear as a result of deforestation also are stunted.

[*See also* **Biodiversity; Endangered species; Forestry; Rain forest; Slash-and-burn agriculture; Tree**]

Formula, chemical

A chemical formula is a combination of chemical symbols that represents the chemical composition of a compound. At a minimum, a formula tells which elements are present in the compound and the relative amount of each element. The chemical formula most familiar to people is probably H_2O, the formula for water. This formula says that water consists of two elements, hydrogen (H) and oxygen (O). Further, it says that the ratio of the two elements is two parts hydrogen and one part oxygen. On a submicroscopic scale, the formula says that a molecule of water contains two atoms of hydrogen and one atom of oxygen.

Determining chemical formulas

A chemical formula can be determined in one of two ways: by experimentation or by prediction. For example, imagine that an entirely new compound has been discovered whose formula must be determined. That compound can be broken down in the laboratory and the elements present determined. Also, the ratio of the elements can be found. The formula obtained in this way shows the simplest possible ratio of the ele-

▼ Words to Know

Atom: The smallest particle of which an element can exist.

Chemical formula: A combination of chemical symbols that shows the composition of a compound.

Compound: A substance that contains two or more elements combined in a fixed proportion.

Empirical: Based on observation or experimentation.

Molecule: A particle formed by the combination of two or more atoms.

Valence: The tendency of an atom to gain or lose electrons in reacting with other atoms.

ments present and is known as the compound's empirical formula. The word empirical means "obtained by means of experimentation."

The empirical formula of a compound may not be its true or correct formula. Consider three different chemical compounds made of carbon and hydrogen only. The first compound contains one carbon atom and one hydrogen atom in each molecule. A molecule of the second compound consists of three carbon atoms and three hydrogen atoms joined to each other. And a molecule of the third compound contains six atoms of carbon and six atoms of hydrogen joined to each other.

The empirical formula for all three compounds is CH because the ratio of carbon to hydrogen is 1:1 in each. But the true formula is different for the three compounds. It is CH for the first compound, C_3H_3 for the second, and C_6H_6 for the third. The true, correct, or molecular formula for most chemical compounds also can be determined experimentally.

A second way of writing the chemical formula of a compound is by making intelligent guesses. When sodium reacts with chlorine to form sodium chloride, for example, each sodium atom loses one electron and each chlorine atom gains one electron. It makes sense to assume that the formula for sodium chloride is NaCl. To form the compound, every sodium atom needs one chlorine atom, so their final ratio should be 1:1.

Chemists now know enough about the chemical elements to use this method with confidence. The tendency of any given element to lose or gain electrons in forming a compound is called its valence. The valence of sodium, for example, is +1, and the valence of chlorine, −1. Using valences, chemists can write the formulas for most chemical compounds with a high degree of accuracy.

Kinds of chemical formulas

Molecular formulas are the simplest kind of formulas to write because they tell only the minimum amount of information: the kind and number of atoms present in a compound. Structural formulas are a more complex type of formula because they also show how the atoms in a molecule are arranged in space.

Structural formulas. The structural formula for water is H—O—H. The dashed lines (—) in this formula are called bonds. They stand for the electrons that hold each hydrogen atom to the oxygen atom.

Another example of a structural formula is the expanded structural formula. It shows not only the elements present (for example, hydrogen, carbon, and oxygen) and the ratio of those elements in the compound (for example, CH_4O), but also the arrangement of those atoms in comparison to each other. Thus, in an expanded structural formula you can see that three hydrogen atoms are attached to the carbon atom and one hydrogen atom is attached to the oxygen atom.

The only disadvantage of an expanded structural formula is the time and space required to write it out. Because of this disadvantage, chemists have developed an abbreviated kind of structural formula known as a condensed structural formula. The condensed structural formula for methanol can be written as:

$$CH_3—OH \text{ or } CH_3OH$$

Both the condensed and structural formulas for methanol provide the same information.

When students are first beginning to study chemistry, they generally have to write expanded structural formulas. With practice, however, they soon develop the ability to write condensed formulas.

Spatial formulas. Other kinds of chemical formulas contain even more information about the structure of a molecule. For example, the structure of the water molecule shown above (H—O—H) is not quite correct. The hydrogen atoms in a water molecule do not really stick out in opposite directions from each other. Instead, the O—H bonds are bent slightly at an angle to each other.

More sophisticated formulas may be necessary for compounds whose three-dimensional shape is important. The compound known as 1,3-dichlorocyclobutane is an example. The compound consists of four carbon atoms connected to each other in a ring. The ring can be thought of as a square piece of cardboard with one carbon atom at each corner. Attached to two carbon atoms at opposite corners are two chlorine atoms. This molecule can be represented in two different ways, with both chlorine atoms on the same side of the carbon ring or on opposite sides of the ring. The two molecules look different from each other, and two different kinds of 1,3-dichlorocyclobutane can actually be found in the laboratory. Formulas that show special three-dimensional shapes are sometimes known as conformational formulas.

[See also **Compound, chemical; Element, chemical; Symbol, chemical**]

Fossil and fossilization

A fossil is the remains or traces of a once-living plant or animal that was preserved in rock or other material before the beginning of recorded history. The term also is used to describe the fossil fuels (oil, coal, petroleum, and natural gas) that have been formed from the remains of ancient plants and animals. It is unusual for complete organisms to be preserved. Fossils usually represent the hard parts, such as bones or shells of animals and leaves, seeds, or woody parts of plants. Fossils occur on every continent and on the ocean floor. Through paleontology (the scientific study of fossils), it is possible to reconstruct ancient communities of living organisms and to trace the evolution of species.

Fossils of single-celled organisms have been recovered from rocks as old as 3.5 billion years. Animal fossils first appear in rocks dating back about 1 billion years. The occurrence of fossils in unusual places, such as dinosaur fossils in Antarctica and fish fossils on the Siberian steppes, is due to the shifting of the plates that make up Earth's crust and environmental changes (such as ice ages) over time. The best explanation for dinosaurs on Antarctica is not that they evolved there, but that Antarctica was once part of a much larger landmass with which it shared many lifeforms.

Formation of fossils

Most fossils are found in sedimentary rocks, those rocks produced by the accumulation of sediment such as sand or mud. Wind and other

▼ Words to Know

Amber: Transparent golden-brown resin fossil formed from hardened pine tree sap.

Cast: Fossil formed when a mold is later filled in by mud or mineral matter.

Geologic time periods: Episodes in Earth's history marked by different climate factors, sea levels, and lifeforms.

Index fossil: A distinctive fossil, common to a particular geological period, that is used to date rocks of that period.

Mold: Fossil formed when acidic water dissolves a shell or bone around which sand or mud has already hardened.

Paleontology: The scientific study of fossils.

Petrifaction: Process of turning organic material into rock by the replacement of that material with minerals.

Sediment: Sand, silt, clay, rock, gravel, mud, or other matter that has been transported by flowing water.

weathering conditions wash away sediment on land, depositing it in bodies of water. For this reason, fossils of sea creatures are more common than those of land creatures. Land animals and plants that have been preserved are found mostly in sediments in calm lakes, rivers, and estuaries.

The likelihood that any living organism will become a fossil is quite low. The path from the organic, living world to the world of rock and mineral is long and indirect. In the best conditions, fossilization will occur if an animal or plant dies and is quickly covered over with moist sediment. This prevents the animal or plant from being eaten by other organisms or from undergoing natural decay through exposure to oxygen and bacteria. The soft parts of an animal or plant decay more quickly than its hard parts. Teeth and bones are therefore more likely to be preserved than skin, tissues, and organs. Because of this fact, most fossils come from the time period dating to almost 600 million years ago, when organisms began to develop skeletons and hard parts.

Successful fossilization or preservation of an organism can occur in several ways: (1) preservation without change; (2) complete replacement by a mineral; (3) filling in of a hollow space by a mineral; (4) formation of a thin film of carbon; and (5) formation of an imprint or the filling in of an imprint.

Bones, shells, and teeth are examples of fossils preserved without change. The entire skeletal remains of animals that fell into ancient asphalt pits and quicksand have been preserved undamaged. Sometimes an entire organism may be preserved whole. An example of an almost perfectly preserved organism is an ancient insect trapped in pine tree sap. Over time, the pine sap hardened into a transparent golden-brown resin called amber, which contains the body of the insect. The remains of animals trapped in ice—such as woolly mammoths—have been found with skin and hair intact.

The process by which an organism is completely replaced by minerals is called petrifaction. The best-known example of this process is petrified wood, as seen in the Petrified Forest National Park in Arizona. Trees in this area were buried in mud and sand that contained the mineral silica. Ground water carried this dissolved mineral into the trees, where it replaced the wood cells so completely the trees became hardened opal.

Sometimes only small open spaces or holes in a shell or bone are filled in by dissolved minerals. The added mineral matter makes the shell or bone more compact and stonelike, preventing it from decaying.

A mosquito in amber, 35 million years old. *(Reproduced by permission of JLM Visuals.)*

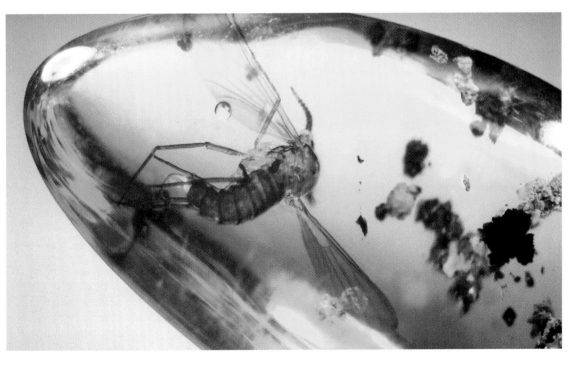

Another type of fossil is the darkened carbon imprint of a buried plant or, more rare, animal. When an organism dies and is buried, pressure underneath Earth's surface compresses the organism between rock faces. The organism decomposes, leaving a thin film of carbon on the rock face in the form of the organism. (All organic matter is made of carbon.) Leaves, insects, and fish are often found preserved this way.

An imprint in rock or the filling in of that imprint are other very common fossils. When an organism trapped in hardening sedimentary rock was dissolved by acidic water percolating through the rock, only the shape or form of the organism remained as an imprint. The cavity remaining in the rock is called a mold. If the mold were later filled in by mud or mineral matter, the resulting fossil is called a cast.

The fossil clock

The principal use of fossils by geologists has been to date rock layers (called strata) that have been deposited on the surface of Earth over millions of years. Different episodes in Earth's history (known as geologic time periods) are marked by different climate factors, sea levels, and lifeforms. Distinctive fossilized lifeforms that are typically associated with a specific geologic time period are known as index fossils. These are fos-

The bottom view of a fossil.
*(Reproduced by permission of
JLM Visuals.)*

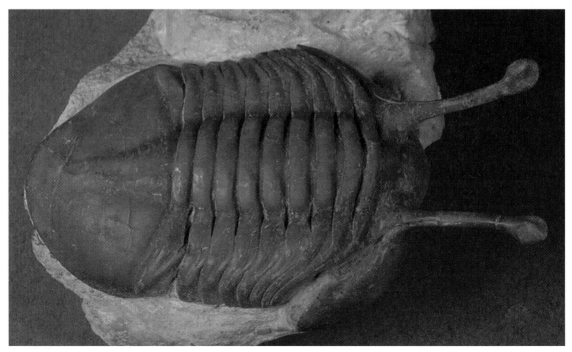

sils of organisms that lived for a short period of time in many areas. Since fossils and the rock they are found in are considered to be the same age, specific index fossils found in different rock layers in different areas indicate that the rock layers are the same age.

[*See also* **Dating techniques; Geologic time; Paleoecology; Paleontology; Rocks**]

Fractal

A fractal is a geometric figure with two special properties. First, it is irregular, fractured, fragmented, or loosely connected in appearance. Second, it is self-similar; that is, the figure looks much the same no matter how far away or how close up it is viewed.

The term fractal was invented by Polish French mathematician Benoit Mandelbrot (1924–) in 1975. He took the word from the Latin word *fractus,* which means "broken."

The idea behind fractals is fairly simple and obvious when explained. But the mathematics used to develop those ideas is not so simple.

Natural fractals

Most objects in nature do not have simple geometric shapes. Clouds, trees, and mountains, for example, usually do not look like circles, triangles, or pyramids. Instead, they can best be described as fractals. Natural objects that can be described as fractals are called natural fractals.

One of the natural objects most often used to explain fractals is a coastline. A coastline has the three properties typical of any fractal figure. First, a coastline is irregular, consisting of bays, harbors, and peninsulas. By definition, any fractal must be irregular in shape.

Second, the irregularity is basically the same at all levels of magnification. Whether viewed from orbit high above Earth, from a helicopter, or from land, whether viewed with the naked eye, or a magnifying glass, every coastline is similar to itself. While the patterns are not precisely the same at each level of magnification, the essential features of a coastline are observed at each level. This property is the self-similar property that also is basic to all fractals.

Third, the length of a coastline depends on the magnification at which it is measured. Measuring the length of a coastline on a photograph taken from space will give only an estimate of its length. Many small

The construction of a well-known fractal, the triadic Koch curve. A line segment (a) has its central one-third removed and replaced with a segment twice as long (b). In order to accomplish this, the replacement segment is "broken" in the middle. The resulting curve has four segments each one-third the length of the original line. Next, the center one-third of *each* of the four segments is replaced with a "broken" line twice as long as the segment that was removed (c). Now the curve has 16 segments, each one-ninth the length of the original line. Repeating this process indefinitely results in a Koch curve which is self-similar because any piece of it can be magnified by a factor of three and look the same as an unmagnified segment. *(Reproduced by permission of The Gale Group.)*

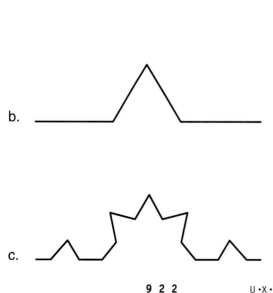

a.

b.

c.

bays and peninsulas will not appear, and the lengths of their perimeters will be excluded from the estimate. A better estimate can be obtained using a photograph taken from a helicopter. Some detail will still be missing, but many of the features missing in the space photo will be included. Thus, the estimate will be longer and closer to what might be termed the actual length of the coastline.

This estimate can be improved further by walking the coastline wearing a pedometer. Again, a longer measurement will result, perhaps more nearly equal to the actual length. But the result is still an estimate because many parts of a coastline are made up of rocks and pebbles that are smaller than the length of an average stride. Successively better estimates can be made by increasing the level of magnification, and each successive measurement will find the coastline longer. Eventually, the level of magnification must achieve atomic or even nuclear resolution to allow measurement of the irregularities in each grain of sand, each clump of dirt, and each tiny pebble, until the length appears to become infinite. This problematic result suggests the length of every coastline is the same.

The resolution of this problem requires that we rethink the way space is described. Standard one-dimensional space (such as a point), two-dimensional space (such as a line), and three-dimensional space (such as a sphere) are not adequate for the analysis of fractals. Instead, noninte-gral dimensions ($1\frac{1}{2}$; $2\frac{1}{3}$; etc.) are needed.

Constructions

Fractals can often be drawn by rather simple rules, as shown in the accompanying illustration. This drawing shows how the pathway taken by a dust particle in air can be modeled by using fractals. We begin in Step A with a straight line. First, the center one-third of the line is removed and broken in half, as shown in Step B. Next, the center one-third of each of the three remaining line segments is removed and broken in half, as shown in Step C. This process is repeated over and over again until a fractal figure is formed that looks like the path followed by a dust particle in air.

Applications

The similarity between fractals and natural objects has resulted in a number of important ap-

Words to Know

Dimension: The number of coordinates required to describe a figure, such as a point (one), line (two), or sphere (three).

Self-similar: Having an appearance that does not change no matter how far away or how close up an object is viewed.

Similarity: Having corresponding shapes.

plications for this field of mathematics. Fractals are used by geologists to model the meandering paths of rivers and the rock formations of mountains; by botanists to model the branching patterns of trees and shrubs; by astronomers to model the distribution of mass in the universe; by physiologists to model the human circulatory system; by physicists and engineers to model turbulence in fluids; and by economists to model the stock market and world economics.

Fraction, common

A fraction is a mathematical expression that states the ratio between two numbers. The adjective common in the term common fraction means that both numbers involved are integers, or whole numbers. The common fraction $\frac{3}{4}$ can be thought of as the whole number 3 being compared to the whole number 4 in some way or another. A common fraction is generally written with the two numbers separated by a diagonal or horizontal line, as $\frac{3}{4}$. The number above the line is the numerator of the fraction, and the number below the line, the denominator of the fraction. The diagonal or horizontal line separating the numerator and denominator is mathematically equivalent to the division sign ($\div$) or the ratio sign (:).

Meanings of fractions

The fraction "3 compared to 4," or $\frac{3}{4}$, can be interpreted in many ways. At a beginning level, one can imagine a whole object—such as a pie—divided into four parts. The common fraction $\frac{3}{4}$, in this instance, refers to 3 parts out of 4. The 4 in the fraction "$\frac{3}{4}$ of a pie" refers to the total number of parts into which the pie is divided. The 3 refers to the

Words to Know

Denominator: The bottom number in a fraction; the number of parts into which the whole has been divided.

Equivalent fractions: Two or more fractions with different numerators and denominators but the same numerical value.

Improper fraction: A fraction in which the numerator is greater than the denominator.

Numerator: The top number in a fraction; that part of a fraction that tells how many parts of the whole are being dealt with.

number of pieces being considered. Thus, $\frac{3}{4}$ means 3 of the 4 pieces cut from one whole pie.

Another way of interpreting fractions is to think of the denominator as a number of whole parts and the numerators as some selection of those parts. In this case, $\frac{3}{4}$ could refer to a set of 4 pies, 3 of which are being considered. In this case, $\frac{3}{4}$ means "3 pies out of a complete set of 4 pies."

Yet a third way of thinking about a fraction is as a division problem. The common fraction $\frac{3}{4}$ also means the number 3 divided by the number 4. Treating a common fraction as a division problem results in the formation of another kind of fraction, a decimal fraction. A decimal fraction is a fraction whose denominator is 10, 100, 1,000, or some other multiple of 10.

Dividing 3 by 4 results in 0.75. The number 0.75 is a decimal fraction because it can be thought of as a fraction whose denominator is 100. That is, 0.75 also can be expressed as the common fraction $\frac{75}{100}$.

Applications

Fractions are numbers that can be manipulated according to the same rules as those used for whole numbers, such as addition, subtraction, multiplication, and division. Fractions are of immense use in mathematics and physics (the science of matter and energy) and in the application of these studies to modern technology. They are used in everyday life as well, for instance when baking a cake or selecting a nut to screw into a bolt.

Frequency

Any process that repeats on a regular basis has an associated frequency. The frequency is the number of repetitions, or cycles, that occur during a given time interval. The inverse of the frequency is called the period of the process.

Suppose you stand on a beach and watch the waves come in. You will notice that the waves arrive in a regular pattern, perhaps one every second. The frequency of that wave motion, then, is one wave per second. The period for the wave motion is the inverse of the frequency, or one second per wave.

All forms of wave motion have some frequency associated with them. That frequency is defined as the number of wave crests (or troughs) that pass a given point per second. Light waves, for example, have a frequency of about 4×10^{14} to 7×10^{14} cycles per second. By comparison, the frequency of X rays is about 10^{18} cycles per second and that of radio waves is about 100 to 1,000 cycles per second.

The frequency of some processes depends on other factors. For example, the frequency with which a string vibrates depends on factors

Harmonics

What makes a note from a musical instrument sound rich and pleasing to the ear? The answer is harmonics.

If you pluck a guitar string, the string vibrates in a very complex way. If you could actually watch that vibration in slow motion, you would see the whole string vibrating at once with a frequency known as the fundamental frequency. At the same time, however, the string would be vibrating in halves (the first overtone), in thirds (the second overtone), and in even smaller segments. The collection of overtones is known as the harmonics of the sound produced by the vibrating string.

The harmonics produced by a vibrating string depend on factors such as the place the string is plucked and how strongly it is pulled. The many different sounds produced from a single guitar string depend on the variety of harmonics that a player can produce from that string.

such as the type of string used and its length. One way to change the frequency of a vibrating string is to change its length. The frequency of a vibrating string determines the pitch of the sound it produces. Thus, when a violinist plays on her instrument, she places her finger on different parts of the string in order to produce sounds of different pitches, or different notes.

Friction

Friction is a force that resists motion when the surface of one object slides over the surface of another. Frictional forces are always parallel to the surfaces in contact, and they oppose any motion or attempted motion. No movement will occur unless a force equal to or greater than the frictional force is applied to the body or bodies that can move.

Friction is often regarded as a nuisance because it reduces the efficiency of machines. It is also, however, an essential force for such items as nails, screws, pliers, bolts, forceps, and matches. Without friction we could not walk, play a violin, or pick up a glass of water.

Gravity and friction are the two most common forces affecting our lives. While we know a good deal about gravitational forces, we know relatively little about friction. Frictional forces are believed to arise from the forces of attraction between the molecules in two surfaces that are pushed together by pressure.

The surface of a given material may feel smooth. But at the atomic level, it is filled with valleys and hills a hundred or more atoms or molecules high. When one object is placed on top of another object, the pressure it exerts squeezes the hills and valleys in the two surfaces together. Molecules on the two surfaces tend to stick to one another, producing friction.

The laws of friction

Three laws apply to frictional forces. First, the force of friction between an object and the surface on which it rests is proportional to the weight of the object. The heavier the object, the greater the frictional force. The lighter the object, the less the frictional force. Second, in most cases, the force of friction between an object and the surface on which it rests is independent of the surface area of the object. Two objects may have very different surface areas, but if they weigh the same amount they will exert the same frictional force. Third, the force of friction between an object and the surface on which it rests is independent of the speed at which the object moves—provided that the speed is not zero.

The third law suggests that two kinds of friction exist, static and kinetic friction. Static friction is the force required to make an object at rest begin to move. In contrast, kinetic friction is the resistance to motion of an object moving across a surface. Static friction always is greater than kinetic friction because fewer areas of the object are in contact with a surface once a body is in motion. Molecules are not in contact long enough to form attractions to each other.

Two kinds of kinetic friction exist: sliding and rolling friction. When you push a book across a table top, the resistance you experience is caused by sliding friction. When you push a wheelbarrow over the ground, the resistance you feel is caused by rolling friction. In general, rolling friction is always less than sliding friction. One reason is that the contact area between a wheel and a surface is very small and brief.

The friction between two surfaces can be reduced by using a lubricant, such as oil. The oil reduces the amount of contact between two surfaces and allows them to slide or roll over each other more smoothly.

Function

A function is a mathematical relationship between two sets of real numbers. These sets of numbers are related to each other by a rule that assigns each value from one set to exactly one value in the other set. For example, suppose we choose the letter x to stand for the numbers in one set and the letter y for the numbers in the second set. Then, for each value we assign to x, we can find one and only one comparable value of y.

An example of a function is the mathematical equation $y = 3x + 2$. For any given value of x, there is one and only one value of y. If we choose 5 for the value of x, then y must be equal to 17 ($3 \cdot 5 + 2 = 17$). Or if we choose 11 for the value of x, then y must be equal to 35 ($3 \cdot 11 + 2 = 35$).

The standard notation for a function is $y = f(x)$ and is read "y equals f of x." Functions can also be represented in other ways, such as by graphs and tables. Functions are classified by the types of rules that govern their relationships: algebraic, trigonometric, logarithmic, and exponential. Mathematicians and scientists have found that elementary functions represent many real-world phenomena.

Characteristics of functions

The idea of a function is very important in mathematics because it describes any situation in which one quantity depends on another. For example, the height of a person depends, to a certain extent, on that person's age. The distance an object travels in four hours depends on its speed. When such relationships exist, one variable is said to be a function of the other. Therefore, height is a function of age and distance is a function of speed.

One way to represent the relationship between the two sets of numbers of a function is with a mathematical equation. Consider the relationship of the area of a square to its sides. This relationship is expressed by the equation $A = x^2$. Here, A, the value for the area, depends on x, the length of a side. Consequently, A is called the dependent variable and x is the independent variable. In fact, for a relationship between two variables to be called a function, every value of the independent variable must correspond to exactly one value of the dependent variable.

The previous equation mathematically describes the relationship between a side of the square and its area. In functional notation, the relationship between any square and its area could be represented by $f(x) = x^2$, where $A = f(x)$. To use this notation, we substitute the value found between the parentheses into the equation. For a square with a side 4 units long, the function of the area is $f(4) = 4^2$ or 16. Using $f(x)$ to describe the function is a matter of tradition. However, we could use almost any combination of letters to represent a function such as $g(s)$, $p(q)$, or even $LMN(z)$.

Just as we add, subtract, multiply, or divide real numbers to get new numbers, functions can be manipulated as such to form new functions.

Consider the functions $f(x) = x^2$ and $g(x) = 4x + 2$. The sum of these functions $f(x) + g(x) = x^2 + 4x + 2$. The difference of $f(x) - g(x) = x^2 - 4x + 2$. The product and quotient can be obtained in a similar way.

In addition to a mathematical equation, graphs and tables can be used to represent a function. Since a function is made up of two sets of numbers—each of which is paired with only one other number—a graph of a function can be made by plotting each pair on an x,y coordinate system known as the Cartesian coordinate system. Graphs are helpful because they make it easier to visualize the relationship between the domain and the range of the function.

Classification of functions

Functions are classified by the type of mathematical equation that represents their relationship. Algebraic functions are the most common type of function. These are functions that can be defined using addition, subtraction, multiplication, division, powers, and roots. Examples of algebraic functions include the following: $f(x) = x + 4$ and $f(x) = x/2$ and $f(x) = x^3$.

Two other common types of functions are trigonometric and exponential (or logarithmic) functions. Trigonometric functions deal with the sizes of angles and include the functions known as the sine, cosine, tangent, secant, cosecant, and cotangent. Exponential functions can be defined by the equation $f(x) = b^x$, where b is any positive number except 1. The variable b is constant and is known as the base.

An example of an exponential function is $f(x) = 10^x$. Notice that for values of x equal to 1, 2, 3, and 4, the values of $f(x)$ are 10, 100, 1,000, and 10,000. One property of exponential functions is that they change very rapidly with changes in the independent variable.

The inverse of an exponential function is a logarithmic function. In the equation $f(x) = 10^x$, one procedure is to set certain values of x (as we did in the example above) and then find the corresponding values of $f(x)$. Another possibility is to set certain values of $f(x)$ and find out what values of x are needed to produce those values. This process is using the exponential function in reverse and is known as a logarithmic function.

Applications

All types of functions have many practical applications. Algebraic functions are used extensively by chemists and physicists. Trigonometric functions are particularly important in architecture, astronomy, and navigation. Financial institutions often use exponential and logarithmic functions.

Fungi

Fungi (plural of fungus) are one of the five kingdoms of organisms. Kingdoms are the main divisions into which scientists classify all living things on Earth. The other kingdoms are: Monera (single-celled organisms without nuclei), Protista (single-celled organisms with a nucleus), Plantae (plants), and Animalia (animals).

Fungi constitute a large and diverse group of organisms. The kingdom of fungi is divided into four major groups: conjugating fungi, sac fungi, club fungi, and imperfect fungi. Mushrooms, molds, yeasts, and mildew are all fungi. Biologists have estimated that there are more than 200,000 species of fungi in nature, although only about 100,000 have been identified so far. The scientific study of fungi is called mycology.

General characteristics

The different groups of fungi have different levels of cellular organization. Some groups consist of single-celled organisms that have a single nucleus per cell. (A nucleus is a membrane-enclosed structure within a cell that contains the cell's genetic material and controls its growth and reproduction.) Other groups consist of single-celled organisms in which each cell has hundreds or thousands of nuclei. Still others consist of multicellular organisms that have one or two nuclei per cell. The bodies of multicellular fungi usually consist of slender, cottony filaments called hyphae. A mass of hyphae is called a mycelium. The mycelium carries on all the life-maintaining processes of the organism, including sexual reproduction (in most species).

Unlike plants, fungi do not contain chlorophyll (green pigment) and thus cannot create their own food through photosynthesis (the chemical process by which plants containing chlorophyll use sunlight to convert carbon dioxide and water to carbohydrates, releasing oxygen as a by-product).

Most species of fungi grow on land and obtain their nutrients from dead organic matter. Most species feed by secreting enzymes, which partially break down the food. The fungi then absorb the partially digested

Words to Know

Carbohydrate: A compound consisting of carbon, hydrogen, and oxygen found in plants and used as a food by humans and other animals.

Hyphae: Slender, cottony filaments making up the body of multicellular fungi.

Nucleus: Membrane-enclosed structure within a cell that contains the cell's genetic material and controls its growth and reproduction.

Parasite: Organism living in or on another organism (called a host) from which it obtains nutrients.

Photosynthesis: Chemical process by which plants containing chlorophyll use sunlight to convert carbon dioxide and water to carbohydrates, releasing oxygen as a by-product.

Symbiosis: Close relationship between two organisms of different species, which often benefits each member.

food to complete digestion internally. Because fungi (along with bacteria) help decompose dead plants, animals, and other organic matter, they serve an important ecological role. They release large amounts of carbon dioxide into the atmosphere and recycle nitrogen and other important nutrients for use by plants and other organisms.

Some fungi are parasites, living in or on another organism (called a host) from which they obtain their nutrients. This relationship usually harms the host. Such parasitic fungi usually have specialized tissues called haustoria that penetrate the host's body. Most of the diseases that afflict agricultural plants are caused by parasitic fungi. Some examples are corn smut, black stem rust of wheat and barley, and cotton root rot. Some species of fungi also can parasitize animals. Fungi that parasitize humans cause diseases such as athlete's foot, ringworm, and yeast infections.

Conjugating fungi

There are about 600 species of conjugating fungi. Most species are land-based and feed on organic matter, although there are a few parasitic species. The algaelike conjugating fungi have a continuous mycelium containing hundreds or thousands of nuclei, with no divisions between them. Species of conjugating fungi cause potato blight, downy mildew, black bread mold, and water mold (which affects dead leaves and sticks in water).

Sac fungi

Sac fungi are so-named because many species in this group reproduce sexually by forming a spore-filled structure called an ascus, which means literally "a sac." This large group of fungi includes many species

An American fly agaric. This mushroom is very common in all of North America, but it is somewhat more rare in the southern states, where specimens are more slender and tinged with a salmonlike color. *(Reproduced by permission of Field Mark Publications.)*

Lichens

A lichen is the product of a symbiotic (mutually beneficial) relationship between fungi and blue-green or green algae. The resulting structure resembles neither species. Typically, the algae supply carbohydrates to the fungi and the fungi supply nitrogen and other nutrients to the algae. Lichens can be very colorful, ranging from bright reds and oranges to yellows and greens, with white, gray, and black hues.

Many lichens can inhabit harsh environments and withstand prolonged periods of drought. In the temperate region of North America, lichens often grow on tree trunks and bare rocks and soil. In Antarctica, they have been found growing upon and within rocks. In the Arctic, the lichen species commonly known as reindeer mosses are important in the diets of caribou and reindeer.

that are beneficial to humans. For example, yeasts are a major group of sac fungi. Different yeasts are used by bakers, brewers, and vintners to make their bread, beer, or wine. Truffles, regarded as a food delicacy, are underground sac fungi that grow in association with tree roots.

Some species of sac fungi appear as blue-green molds on fruits, vegetables, and cheeses. Several other species are important for the making of cheeses, such as blue cheese.

Some other sac fungi cause plant diseases. These include chestnut blight (a disease that virtually wiped out the American chestnut as a mature forest tree) and Dutch elm disease.

Club fungi

Club fungi species reproduce sexually by forming spores on top of club-shaped structures called basidia. The club fungi are believed to be closely related to the sac fungi. This large group includes species that are known as mushrooms, toadstools, earthstars, stinkhorns, puffballs, jelly fungi, coral fungi, and many other interesting names. Some species, such as the rusts and smuts, cause disease in agricultural grains. Other species, such as the fly agaric, produce chemical hallucinogens (chemicals that induce visions) and have been used by numerous cultures in their religious ceremonies.

A significant species of club fungi is called mycorrhizae, which means "fungus root." Mycorrhizal fungus form a symbiotic relationship with many types of plant roots. (Symbiosis is the close association between two organisms of different species, which often benefits each member.) The fungus typically supplies nitrogen-containing compounds to the plant, and the plant supplies carbohydrates and other organic compounds to the fungus. Mycorrhizal fungus are very important for the growth of orchids and many trees, including pines and beeches.

Imperfect fungi

Mycologists have never observed the sexual reproduction of fungi in the imperfect fungi group. Since this part of their life cycle is missing, they are referred to as imperfect fungi. These fungi may have lost their sexual phase through the course of evolution. Species in this group produce plant and animal diseases. Athlete's foot and ringworm in humans are caused by imperfect fungi.

Some species in this group appear as blue-green molds on fruits, vegetables, and cheeses. Several other species are important for the making of cheeses such as blue cheese, Roquefort, and Camembert. Certainly the best known product obtained from this group of fungi is penicillin, the first widely used antibiotic. Penicillin was first discovered in the mold *Penicillium notatum* by Scottish bacteriologist Alexander Fleming (1881–1955) in 1928. Scientists now know it is produced by other species in this group, as well.

[*See also* **Fermentation; Hallucinogens; Parasite; Yeast**]

G

Gaia hypothesis

The Gaia (pronounced GAY-ah) hypothesis is the idea that Earth is a living organism and can regulate its own environment. This idea argues that Earth is able to maintain conditions that are favorable for life to survive on it, and that it is the living things on Earth that give the planet this ability.

Mother Earth

The idea that Earth and its atmosphere are some sort of "superorganism" was actually first proposed by Scottish geologist (a person specializing in the study of Earth) James Hutton (1726–1797), although this was not one of his more accepted and popular ideas. As a result, no one really pursued this notion until some 200 years later, when the English chemist James Lovelock (1919–) put forth a similar idea in his 1979 book, *Gaia: A New Look at Life on Earth*. Gaia is the name of the Greek goddess of Earth and mother of the Titans. In modern times, the name has come to symbolize "Earth Mother" or "Living Earth." In this book, Lovelock proposed that Earth's biosphere (all the parts of Earth that make up the living world) acts as a single living system that if left alone, can regulate itself.

As to the name Gaia, the story goes that Lovelock was walking in the countryside surrounding his home in Wilshire, England, and met his neighbor, English novelist William Golding (1911–1993), author of *Lord of the Flies* and several other books. Telling Golding of his new theory, he then asked his advice about choosing a suitable name for it, and the result of this meeting was that the term "Gaia" was chosen because of its

Words to Know

Biosphere: The sum total of all lifeforms on Earth and the interaction among those lifeforms.

Feedback: Information that tells a system what the results of its actions are.

Homeostasis: State of being in balance; the tendency of an organism to maintain constant internal conditions despite large changes in the external environment.

Photosynthesis: Chemical process by which plants containing chlorophyll use sunlight to manufacture their own food by converting carbon dioxide and water to carbohydrates, releasing oxygen as a by-product.

Symbiosis: A pattern in which two or more organisms live in close connection with each other, often to the benefit of both or all organisms.

real connection to the Greek goddess who pulled the living world together out of chaos or complete disorder.

Origin of Earth's atmosphere

Lovelock arrived at this hypothesis by studying Earth's neighboring planets, Mars and Venus. Suggesting that chemistry and physics seemed to argue that these barren and hostile planets should have an atmosphere just like that of Earth, Lovelock stated that Earth's atmosphere is different because it has life on it. Both Mars and Venus have an atmosphere with about 95 percent carbon dioxide, while Earth's is about 79 percent nitrogen and 21 percent oxygen. He explained this dramatic difference by saying that Earth's atmosphere was probably very much like that of its neighbors at first, and that it was a world with hardly any life on it. The only form that did exist was what many consider to be the first forms of life—anaerobic (pronounced ANN-ay-roe-bik) bacteria that lived in the ocean. This type of bacteria cannot live in an oxygen environment, and its only job is to convert nitrates to nitrogen gas. This accounts for the beginnings of a nitrogen build-up in Earth's atmosphere.

The oxygen essential to life as we know it did not start to accumulate in the atmosphere until organisms that were capable of photosynthesis evolved. Photosynthesis is the process that some algae and all plants use to convert chemically the Sun's light into food. This process uses carbon dioxide and water to make energy-packed glucose, and it gives off oxygen as a by-product. These very first photosynthesizers were a blue-green algae called cyanobacteria (pronounced SIGH-uh-no-bak-teer-eea) that live in water. Eventually, these organisms produced so much oxygen that they put the older anaerobic bacteria out of business. As a result, the only place that anaerobic bacteria could survive was on the deep-sea floor (as well as in heavily water-logged soil and in our own intestines). Lovelock's basic point was that the existence of life (bacteria) eventually made Earth a very different place by giving it an atmosphere.

Lovelock eventually went beyond the notion that life can change the environment and proposed the controversial Gaia hypothesis. He said that Gaia is the "Living Earth" and that Earth itself should be viewed as being alive. Like any living thing, it always strives to maintain constant or stable conditions for itself, called homeostasis (pronounced hoe-mee-o-STAY-sis). In the Gaia hypothesis, it is the presence and activities of life that keep Earth in homeostasis and allow it to regulate its systems and maintain steady-state conditions.

Cooperation over competition

Lovelock was supported in his hypothesis by American microbiologist Lynn Margulis (1918–) who became his principal collaborator. Margulis not only provided support, but she brought her own scientific ability and achievements to the Gaia hypothesis. In her 1981 book, *Symbiosis in Cell Evolution*, Margulis had put forth the then-unheard of theory that life as we know it today evolved more from cooperation than from competition. She argued that the cellular ancestors of today's plants and animals were groups of primitive, formless bacteria cells called prokaryotes (pronounced pro-KAR-ee-oats). She stated that these simplest of bacteria formed symbiotic relationships—relationships that benefitted both organisms—which eventually led to the evolution of new lifeforms. Her theory is called endosymbiosis (pronounced en-doe-sim-bye-O-sis) and is based on the fact that bacteria routinely take and transfer bits of genetic material from each other.

Margulis then argued that simple bacteria eventually evolved into more complex eukaryotic (pronounced you-kar-ee-AH-tik) cells or cells with a nucleus. These types of cells form the basic structure of plants and animals. Her then-radical but now-accepted idea was that life evolved more out of cooperation (which is what symbiosis is all about) than it did out of competition (in which only the strong survive and reproduce).

The simple prokaryotes did this by getting together and forming symbiotic groups or systems that increased their chances of survival. According to Margulis then, symbiosis, or the way different organisms adapt to living together to the benefit of each, was the major mechanism for change on Earth.

Most scientists now agree with her thesis that oxygen-using bacteria joined together with fermenting bacteria to form the basis of a type of new cell that eventually evolved into complex eukaryotes. For the Gaia hypothesis, the Margulis concept of symbiosis has proven to be a useful explanatory tool. Since it explains the origin and the evolution of life on Earth (by stating that symbiosis is the mechanism of change), it applies also to what continues to happen as the process of evolution goes on and on.

Gaia explained

The main idea behind the Gaia hypothesis can be both simple and complex. Often, several similar examples or analogies concerning the bodies of living organisms are used to make the Gaia concept easier to understand. One of these states that we could visualize Earth's rain forests as the lungs of the planet since they exchange oxygen and carbon dioxide. Earth's atmosphere could be thought of as its respiratory system, and its streams of moving water and larger rivers like its circulatory system, since they bring in clean water and flush out the system. Some say that the planet actually "breathes" because it contracts and expands with the Moon's gravitational pull, and the seasonal changes we all experience are said to reflect our own rhythmic bodily cycles.

Many of these analogies are useful in trying to explain the general idea behind the Gaia hypothesis, although they should not be taken literally. Lovelock, however, has stated that Earth is very much like the human body in that both can be viewed as a system of interacting components. He argues that just as our bodies are made up of billions of cells working together as a single living being, so too are the billions of different lifeforms on Earth working together (although unconsciously) to form a single, living "superorganism." Further, just as the processes or physiology of our bodies has its major systems (such as the nervous system, circulatory system, respiratory system, etc.), so, says Lovelock, Earth has its own "geophysiology." This geophysiology is made up of four main components: atmosphere (air), biosphere (all lifeforms), geosphere (soil and rock), and hydrosphere (water). Finally, just as our own physiological health depends on all of our systems being in good working condition and, above all, working together well, so, too, does Earth's geophysiology depend on its systems working in harmony.

Life is the regulating mechanism

Lovelock claims that all of the living things on Earth provide it with this necessary harmony. He states that these living things, altogether, control the physical and chemical conditions of the environment, and therefore it is life itself that provides the feedback that is so necessary to regulating something. Feedback mechanisms can detect and reverse any unwanted changes. A typical example of feedback is the thermostat in most homes. We set it to maintain a comfortable indoor temperature, usually somewhere in the range between 65°F (18°C) and 70°F (21°C). The thermostat is designed so that when the temperature falls below a certain setting, the furnace is turned on and begins to heat the house. When that temperature is reached and the thermostat senses it, the furnace is switched off. Our own bodies have several of these feedback mechanisms, all of which are geared to maintaining conditions within a certain proper and balanced range.

For Earth's critical balance, Lovelock says that it is the biosphere, or all of life on Earth, that functions as our thermostat or regulator. He says that the atmosphere, the oceans, the climate, and even the crust of Earth are regulated at a state that is comfortable for life *because of the behavior of living organisms*. This is the revolutionary lesson that the Gaia hypothesis wants to teach. It says that all of Earth's major components, such as the amount of oxygen and carbon dioxide in the atmosphere, the

The elongated globe view of the Earth. *(Reproduced by permission of The Stock Market.)*

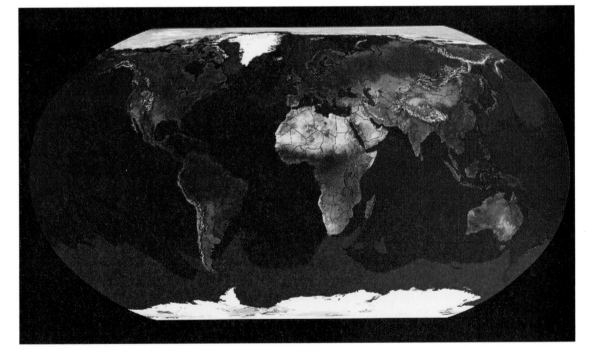

saltiness of the oceans, and the temperature of our surface is regulated or kept in proper balance by the activities of the life it supports. He also states that this feedback system is self-regulating and that it happens automatically. As evidence that, if left alone, Earth can regulate itself, he asserts that it is the activity of living organisms that maintain the delicate balance between atmospheric carbon dioxide and oxygen. In a way, Lovelock argues that it is life itself that maintains the conditions favorable for the continuation of life. For example, he contends that it is no accident that the level of oxygen is kept remarkably constant in the atmosphere at 21 percent. Lovelock further offers several examples of cycles in the environment that work to keep things on an even keel.

Lovelock also warns that since Earth has the natural capacity to keep things in a stable range, human tampering with Earth's environmental balancing mechanisms places everyone at great risk. While environmentalists insist that human activity (such as industrial policies that result in harming Earth's ozone layer) is upsetting Earth's ability to regulate itself, others who feel differently argue that Earth can continue to survive very well no matter what humans do exactly because of its built-in adaptability.

Earth as seen from space

An important aspect about the Gaia hypothesis is that it offers scientists a new model to consider. Most agree that such a different type of model was probably not possible to consider seriously until humans went into space. However, once people could travel beyond the atmosphere of Earth and put enough distance between them and their planet, then they could view their home from an extra-terrestrial viewpoint. No doubt that the 1960s photographs of the blue, green, and white ball of life floating in the total darkness of outer space made both scientists and the public think of their home planet a little differently than they ever had before. These pictures of Earth must have brought to mind the notion that it resembled a single organism.

Although the Gaia hypothesis is still very controversial and has not been established scientifically (by being tested and proven quantitatively), it has already shown us the valuable notion of just how interdependent everything is on Earth. We now recognize that Earth's biological, physical, and chemical components or major parts regularly interact with and mutually affect one another, whether by accident or on purpose. Finally, it places great emphasis on what promises to be the planet's greatest future problem—the quality of Earth's environment and the role humans will play in Earth's destiny.

[*See also* **Biosphere; Ecosystem**]

Galaxy

A galaxy is a large collection of stars, glowing nebulae (clouds), gas, and dust bound together by gravity. Many scientists now believe that a black hole, the remains of a massive star, lies at the center of many galaxies. Galaxies are as plentiful in the universe as grains of sand on a beach. The galaxy that contains our solar system is called the Milky Way. The Milky Way is part of a cluster of some 30 galaxies known as the Local Group, and the Local Group is part of a local supercluster that includes many clusters.

A photograph of the Andromeda galaxy (M31). Also seen, as the bright spot below and to the left of Andromeda, is one of its two dwarf elliptical satellite galaxies, M32 (NGC 221). Andromeda is a spiral galaxy some 2.2 million light-years from our own galaxy, the Milky Way. It measures approximately 170,000 light-years across, and as the largest of the nearby galaxies is faintly visible to the naked eye. *(Reproduced by permission of Photo Researchers, Inc.)*

Words to Know

Barred spiral galaxy: A spiral galaxy in which the spiral arms start at the end of a central bar structure rather than the nucleus.

Black hole: The remains of a massive star that has burned out its nuclear fuel and collapsed under tremendous gravitational force into a single point of infinite mass and gravity.

Dark matter: Unseen matter that has a gravitational effect on the motions of galaxies within clusters of galaxies.

Halo: A distribution of older stars and clusters of stars surrounding the nucleus of a spiral galaxy.

Irregular galaxy: A galaxy that does not fit into the shape categories of elliptical and spiral galaxies.

Light-year: The distance light travels in one year, roughly 5.88 trillion miles (9.46 trillion kilometers).

Milky Way: The galaxy in which we are located.

Nebulae: Bright or dark clouds, often composed of gases, hovering in the space between the stars.

Nucleus: The central core of a galaxy.

Radio waves: Electromagnetic radiation, or energy emitted in the form of waves or particles.

Spiral arms: The regions where stars are concentrated that spiral out from the center of a spiral galaxy.

Spiral galaxy: A galaxy in which spiral arms wind outward from the nucleus.

Although astronomers are not yet sure how galaxies formed and evolved, the process must have occurred quickly very early in the history of the universe. The age of the oldest galaxies appears to be about the same age as the universe, which is estimated to be 10 to 13 billion years old.

The shape of galaxies

Galaxies can be spiral, elliptical, or irregular in shape. The Milky Way and nearby Andromeda galaxy are both spiral shaped. They have a group of objects at the center (stars and possibly a black hole) surrounded by a halo of stars and an invisible cloud of dark matter. From this nucleus or center, arms spiral out like a pinwheel. The spiral shape is formed because the entire galaxy is rotating, with the stars at the outer edges forming the arms. Most spiral galaxies have just one arm wrapped around the nucleus, although some have two or even three arms.

Spiral galaxies are divided into two types: barred and unbarred. In barred spirals, a thick bar of stars crosses the center of the galaxy. Unbarred spirals have no such feature.

An elliptical galaxy contains mostly older stars, with very little dust or gas. It can be round or oval, flattened or spherical, and resembles the nucleus of a spiral galaxy without the arms. Astronomers do not yet know whether elliptical galaxies eventually form arms and become spirals, or if spiral galaxies lose their arms to become elliptical.

About one-quarter of all galaxies are irregular in shape and are much smaller than spiral galaxies. The irregular shape may be caused by the formation of new stars in these galaxies or by the pull of a neighboring galaxy's gravitational field. Two examples of an irregular galaxy are the Large and Small Magellanic Clouds, visible in the night sky from the Southern Hemisphere.

A fish-eye lens view of the southern Milky Way. *(Reproduced by permission of Photo Researchers, Inc.)*

Active Galaxies

An active galaxy is one that emits far more energy than a normal galaxy. The Milky Way, like most galaxies, is relatively stable and quiet. Active galaxies, on the other hand, give off more than 100 times the energy of the Milky Way. Explosions at the nucleus of active galaxies spew huge jets of material hundreds of thousands of light-years into space. The energy is emitted as radio waves (electromagnetic radiation) rather than optical light. There are several varieties of active galaxies, including Seyfert galaxies and quasars.

Seyfert galaxies look like spiral galaxies with a hyperactive nucleus. The normal-looking spiral arms surround an abnormally bright nucleus. Quasars are the most interesting of active galaxies. A quasar can emit more energy in one second than our sun has in its entire lifetime. Quasars, which look like stars, are the most distant and energetic objects in the universe known so far. Most astronomers consider a quasar to be the very active nucleus of a distant galaxy in the early stages of evolution. The light from a quasar has been traveling toward Earth for billions of years, perhaps from the very beginning of the universe.

Some galaxies are variations of these types. There are the Seyfert galaxies (violent, fast-moving spirals); bright elliptical galaxies of supergiants that often consume other galaxies; ring galaxies that seem to have no nucleus; twisted starry ribbons formed when two galaxies collide; and others.

The Milky Way

The Milky Way is a barred spiral galaxy about 100,000 light-years across. Its disklike nucleus, which bulges to about 30,000 light-years thick, contains billions of old stars and maybe even a black hole. It has four spiral arms. Our solar system is located in the Orion arm, about 30,000 light-years from the center of the galaxy.

Just as Earth revolves around the Sun, the Sun revolves around the nucleus of the galaxy. Traveling at a speed of about 155 miles (250 kilometers) per second, the Sun completes one revolution around the galactic center in about 220 million years.

In ancient times, people looked into space and saw a glowing band of light. They thought it resembled a river of milk and called it the Milky

Way. In the late 1500s, Italian physicist and astronomer Galileo Galilei (1564–1642) first examined the Milky Way through a telescope and saw that the glowing band was made up of countless stars. As early as 1755, German philosopher Immanuel Kant (1724–1804) suggested that the Milky Way was a lens-shaped group of stars, and that many other such groups existed in the universe.

Over the years, astronomers learned more about the shape of the Milky Way, but they continued to place our solar system at the center. In 1918, American astronomer Harlow Shapley (1885–1972) studied the distribution of star clusters and determined that our solar system was not at the center, but on the fringes of the galaxy.

Hubble and the expanding universe

In 1924, American astronomer Edwin Hubble (1889–1953) first proved the existence of other galaxies. Using a very powerful 100-inch (254-centimeter) telescope at Mount Wilson Observatory in California, he discovered that a group of stars long thought to be part of the Milky Way was actually a separate galaxy, now known as the Andromeda galaxy. Modern estimates place Andromeda 2.2 million light-years away from the Milky Way. Hubble also discovered many other spiral-shaped galaxies. In 1927, Dutch astronomer Jan Oort (1900–1992) showed that galaxies rotate about their center.

Beyond these important discoveries, Hubble found that more distant galaxies are moving away from us at a faster rate. From this observation, known as Hubble's Law, he deduced that the universe is expanding, a fundamental fact about the nature of the universe.

In early 1996, the Hubble Space Telescope sent back photographs of 1,500 very distant galaxies in the process of forming, indicating that the number of galaxies in the universe is far greater than previously thought. Based on this and other discoveries in the late 1990s, astronomers have estimated the number of galaxies to be 50 billion.

[See also **Quasar; Radio astronomy; Solar system; Star; Starburst galaxy**]

Game theory

Game theory is a branch of mathematics concerned with the analysis of conflict situations. The term conflict situation refers to a condition

Words to Know

Game: A situation in which a conflict arises between two or more players.

Nonzero-sum game: A game in which the amount lost by all players is not equal to the amount won by all other players.

Zero-sum, two-player games: A game in which the amount lost by one player is equal to the amount won by the other player.

involving two or more people or groups of people trying to achieve some goal. A simple example of a conflict situation is the game of tic-tac-toe. In this game, two people take turns making Xs or Os in a #-shaped grid. The first person to get three Xs or Os in a straight line wins the game. It is possible, however, that neither person is able to achieve this goal, and the game then ends in a tie or a stand-off.

The variety of conditions described by the term conflict situation is enormous. They range from board and card games such as poker, bridge, chess and checkers; to political contests such as elections; to armed conflicts such as battles and wars.

Mathematicians have long been intrigued by games and other kinds of conflict situations. Is there some mathematical system for winning at bridge? at poker? in a war? One of the earliest attempts to answer this question was the probability theory, developed by French mathematician and physicist (one who studies the science of matter and energy) Blaise Pascal (1623–1662) and his colleague Pierre de Fermat (1601–1665). At the request of a gentleman gambler, Pascal and Fermat explored the way to predict the likelihood of drawing certain kinds of hands (a straight, a flush, or three-of-a-kind, for example) in a poker game. In their attempts to answer such questions, Pascal and Fermat created a whole new branch of mathematics.

The basic principles of game theory were first suggested by Hungarian American mathematician and physicist John von Neumann (1903–1957) in 1928. The theory received little attention until 1944, when Neumann and economist Oskar Morgenstern (1902–1977) wrote the classic treatise *Theory of Games and Economic Behavior*. Since then, many economists and scientists have expanded and applied the theory.

Characteristics of games

The mathematical analysis of games begins by recognizing certain basic characteristics of all conflict situations. First, games always involve at least two people or two groups of people. In most cases, the game results in a win for one side of the game and a loss for the other side. Second, games always begin with certain set conditions, such as the dealing of cards or the placement of soldiers on a battlefield. Third, choices always have to be made. Some choices are made by the players themselves ("where shall I place my next X"?) and some choices are made by chance

Chess is considered a game of perfect information because both players know exactly where all the pieces are located and what moves they can make. *(Reproduced by permission of Field Mark Publications.)*

(such as rolling dice). Finally, the game ends after a set number of moves and a winner is declared.

Types of games

Games can be classified in a variety of ways. One method of classification depends on the amount of information players have. In checkers and chess, for example, both players know exactly where all the pieces are located and what moves they can make. There is no hidden information that neither player knows about. Games such as these are known as games of perfect information.

The same cannot be said for other games. In poker, for example, players generally do not know what cards their opponents are holding, and they do not know what cards remain to be dealt. Games like poker are known as games of imperfect knowledge. The mathematical rules for dealing with these two kinds of games are very different. In one case, one can calculate all possible moves because everything is known about a situation. In the other case, one can only make guesses based on probability as to what might happen next. Nonetheless, both types of games can be analyzed mathematically and useful predictions about future moves can be made.

Games also can be classified as zero-sum or nonzero-sum games. A zero-sum game is a game in which one person wins. Everything lost by the loser is given to the winner. For example, suppose that two players decide to match pennies. The rule is that each player flips a penny. If both pennies come up the same (both heads or both tails), player A wins both pennies. If both pennies come up opposite (one head and one tail), player B wins both pennies. This game is a zero-sum game because one player wins everything (both pennies) on each flip, while the other player loses everything. Game theory often begins with the analysis of zero-sum games between two players because they are the simplest type of conflict situation to analyze.

Most conflict situations in real life are not zero-sum games. At the end of a game of Monopoly™, for example, one player may have most of the property, but a second player may still own some property on the board. Also, the game may involve more than two people with almost any type of property distribution.

Application of game theory

Game theory is a powerful tool that can suggest the best strategy or outcome in many different situations. Economists, political scientists, the military, and sociologists have all used it to describe situations in their various fields. A recent application of game theory has been in the study of the behavior of animals in nature. Here, researchers are applying the notions of game theory to describe the many aspects of animal behavior including aggression, cooperation, and hunting methods. Data collected from these studies may someday result in a better understanding of our own human behaviors.

Gamma ray

Gamma rays are high-energy subatomic particles formed either by the decay of radioactive elements or by nuclear reactions. The wavelength of a gamma ray is very short—less than the radius of an atom—and the energy they carry can measure millions of electron volts.

Terrestrial gamma rays—those produced on Earth—are the only gamma rays we can observe here. A second class of gamma rays, called cosmic gamma rays, do not penetrate to the surface of Earth because the ozone layer absorbs high-energy radiation. The only way to detect cosmic gamma rays, which are created by nuclear fusion reactions that occur within the core of stars, is by sending a satellite-observatory into space.

First detection

Cosmic gamma rays were first discovered in 1967 by small satellites called Velas. These military satellites had been put into orbit to monitor nuclear weapon explosions on Earth, but they found gamma ray bursts from outside our solar system as well.

Several other small satellites launched in the early 1970s gave pictures of the whole gamma-ray sky. These pictures reveal hundreds of previously unknown stars and several possible black holes, the remains of massive stars. Thousands more stars were discovered in 1977 and 1979 by three large satellites called High Energy Astrophysical Observatories. They found that the entire Milky Way galaxy shines with gamma rays.

The Compton Gamma Ray Observatory

Then, on April 5, 1991, the National Aeronautics and Space Administration (NASA) sent the Compton Gamma Ray Observatory (CGRO) into space aboard the space shuttle *Atlantis*. During its nine-year mission, this 17-ton (15.4-metric ton) observatory provided scientists with an

↓ Words to Know

Antimatter: Matter composed of antiparticles, or subatomic particles identical to one another in mass but opposite in electric and magnetic charge. When an electron (with a negative charge) is brought together with its counterpart positron (with a positive charge), they destroy each other and are converted into energy.

Black hole: The remains of a massive star that has burned out its nuclear fuel and collapsed under tremendous gravitational force into a single point of infinite mass and gravity.

Interstellar medium: The space between the stars, consisting mainly of empty space with a very small concentration of gas atoms and tiny solid particles.

Nuclear reaction: The processes by which an atomic nucleus is split (fission) or joined with another (fusion), resulting in the release of great amounts of energy.

Ozone layer: The atmospheric layer of approximately 15 to 30 miles (24 to 48 kilometers) above Earth's surface that protects the lower atmosphere from harmful solar radiation.

Pulsar: Rapidly rotating star that emits varying radio waves at precise intervals; also known as a neutron star because much of the matter within has been compressed into neutrons.

all-sky map of cosmic gamma-ray emissions, as well as new information about supernovas, young star clusters, pulsars, black holes, quasars, solar flares, and gamma-ray bursts. Gamma-ray bursts are intense flashes of gamma rays that occur uniformly across the sky and are of unknown origin. The energy of just one of these bursts has been calculated to be more than 1,000 times the energy that our Sun will generate in its entire ten-billion-year lifetime.

A major discovery of the CGRO was the class of objects called gamma-ray blazars, quasars that emit most of their energy as gamma rays and vary in brightness over a period of days. Scientists also have found evidence for the existence of antimatter based on the presence of gamma rays given off by the mutual destruction of electrons and positrons in the interstellar medium, or the space between the stars.

Quasar: Extremely bright, starlike sources of radio waves that are the oldest known objects in the universe.

Radiation: Energy emitted in the form of waves or particles.

Radioactivity: The property possessed by some elements of spontaneously emitting energy in the form of particles or waves by disintegration of their atomic nuclei.

Radio waves: Electromagnetic radiation, or energy emitted in the form of waves or particles.

Solar flare: Sudden outbursts of light extending from the Sun that last only five to ten minutes and produce an incredible amount of energy.

Subatomic particle: Basic unit of matter and energy smaller than an atom.

Supernova: The explosion of a massive star at the end of its lifetime, causing it to shine more brightly than the rest of the stars in the galaxy put together.

Wavelength: The distance between one peak of a wave of light, heat, or energy and the next corresponding peak.

NASA decided to end the CGRO's mission after one of its three gyroscopes failed in December 1999. The observatory, which cost $670 million, could have been kept aloft for eleven more years, but NASA decided that if more equipment had failed, they could not control its return to Earth. So, on June 4, 2000, after completing 51,658 orbits of the planet, the CGRO re-entered Earth's atmosphere and broke apart. The charred remains of the craft—roughly 6 tons (5.4 metric tons) of superheated metal—splashed into the Pacific Ocean about 2,500 miles (4,020 kilometers) southeast of Hawaii.

To study gamma rays further, NASA plans to launch the Gamma Ray Large Area Telescope in 2005.

[*See also* **Gamma-ray burst; Radioactivity; Star**]

Gamma-ray burst

Gamma-ray bursts are unexplained intense flashes of light that occur several times a day in distant galaxies. The bursts give off more light than anything else in the universe and then quickly fade away. They were first detected in the late 1960s when instruments on orbiting satellites picked them up. No known explosion besides the big bang is more powerful than a gamma-ray burst. (The big bang is a theory that explains the beginning of the universe as a tremendous explosion from a single point that occurred 12 to 15 billion years ago.) Gamma-ray bursts are mysterious because scientists do not know for sure what causes them or where in the sky they will occur.

Types of bursts

There are two types of gamma-ray bursts: short and long. Short bursts last no more than two seconds. Long bursts can last up to just over fifteen minutes. The shorter life of a short gamma-ray burst makes it more difficult for astronomers to study. Short bursts leave no trace of light because they have no detectable afterglow (a gleam of light that remains briefly after the original light has dissipated). In addition, weaker gamma-

This photo taken by the Hubble Space Telescope on January 23, 1999, shows the remains of the most powerful cosmic explosion recorded to date. *(Reproduced by permission of the Corbis Corporation [Bellevue].)*

Words to Know

Big bang theory: Theory that explains the beginning of the universe as a tremendous explosion from a single point that occurred 12 to 15 billion years ago.

Black hole: Single point of infinite mass and gravity formed when a massive star burns out its nuclear fuel and collapses under its own gravitational force.

Gamma ray: Short-wavelength, high-energy radiation formed either by the decay of radioactive elements or by nuclear reactions.

Neutron star: The dead remains of a massive star following a supernova. It is composed of an extremely dense, compact, rapidly rotating core composed of neutrons that emits varying radio waves at precise intervals.

Supernova: The explosion of a massive star at the end of its lifetime, causing it to shine more brightly than the rest of the stars in the galaxy put together.

ray bursts tend to be observed as shorter, since only the higher parts of the emission are observable.

Astronomers believe that each type of burst may come from a different type of cosmic explosion. To learn more about the sources of gamma-ray bursts, scientists at the National Aeronautics and Space Administration (NASA) studied the time histories of short and long bursts. They did this by counting the number of gamma-ray pulses (particles of light, called photons, that arrive at about the same time) in each burst, and by measuring the arrival time of lower-energy and high-energy pulses. The astronomers learned that short bursts had fewer pulses than long bursts and that their lag times were twenty times shorter than those of longer bursts. This suggested that both long and short bursts were produced in physically different objects.

Theories of gamma-ray burst origin

Scientists' theories about the source of gamma-ray bursts are many. Some believe that they are a result of a fusion of black holes or neutron stars. (A black hole is the remains of a massive star that has burned out its nuclear fuel and collapsed under tremendous gravitational force into a single point of infinite mass and gravity. A neutron star is a dead remnant of a massive star; a star dies when it uses up all of its nuclear fuel.) Others believe that supernovae or hypernovae are the cause of a gamma-ray burst. (A supernova is a typical exploding star; a hypernova also is an exploding star, but with about 100 times more power as that of supernova.) In 2000, two sets of astronomers found evidence of an iron-rich cloud near gamma-ray bursts. Since stars at the supernova stage produce iron, the scientists theorized that a supernova emitted the iron cloud just before the gamma-ray burst.

The power of a gamma-ray burst is astounding. A satellite launched by NASA in 1991 detected gamma-ray bursts at a rate of nearly one a day for almost two years. The energy of just one burst was calculated to be more than 1,000 times the energy that the Sun would generate in its almost 10-billion-year lifetime.

The most distant gamma-ray burst measured so far is one that scientists detected on January 31, 2000. To determine how far the gamma-ray burst had traveled, astronomers measured the burst's spectrum (the range of individual wavelengths of radiation produced when light is broken down by the process of spectroscopy). Astronomers estimated that the explosion that caused the burst took place near the time the Milky Way

This image is made up of data taken by the first four years of the Compton Gamma-Ray Observatory spacecraft's telescope. The bright horizontal band along the center is the gamma-ray emission from the Milky Way galaxy. *(Reproduced by permission of the Corbis Corporation [Bellevue].)*

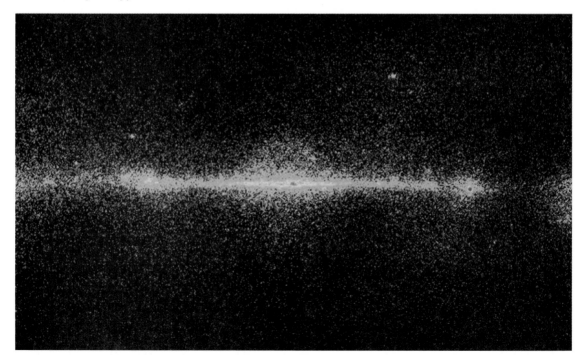

(a galaxy that includes a few hundred billion stars, the Sun, and our solar system) was formed, or 6 billion years before our solar system was born. Viewed another way, this particular gamma-ray burst has traveled through 90 percent of the age of the universe.

Scientists study gamma-ray bursts as a way of helping to better understand the evolution of the universe.

[*See also* **Gamma ray; Star**]

Gases, liquefaction of

Liquefaction of gases is the process by which a gas is converted to a liquid. For example, oxygen normally occurs as a gas. However, by applying sufficient amounts of pressure and by reducing the temperature by a sufficient amount, oxygen can be converted to a liquid.

Liquefaction is an important process commercially because substances in the liquid state take up much less room than they do in their gaseous state. As an example, oxygen is often used in space vehicles to burn the fuel on which they operate. If the oxygen had to be carried in its gaseous form, a space vehicle would have to be thousands of times larger than anything that could possibly fly. In its liquid state, however, the oxygen can easily fit into a space vehicle's structure.

Liquefaction of a gas occurs when its molecules are pushed closer together. The molecules of any gas are relatively far apart from each other, while the molecules of a liquid are relatively close together. Gas molecules can be squeezed together by one of two methods: by increasing the pressure on the gas or by lowering the temperature of the gas.

Critical temperature and pressure

Two key properties of gases are important in developing methods for their liquefaction: critical temperature and critical pressure. The critical temperature of a gas is the temperature at or above which no amount of pressure, however great, will cause the gas to liquefy. The minimum pressure required to liquefy the gas at the critical temperature is called the critical pressure.

For example, the critical temperature for carbon dioxide is 88°F (31°C). That means that no amount of pressure applied to a sample of carbon dioxide gas at or above 88°F will cause the gas to liquefy. At

↓ Words to Know

Critical pressure: The minimum pressure required to liquefy a gas at its critical temperature.

Critical temperature: The temperature at or above which no amount of pressure, however great, will cause a gas to liquefy.

Cryogenics: The production and maintenance of low temperature conditions and the study of the behavior of matter under such conditions.

Liquefied natural gas (LNG): A mixture of gases obtained from natural gas or petroleum from which almost everything except methane has been removed before it is converted to the liquid state.

Liquefied petroleum gas (LPG): A mixture of gases obtained from natural gas or petroleum that has been converted to the liquid state.

or below that temperature, however, the gas can be liquefied provided sufficient pressure is applied. The corresponding critical pressure for carbon dioxide at 88°F is 72.9 atmospheres. In other words, the application of a pressure of 72.9 atmospheres on a sample of carbon dioxide gas at 88°F will cause the gas to liquefy. (An atmosphere is a unit of pressure equal to the pressure of the air at sea level, or approximately 14.7 pounds per square inch.)

A difference in critical temperatures among gases means that some gases are easier to liquefy than are others. The critical temperature of carbon dioxide is high enough so that it can be liquefied relatively easily at or near room temperature. By comparison, the critical temperature of nitrogen gas is −233°F (−147°C) and that of helium is −450°F (−268°C). Liquefying gases such as nitrogen and helium present much greater difficulties than does the liquefaction of carbon dioxide.

Methods of liquefaction

In general, gases can be liquefied by one of three general methods: (1) by compressing the gas at temperatures less than its critical temperature; (2) by making the gas do some kind of work against an external force, causing the gas to lose energy and change to the liquid state; and (3) by using the Joule-Thomson effect.

Compression. In the first approach, the application of pressure alone is sufficient to cause a gas to change to a liquid. For example, ammonia has a critical temperature of 271°F (133°C). This temperature is well above room temperature. Thus, it is relatively simple to convert ammonia gas to the liquid state simply by applying sufficient pressure. At its critical temperature, that pressure is 112.5 atmospheres.

Making a gas work against an external force. A simple example of the second method for liquefying gases is the steam engine. A series of steps must take place before a steam engine can operate. First, water is boiled and steam is produced. That steam is then sent into a cylinder. Inside the cylinder, the steam pushes on a piston. The piston, in turn, drives some kind of machinery, such as a railroad train engine.

As the steam pushes against the piston, it loses energy. Since the steam has less energy, its temperature drops. Eventually, the steam cools off enough for it to change back to water.

This example is not a perfect analogy for the liquefaction of gases. Steam is not really a gas but a vapor. A vapor is a substance that is normally a liquid at room temperature but that can be converted to a gas quite easily. The liquefaction of a true gas, therefore, requires two steps. First, the gas is cooled. Next, the cool gas is forced to do work against some external system. It might, for example, be driven through a small turbine. A turbine is a device consisting of blades attached to a central rod. As the cooled gas pushes against the turbine blades, it makes the rod rotate. At the same time, the gas loses energy, and its temperature drops even further. Eventually the gas loses enough energy for it to change to a liquid.

This process is similar to the principle on which refrigeration systems work. The coolant in a refrigerator is first converted from a gas to a liquid by one of the methods described above. The liquid formed then absorbs heat from the refrigerator box. The heat raises the temperature of the liquid, eventually changing it back to a gas.

There is an important difference between liquefaction and refrigeration, however. In the former process, the liquefied gas is constantly removed from the system for use in some other process. In the latter process, however, the liquefied gas is constantly recycled within the refrigeration system.

Using the Joule-Thomson effect. Gases also can be made to liquefy by applying a principle discovered by English physicists James Prescott Joule (1818–1889) and William Thomson (later known as Lord

Kelvin; 1824–1907) in 1852. The Joule-Thomson effect depends on the relationship of volume, pressure, and temperature in a gas. Change any one of these three variables, and at least one of the other two (or both) will also change. Joule and Thomson found, for example, that allowing a gas to expand very rapidly causes its temperature to drop dramatically. Reducing the pressure on a gas accomplishes the same effect.

To cool a gas using the Joule-Thomson effect, the gas is first pumped into a container under high pressure. The container is fitted with a valve with a very small opening. When the valve is opened, the gas escapes from the container and expands quickly. At the same time, its temperature drops.

In some cases, the cooling that occurs during this process may not be sufficient to cause liquefaction of the gas. However, the process can be repeated more than once. Each time, more energy is removed from the gas, its temperature falls further, and it eventually changes to a liquid.

Practical applications

The most common practical applications of liquefied gases are the compact storage and transportation of combustible fuels used for heating, cooking, or powering motor vehicles. Two kinds of liquefied gases are widely used commercially for this reason: liquefied natural gas (LNG) and liquefied petroleum gas (LPG). LPG is a mixture of gases obtained from natural gas or petroleum that has been converted to the liquid state. The mixture is stored in strong containers that can withstand very high pressures.

Liquefied natural gas (LNG) is similar to LPG, except that it has had almost everything except methane removed. LNG and LPG have many similar uses.

In principle, all gases can be liquefied, so their compactness and ease of transportation make them popular for a number of other applications. For example, liquid oxygen and liquid hydrogen are used in rocket engines. Liquid oxygen and liquid acetylene can be used in welding operations. And a combination of liquid oxygen and liquid nitrogen can be used in Aqua-Lung™ devices (an underwater breathing apparatus).

Liquefaction of gases also is important in the field of research known as cryogenics (the branch of physics that deals with the production and effects of extremely low temperatures). Liquid helium is widely used for the study of behavior of matter at temperatures close to absolute zero, 0 K (−459°F; −273°C).

[*See also* **Cryogenics; Gases, properties of**]

Gases, properties of

Gases are a state of matter characterized by two properties: their lack of definite volume and their lack of definite shape. This definition suggests, in the first place, that a given mass of gas can occupy any volume whatsoever. Imagine a cylindrical tank filled with a small amount of hydrogen gas placed in a chemistry laboratory. If the top is removed from that tank in a room, the gas escapes from the tank to fill the room. If the door to the room is opened, the gas then escapes to fill the building. If the building door also is opened, the gas escapes into the outside environment and, at least in theory, then expands throughout the universe. Neither solids nor liquids, the other two common forms of matter, display this property.

Gases also take the shape of the container in which they are placed. Suppose the valve of the tank of hydrogen gas is fitted with a rubber hose that leads to a cubic box. When the valve is opened, the hydrogen gas fills the cubic box. Its shape changes from cylindrical to cubic. Liquids also take the shape of their container, although solids do not.

Kinetic theory of matter

Our understanding of the properties of gases arises from the kinetic theory of matter. The kinetic theory of matter says that all matter is made

Solid carbon dioxide, known as dry ice, passes directly into a gaseous state at room temperature. *(Reproduced by permission of Photo Researchers, Inc.)*

Words to Know

Direct proportion: A mathematical relationship between two variables such that a change in one produces a corresponding change in the other in the same direction.

Gas law: A statement that shows the mathematical relationship of the volume, pressure, and temperature of a gas.

Ideal gas: A gas in which the particles of the gas have no effect on each other.

Inverse proportion: A mathematical relationship between two variables such that a change in one produces a corresponding change in the other, but in the opposite direction.

Kinetic theory of matter: A scientific theory that says that all matter is made up of tiny particles that are constantly in motion.

up of tiny particles that are constantly in motion. In solids, those particles are relatively close together and move relatively slowly. In liquids, they are somewhat farther apart and move more rapidly. In gases, those particles are very far apart and move with much greater speed than in solids or liquids.

The rapid speed with which gas particles move explains their tendency to fly away from each other and fill any container in which they are placed. Their relatively great distance from each other explains the other properties of gases explained below.

Gas laws

Most of the fundamental laws describing the properties of gases were discovered in the eighteenth and early nineteenth centuries. Those laws deal primarily with three properties of gases: their volume, pressure, and temperature.

Boyle's law. The volume of a gas depends on the pressure exerted on it. When you pump up a bicycle tire, you push down on a handle that squeezes the gas inside the pump. You can squeeze a balloon and reduce its size (the volume it occupies). In general, the greater the pressure exerted on a gas, the less its volume. Conversely, the less pressure on a gas,

Some Gases and Their Properties

Name	Formula	Content % in atm	Color	Odor	Toxicity
Ammonia	NH_3	—	Colorless	Penetrating	Toxic
Argon	Ar	0.93	Colorless	Odorless	Nontoxic
Carbon dioxide	CO_2	0.03	Colorless	Odorless	Nontoxic
Carbon monoxide	CO	—	Colorless	Odorless	Very toxic
Chlorine	Cl_2	—	Pale green	Irritating	Very toxic
Helium	He	0.00052	Colorless	Odorless	Nontoxic
Hydrogen	H_2	0.0005	Colorless	Odorless	Nontoxic
Hydrochloric acid	HCl	—	Colorless	Irritating	Corrosive
Hydrogen sulfide	H_2S	—	Colorless	Foul	Very toxic
Krypton	Kr	0.00011	Colorless	Odorless	Nontoxic
Methane	CH_4	0.0002	Colorless	Odorless	Nontoxic
Neon	Ne	0.0018	Colorless	Odorless	Nontoxic
Nitrogen	N_2	78.1	Colorless	Odorless	Nontoxic
Nitrogen dioxide	NO_2	—	Red brown	Irritating	Very toxic
Nitric oxide	NO	—	Colorless	Odorless	Very toxic
Ozone	O_3	Varied	Bluish	Sharp	Sharp
Oxygen	O_2	20.9	Colorless	Odorless	Nontoxic
Radon	Rd		Colorless	Odorless	Toxic
Sulfur dioxide	SO_2	—	Colorless	Choking	Toxic
Xenon	Xe	0.0000087	Colorless	Odorless	Nontoxic

the greater its volume. A relationship of this kind is said to be an inverse proportion. Increasing one variable (such as the pressure) causes a decrease in the other variable. This mathematical relationship between volume and pressure was discovered in 1662 by English chemist Robert Boyle (1627–1691). This relationship is true *only* if the temperature of the gas remains constant while the pressure is changed.

Charles's law. If a balloon is taken from inside a warm house to much cooler air outside, the balloon will appear to collapse. Volume and temperature have a direct relationship to each other. When temperature increases, so does volume; when temperature decreases, so does volume. The mathematical relationship between gas volume and temperature was first derived in 1787 by French physicist Jacques Alexandre Charles (1746–1823). Charles's law is valid *only* when the pressure on the gas is constant.

Gay-Lussac's law.   The relationship between temperature and pressure can be observed when pumping up a bicycle or car tire. The tire gets warmer as more air is added to it. The reason for this change is that increasing the pressure on a gas also increases its temperature. This relationship was first expressed mathematically by French chemist Gay-Lussac (1778–1850) around 1802. Again, this law is valid *only* when the volume of a gas remains constant (as when it's trapped in a tire).

The combined gas law.   The final gas law—one that shows how volume, pressure, and temperature are related to each other—is called the combined gas law. The value of the gas laws is that one can find any one of the variables, assuming that the others are known.

Ideal and real gases

All four of the gas laws previously discussed apply only to ideal gases. An ideal gas is a theoretical concept developed by scientists to learn more about gases. The particles of which an ideal gas is made have no effect on each other. That is, they do not exert gravitational attraction on each other, and they bounce off each other without losing any energy.

If one makes these assumptions about gases, it is much easier to develop laws describing their behavior. There is, however, one problem with this concept: there is no such thing as an ideal gas in the real world. All gas particles really do interact with each other in some way or another.

That fact doesn't mean that the gas laws are useless. Instead, it warns us that the predictions made by the gas laws may be more or less incorrect. The more or less depends on how closely the gas under consideration resembles an ideal gas. Some gases, like hydrogen and helium, match the description of an ideal gas quite well; other gases do not even come close.

Properties of real gases

Gases, like other forms of matter, have physical properties such as color, odor, and taste. In general, gases tend to be colorless and odorless, although some important exceptions exist. Also, most gases are transparent: that is, it is possible to see objects through them rather clearly.

Generator

A generator is a machine that converts mechanical energy into electrical energy. Generators can be subdivided into two major categories depending on whether the electric current produced is alternating current (AC)

Words to Know

Alternating current (AC): Electric current in which the direction of flow changes back and forth rapidly and at a regular rate.

Armature: A part of a generator consisting of an iron core around which is wrapped a wire.

Commutator: A slip ring that serves to reverse the direction in which an electrical current flows in a generator.

Direct current (DC): Electrical current that always flows in the same direction.

Electromagnetic induction: The production of an electromotive force (something that moves electricity) in a closed electrical circuit as a result of a changing magnetic field.

Slip ring: The device in a generator that provides a connection between the armature and the external circuit.

or direct current (DC). The basic principle on which both types of generators work is the same, although the details of construction of the two may differ somewhat.

Principle of operation

In 1820, Danish physicist Hans Christian Oersted (1777–1851) discovered that an electric current created a magnetic field around it. French physicist André Marie Amperè (1775–1836) then found that a coil of wire with current running through it behaved just like a magnet.

In about 1831, English physicist Michael Faraday (1791–1867) discovered the scientific principle on which generators operate: electromagnetic induction. By reversing the work of Oersted and extending the work of Amperè, Faraday reasoned that if a current running through a coiled wire could produce a magnetic field, then a magnetic field could induce (generate) a current of electricity in a coil of wire. By moving a magnet back and forth in or near a coil of wire, he created an electrical current without any other source of voltage feeding the wire.

Faraday also discovered that it makes no difference whether the coil rotates within the magnetic field or the magnetic field rotates around the coil. The important factor is that the wire and the magnetic field are in motion in relation to each other. In general, most AC generators have a stationary (fixed) magnetic field and a rotating coil, while most DC generators have a stationary coil and a rotating magnetic field.

Alternating current (AC) generators

A magnet creates magnetic lines of force on either side of it that move in opposite directions. As the metal coil passes through the magnetic field

Serbian-born American electrical engineer Nikola Tesla (1856–1943) with one of his early electrical generators. *(Reproduced by permission of The Granger Collection, Ltd.)*

in a generator, the electrical power that is produced constantly changes. At first, the generated electric current moves in one direction (as from left to right). Then, when the coil reaches a position where it is parallel to the magnetic lines of force, no current at all is produced. As the coil continues to rotate, it cuts through magnetic lines of force in the opposite direction, and the electrical current generated travels in the opposite direction (as from right to left). The ends of the coil are attached to metal slip rings that collect the electrical current. Each slip ring, in turn, is attached to a metal brush, which transfers the current to an external circuit.

Thus, a spinning coil in a fixed magnetic field will produce an alternating current, one that travels first in one direction and then in the opposite. The rate at which the current switches back and forth is known as its frequency. Ordinary household current alternates at a frequency of 60 times per second (or 60 hertz).

The efficiency of an AC generator can be increased by substituting an armature for the wire coil. An armature consists of a cylinder-shaped iron core with a long piece of wire wrapped around it. The longer the piece of wire, the greater the electrical current that can be generated by the armature.

Commercial generators. One of the most important uses of generators is the production of large amounts of electrical energy for use in industry and homes. The two most common energy sources used in operating AC generators are water and steam. Both of these energy sources have the ability to drive generators at the very high speeds at which they operate most efficiently, usually no less than 1,500 revolutions per minute.

In order to generate hydroelectric (water) power, a turbine is needed. A turbine consists of a large central shaft on which are mounted a series of fanlike vanes. As moving water strikes the vanes, it causes the central shaft to rotate. If the central shaft is then attached to a very large magnet, it causes the magnet to rotate around a central armature, generating electricity.

Steam power is commonly used to run electrical generating plants. Coal, oil, or natural gas is burned—or the energy from a nuclear reactor is harnessed—to boil water to create steam. The steam is then used to drive a turbine which, in turn, spins a generator.

Direct current (DC) generators

An AC generator can be modified to produce direct current (DC) electricity also. This change requires a commutator. A commutator is simply a slip ring that has been cut in half, with both halves insulated from each other. The brushes attached to each half of the commutator are arranged so that at the moment the direction of the current in the coil reverses, they slip from one half of the commutator to the other. The current that flows into the external circuit, therefore, is always traveling in the same direction. This results in a steadier current.

[*See also* **Electric current; Electromagnetic field; Electromagnetic induction**]

Genetic disorders

Genetic disorders are conditions that have some origin in an individual's genetic make-up. Many of these disorders are inherited and are governed by the same genetic rules that determine dimples and red hair. However, some genetic disorders—such as Down syndrome, characterized by heart malformation, poor muscle tone, and a flattened face—result from a spontaneous mutation (gene change) that takes place during embryonic (earliest life) development.

Genetic disorders can be classified according to the way in which they develop. If the disorder is transmitted by genes inherited from only one parent, it is said to be an autosomal dominant disorder. The term autosome applies to any of the 22 chromosomes that are identical in human males and females. (Chromosomes are structures that organize genetic information in the nucleus of cells.) By contrast, disorders that can be inherited only by the transmission of genes from both parents is called an autosomal recessive disorder.

Other genetic disorders are associated with the X (female) or Y (male) chromosome and are called sex-linked disorders because the X and Y chromosomes are related to sexual characteristics in humans. Finally, the development of some genetic disorders involves environmental factors, factors present outside the organism itself. Such disorders are known as multifactorial genetic disorders.

Principles of genetic inheritance

Genetic information in humans is stored in units known as genes located on large complex molecules called chromosomes. A vast range of human characteristics, from eye and hair color to musical and literary talents, are controlled by genes. To say that a person has red hair color,

Words to Know

Chromosomes: Structures that organize genetic information in the nucleus of cells.

Dominant trait: A trait that can manifest (be expressed) when inherited from one parent.

Gene: A section of a chromosome that carries instructions for the formation, functioning, and transmission of specific traits from one generation to another.

Multifactorial trait: A trait that results from both genetic and environmental influences.

Proteins: Large molecules that are essential to the structure and functioning of all living cells.

Recessive trait: A trait that is expressed in offspring only when identical genes for the trait are inherited from both parents.

Sex-linked disorder: A disorder that generally affects only one sex (male or female).

for example, is simply to say that that person's body contains genes that tell hair cells how to make red hair.

Reproduction in humans occurs when a sperm cell from a male penetrates and fertilizes an egg cell from a female. The fertilized egg cell, called a zygote, contains genes from both parents. For example, the zygote will contain two genes that control hair color, one gene from the mother and one gene from the father.

In some cases, both genes carry the same message. For example, the zygote might contain two genes that act as a kind of code that tells a cell to make red hair, one from each parent. In that case, the child will be born with red hair.

In other cases, two genes may carry different messages. The zygote might, for instance, carry a gene for red hair from the mother and for brown hair from the father. In such cases, one gene is dominant and the other recessive. As these terms suggest, one gene will "win out" over the other and determine the offspring's hair color. In this example, the gene for brown hair is dominant over the gene for red hair, and the offspring will have brown hair.

Dominant genetic disorders

If one parent has an autosomal dominant disorder, then offspring have a 50 percent chance of inheriting that disease. Approximately 2,000 autosomal dominant disorders (ADDs) have been identified. These disorders have effects that range from inconvenience to death. ADDs include Huntington's disorder, polydactyly (extra toes or fingers), Marfan's syndrome (extra long limbs), achondroplasia (a type of dwarfism), some forms of glaucoma (a vision disorder), and hypercholesterolemia (high blood cholesterol).

ADDs may occur early or late in life. People with ADDs that are diagnosed at older ages are faced with very special problems. They may already have had children of their own and transmitted the genetic trait that caused their disorder to their offspring.

Huntington's disease (also known as Huntington's chorea) is an example of an ADD that is typically diagnosed relatively late in life. The

A young girl with the genetic disorder Down syndrome. *(Reproduced by permission of Photo Researchers, Inc.)*

disorder is characterized by progressive involuntary, rapid, jerky motions and mental deterioration. It usually appears in affected individuals between the ages of 30 and 50, and leads to dementia and eventual death in about 15 years.

Marfan's syndrome, also called arachnodactyly, is an ADD characterized by long, thin arms, legs, and fingers. People with Marfan's syndrome also tend to be stoop-shouldered and have a bluish tint to their eyeballs. In addition, these individuals have a high incidence of eye and heart problems. Abraham Lincoln is believed to have had Marfan's syndrome.

Recessive genetic disorders

Recessive genetic disorders (RGD) are caused when both parents supply a recessive gene to their offspring. The probability of such an event's occurring is 25 percent each time the parents conceive. About 1,000 confirmed RGDs exist. Some of the better known examples of the

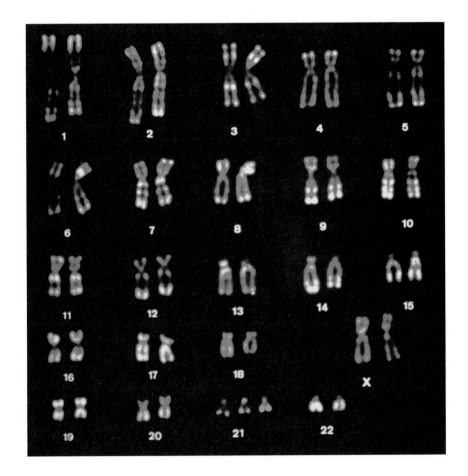

Down syndrome is a genetic disorder resulting from three chromosomes instead of two in chromosome pair 21. (Reproduced by permission of Custom Medical Stock Photo, Inc.)

condition include cystic fibrosis, sickle-cell anemia, Tay-Sachs disease, galactosemia, phenylketonuria (PKU), adenosine deaminase deficiency, growth hormone deficiency, Werner's syndrome (juvenile muscular dystrophy), albinism (lack of skin pigment), and autism.

Some RGDs tend to affect people of one particular ethnic background at a higher rate than the rest of the population. Three such RGDs are cystic fibrosis, sickle-cell anemia, and Tay-Sachs disease. Cystic fibrosis is one of the most common autosomal recessive diseases in Caucasian children in the United States. About 5 percent of Caucasians carry this recessive gene. Cystic fibrosis is characterized by excessive secretion of an unusually thick mucus that clogs respiratory ducts and collects in lungs and other body areas. Cystic fibrosis patients usually die before the age of 20, although some individuals live to the age of 30.

Sickle-cell anemia occurs with an unusually high incidence among the world's black and Hispanic populations. However, some cases also occur in Italian, Greek, Arabian, Maltese, southern Asian, and Turkish people. About 1 in 12 blacks carry the gene for this disorder. Sickle-cell anemia is caused by mutations in the genes responsible for the production of hemoglobin. (Hemoglobin is the compound that carries oxygen in red blood cells to tissues and organs throughout the body.) Sickle-cell anemia patients have red blood cells that live only a fraction of the normal life span of 120 days. The abnormal blood cells have a sickled appearance, which led to the disease's name. Sickle-cell patients also die early, before the age of 30.

The Tay-Sachs gene is carried by 1 in 30 Ashkenazi Jews. Children born with Tay-Sachs disorder seem normal for the first 5 months of their lives. But afterwards, they begin to express symptoms of the disorder. Eventually, the condition leads to blindness and death before the age of four.

Galactosemia and PKU are examples of metabolic RGDs. A metabolic RGD is one in which a person's body is unable to carry out functions that are normal and essential to the body. For example, people with galactosemia lack an enzyme (chemical) needed to metabolize (break down) galactose, a sugar found in milk. If people with galactosemia do not avoid normal milk, mental retardation will eventually develop. People with PKU have a similar problem. They lack an enzyme needed to convert the amino acid phenylalanine to the amino acid tyrosine. The build-up of phenylalanine in the body leads to severe mental retardation.

Adenosine deaminase deficiency is one of few "curable" genetic diseases. It is caused by a mutation in a single gene essential to normal development of the immune system. Bone marrow transplants have been found to be of some value to patients. In addition, gene therapy has been

Color Blindness

Is the traffic light red or green? Most humans have the ability to distinguish the color we call red from the color we call green. But some people cannot. Such people are said to be color-blind. Color blindness is a defect in vision that makes it difficult or impossible for a person to distinguish between or among certain colors.

Color-blindness is usually passed on genetically, and is more common in men than in women. About 6 percent of all men and roughly one-tenth of that many women inherit the condition. Individuals also can acquire the condition through various eye diseases. There is no treatment for color blindness.

The most common form of color-blindness involves the inability to distinguish reds from greens. A less common condition involves the inability to distinguish green from yellow.

Color blindness is caused by a lack of pigment in the retina of the eye. Normally, the retina contains molecules capable of detecting every color in the spectrum. However, if some of these molecules are not present, the various colors in the spectrum can not be distinguished from each other, and the person is color-blind.

Color blindness is a sex-linked characteristic. The gene involved in the disorder occurs only on the X chromosome, which is passed to the child by the mother. The Y chromosome, which is passed to the child by the father, does not carry the defective gene. As a result, children inherit color blindness only from their mothers.

successful at replacing these patients' defective gene with a copy of a correct gene that enables their immune system to function effectively.

Sex-linked genetic disorders

Sex-linked genetic disorders (XLGDs) can be either dominant or recessive. Dominant XLGDs affect females, are usually fatal, and cause severe disorders in males who survive. A high percentage of male embryos with dominant XLGD spontaneously abort early in a pregnancy. Dominant XLGD's include conditions such as Albright's hereditary osteodystrophy (seizures, mental retardation, stunted growth), Goltz's syndrome (mental retardation), cylindromatosis (deafness and upper body tumors), oral-facial-digital syndrome (no teeth, cleft tongue, some mental retardation), and incontinentia pigmenti (abnormal swirled skin pigmentation).

Recessive XLGDs are passed to sons through their mothers. Major XLGDs include severe combined immune deficiency syndrome (SCID), color blindness, hemophilia, Duchenne's muscular dystrophy (DMD), some spinal ataxias, and Lesch-Nyhan syndrome. Roughly one-third of these XLGDs result from a spontaneous mutation. Of these disorders, color blindness is the least harmful.

Hemophilia is an example of a serious XLGD. This disorder is caused by the absence of a protein responsible for the clotting of blood. Lacking this protein, a person with hemophilia may easily bleed to death from simple cuts and injuries that would be of little danger to the average person. Hemophilia A is the most severe form of this disease, and is characterized by extreme bleeding. It affects males primarily, although it has been known to occur in females. The disorder has often been associated with royalty. England's Queen Victoria was a carrier whose descendants became rulers in several European countries.

Other usually fatal XLGDs affect the immune, muscular, and nervous systems. SCID, for example, is a disorder affecting the immune system. It is characterized by a very poor ability to combat infection. One way to treat patients with SCID is to completely enclose them in a large plastic bubble that protects them from germs present in the air. The only known cure for SCID involves a bone marrow transplant from a close relative.

DMD afflicts young boys and is apparent by age three or four. It is characterized by wasting leg and pelvic muscles. Patients with DMD are usually wheelchair-bound by the age of 12, and die before the age of 20, often as the result of heart problems.

Multifactorial genetic disorders

Scientists often find it difficult to determine the relative role of heredity and environment in certain medical disorders. One way to answer this question is with statistical and twin studies. Identical and fraternal twins who have been raised in different and identical homes are evaluated for these MFGDs. If fraternal twins have a higher than normal incidence of a disorder and identical twins show an even higher rate of the disorder, then genetic inheritance is believed to contribute to development of the disorder.

Among the most likely candidates for multifactorial genetic disorders are certain medical conditions associated with diet and metabolism, such as obesity, diabetes, alcoholism, rickets, and high blood pressure;

some infectious diseases, such as measles, scarlet fever, and tuberculosis; schizophrenia and some other psychological illnesses; club foot and cleft lip; and various forms of cancer.

The tendency of some people to be more susceptible to a particular MFGD and not another is characteristic of human genetics. All healthy humans have a similar body form with very similar physiological functions. Still, it is easy to see tremendous human diversity that results from a diverse gene pool. This diversity explains why certain groups of people with similar kinds of genes are more prone to some disorders, whereas others have resistance to the same disorders. This diversity protects the human race from being wiped out by a single kind of medical problem.

[*See also* **Birth defects; Cancer; Chromosome; Embryo and embryonic development; Gene; Genetic engineering; Human Genome Project; Mendelian laws of inheritance; Mutation; Nucleic acid**]

Genetic engineering

Genetic engineering is any process by which genetic material (the building blocks of heredity) is changed in such a way as to make possible the production of new substances or new functions. As an example, biologists have now learned how to transplant the gene that produces light in a firefly into tobacco plants. The function of that gene—the production of light—has been added to the normal list of functions of the tobacco plants.

The chemical structure of genes

Genetic engineering became possible only when scientists had discovered exactly what is a gene. Prior to the 1950s, the term gene was used to stand for a unit by which some genetic characteristic was transmitted from one generation to the next. Biologists talked about a "gene" for hair color, although they really had no idea as to what that gene was or what it looked like.

That situation changed dramatically in 1953. The English chemist Francis Crick (1916–) and the American biologist James Watson (1928–) determined a chemical explanation for a gene. Crick and Watson discovered the chemical structure for large, complex molecules that occur in the nuclei of all living cells, known as deoxyribonucleic acid (DNA).

DNA molecules, Crick and Watson announced, are very long chains or units made of a combination of a simple sugar and a phosphate group.

▼ Words to Know

Amino acid: An organic compound from which proteins are made.

DNA (deoxyribonucleic acid): A large, complex chemical compound that makes up the core of a chromosome and whose segments consist of genes.

Gene: A segment of a DNA molecule that acts as a kind of code for the production of some specific protein. Genes carry instructions for the formation, functioning, and transmission of specific traits from one generation to another.

Gene splicing: The process by which genes are cut apart and put back together to provide them with some new function.

Genetic code: A set of nitrogen base combinations that act as a code for the production of certain amino acids.

Host cell: The cell into which a new gene is transplanted in genetic engineering.

Human gene therapy (HGT): The application of genetic engineering technology for the cure of genetic disorders.

Nitrogen base: An organic compound consisting of carbon, hydrogen, oxygen, and nitrogen arranged in a ring that plays an essential role in the structure of DNA molecules.

Plasmid: A circular form of DNA often used as a vector in genetic engineering.

Protein: Large molecules that are essential to the structure and functioning of all living cells.

Recombinant DNA research (rDNA research): Genetic engineering; a technique for adding new instructions to the DNA of a host cell by combining genes from two different sources.

Vector: An organism or chemical used to transport a gene into a new host cell.

Attached at regular positions along this chain are nitrogen bases. Nitrogen bases are chemical compounds in which carbon, hydrogen, oxygen, and nitrogen atoms are arranged in rings. Four nitrogen bases occur in DNA: adenine (A), cytosine (C), guanine (G), and thymine (T).

The way in which nitrogen bases are arranged along a DNA molecule represents a kind of genetic code for the cell in which the molecule occurs. For example, the sequence of nitrogen bases T-T-C tells a cell that it should make the amino acid known as lysine. The sequence C-C-G, on the other hand, instructs the cell to make the amino acid glycine.

A very long chain (tens of thousands of atoms long) of nitrogen bases tells a cell, therefore, what amino acids to make and in what sequence to arrange those amino acids. A very long chain of amino acids arranged in a particular sequence, however, is what we know of as a protein. The specific sequence of nitrogen bases, then, tells a cell what kind of protein it should be making.

Furthermore, the instructions stored in a DNA molecule can easily be passed on from generation to generation. When a cell divides (reproduces), the DNA within it also divides. Each DNA molecule separates into two identical parts. Each of the two parts then makes a copy of itself. Where once only one DNA molecule existed, now two identical copies of the molecule exist. That process is repeated over and over again, every time a cell divides.

This discovery gave a chemical meaning to the term gene. According to our current understanding, a specific arrangement of nitrogen bases forms a code, or set of instructions, for a cell to make a specific protein. The protein might be the protein needed to make red hair, blue eyes, or wrinkled skin (to simplify the possibilities). The sequence of bases, then, holds the code for some genetic trait.

Gene splicing

The Crick-Watson discovery opened up unlimited possibilities for biologists. If genes are chemical compounds, then they can be manipulated just as any other kind of chemical compound can be manipulated. Since DNA molecules are very large and complex, the actual task of manipulation may be difficult. However, the principles involved in working with DNA molecule genes is no different than the research principles with which all chemists are familiar.

For example, chemists know how to cut molecules apart and put them back together again. When these procedures are used with DNA molecules, the process is known as gene splicing. Gene splicing is a process that takes place naturally all the time in cells. In the process of division or repair, cells routinely have to take genes apart, rearrange their components, and put them back together again.

Scientists have discovered that cells contain certain kinds of enzymes that take DNA molecules apart and put them back together again.

Endonucleases, for example, are enzymes that cut a DNA molecule at some given location. Exonucleases are enzymes that remove one nitrogen base unit at a time. Ligases are enzymes that join two DNA segments together.

It should be obvious that enzymes such as these can be used by scientists as submicroscopic scissors and glue with which one or more DNA molecules can be cut apart, rearranged, and the put back together again.

Genetic engineering procedures

Genetic engineering requires three elements: the gene to be transferred, a host cell into which the gene is inserted, and a vector to bring about the transfer. Suppose, for example, that one wishes to insert the gene for making insulin into a bacterial cell. Insulin is a naturally occurring protein made by cells in the pancreas in humans and other mammals. It controls the breakdown of complex carbohydrates in the blood to glucose. People whose bodies have lost the ability to make insulin become diabetic.

The first step in the genetic engineering procedure is to obtain a copy of the insulin gene. This copy can be obtained from a natural source

DNA being injected into a mouse embryo. (Reproduced by permission of Phototake.)

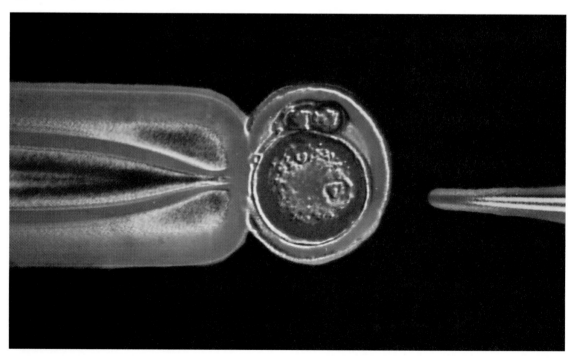

(from the DNA in a pancreas, for example), or it can be manufactured in a laboratory.

The second step in the process is to insert the insulin gene into the vector. The term vector means any organism that will carry the gene from one place to another. The most common vector used in genetic engineering is a circular form of DNA known as a plasmid. Endonucleases are used to cut the plasmid molecule open at almost any point chosen by the scientist. Once the plasmid has been cut open, it is mixed with the insulin gene and a ligase enzyme. The goal is to make sure that the insulin gene attaches itself to the plasmid before the plasmid is reclosed.

The hybrid plasmid now contains the gene whose product (insulin) is desired. It can be inserted into the host cell, where it begins to function just like all the other genes that make up the cell. In this case, however, in addition to normal bacterial functions, the host cell also is producing insulin, as directed by the inserted gene.

Notice that the process described here involves nothing more in concept than taking DNA molecules apart and recombining them in a different arrangement. For that reason, the process also is referred to as recombinant DNA (rDNA) research.

Applications of genetic engineering

The possible applications of genetic engineering are virtually limitless. For example, rDNA methods now enable scientists to produce a number of products that were previously available only in limited quantities. Until the 1980s, for example, the only source of insulin available to diabetics was from animals slaughtered for meat and other purposes. The supply was never large enough to provide a sufficient amount of affordable insulin for everyone who needed insulin. In 1982, however, the U.S. Food and Drug Administration approved insulin produced by genetically altered organisms, the first such product to become available.

Since 1982, the number of additional products produced by rDNA techniques has greatly expanded. Among these products are human growth hormone (for children whose growth is insufficient because of genetic problems), alpha interferon (for the treatment of diseases), interleukin-2 (for the treatment of cancer), factor VIII (needed by hemophiliacs for blood clotting), erythropoietin (for the treatment of anemia), tumor necrosis factor (for the treatment of tumors), and tissue plasminogen activator (used to dissolve blood clots).

Genetic engineering also promises a revolution in agriculture. Recombinant DNA techniques enable scientists to produce plants that are resistant to herbicides and freezing temperatures, that will take longer to ripen, and that will manufacture a resistance to pests, among other characteristics.

Today, scientists have tested more than two dozen kinds of plants engineered to have special properties such as these. As with other aspects of genetic engineering, however, these advances have been controversial. The development of herbicide-resistant plants, for example, means that farmers are likely to use still larger quantities of herbicides. This trend is not a particularly desirable one, according to some critics. How sure can we be, others ask, about the risk to the environment posed by the introduction of "unnatural," engineered plants?

The science and art of animal breeding also are likely to be revolutionized by genetic engineering. For example, scientists have discovered that a gene in domestic cows is responsible for the production of milk. Genetic engineering makes it possible to extract that gene from cows who produce large volumes of milk or to manufacture that gene in the laboratory. The gene can then be inserted into other cows whose milk production may increase by dramatic amounts because of the presence of the new gene.

Human gene therapy

One of the most exciting potential applications of genetic engineering involves the treatment of human genetic disorders. Medical scientists know of about 3,000 disorders that arise because of errors in an individual's DNA. Conditions such as sickle-cell anemia, Tay-Sachs disease, Duchenne muscular dystrophy, Huntington's chorea, cystic fibrosis, and Lesch-Nyhan syndrome result from the loss, mistaken insertion, or change of a single nitrogen base in a DNA molecule. Genetic engineering enables scientists to provide individuals lacking a particular gene with correct copies of that gene. If and when the correct gene begins functioning, the genetic disorder may be cured. This procedure is known as human gene therapy (HGT).

The first approved trials of HGT with human patients began in the 1980s. One of the most promising sets of experiments involved a condition known as severe combined immune deficiency (SCID). Individuals with SCID have no immune systems. Exposure to microorganisms that would be harmless to the vast majority of people will result in diseases that can cause death. Untreated infants born with SCID who are not kept in a sterile bubble become ill within months and die before their first birthday.

In 1990, a research team at the National Institutes of Health (NIH) attempted HGT on a four-year-old SCID patient. The patient received about one billion cells containing a genetically engineered copy of the gene that his body lacked. Another instance of HGT was a procedure, approved in 1993 by NIH, to introduce normal genes into the airways of cystic fibrosis patients. By the end of the 1990s, according to the NIH, more than 390 gene therapy studies had been initiated. These studies involved more than 4,000 people and more than a dozen medical conditions.

In 2000, doctors in France claimed they had used HGT to treat three babies who suffered from SCID. Just ten months after being treated, the babies exhibited normal immune systems. This marked the first time that HGT had unequivocally succeeded.

Controversy remains. Human gene therapy is the source of great controversy among scientists and nonscientists alike. Few individuals maintain that the HGT should not be used. If we could wipe out sickle-cell anemia, most agree, we should certainly make the effort. But HGT raises other concerns. If scientists can cure genetic disorders, they can also design individuals in accordance with the cultural and intellectual fashions of the day. Will humans know when to say "enough" to the changes that can be made with HGT?

Genetically engineered sheep with the human gene responsible for the production of alpha-1-antitrypsin (AAT) transferred into their DNA. When the AAT is eventually extracted from their milk, it will be used as therapy for humans deficient in AAT. The deficiency causes emphysema (a breathing disorder) in approximately 100,000 people in the western world. *(Reproduced by permission of Photo Researchers, Inc.)*

Despite recent successes, most results in HGT since the first experiment was conducted in 1990 have been largely disappointing. And in 1999, research into HGT was dealt a blow when an eighteen-year-old from Tucson, Arizona, died in an experiment at the University of Pennsylvania. The young man, who suffered from a metabolic disorder, had volunteered for an experiment to test gene therapy for babies with a fatal form of that disease. Citing the spirit of this young man, researchers remain optimistic, vowing to continue work into the possible lifesaving opportunities offered by HGT.

The commercialization of genetic engineering

The commercial potential of genetically engineered products was not lost on entrepreneurs in the 1970s. A few individuals believed that the impact of rDNA on American technology would be comparable to that of computers in the 1950s. In many cases, the first genetic engineering firms were founded by scientists involved in fundamental research. The American biologist Herbert Boyer, for example, teamed up with the venture capitalist Robert Swanson in 1976 to form Genentech (Genetic Engineering Technology). Other early firms like Cetus, Biogen, and Genex were formed similarly through the collaboration of scientists and businesspeople.

The structure of genetic engineering (biotechnology) firms has, in fact, long been a source of controversy. Many observers have questioned the right of a scientist to make a personal profit by running companies that benefit from research that had been carried out at publicly funded universities. The early 1990s saw the creation of formalized working relations between universities, individual researchers, and the corporations founded by these individuals. Despite these arrangements, however, many ethical issues remain unresolved.

[*See also* **Birth defects; Chromosome; Diabetes mellitus; Gene; Genetic disorders; Genetics; Human Genome Project; Nucleic acid**]

Genetics

Genetics is the branch of biology concerned with the science of heredity. The term heredity refers to the way in which specific characteristics are transmitted from one generation to the next. For example, we know that a tall mother and a tall father tend to have children that are tall. Geneticists (scientists who study genetics) are interested in finding out two things about this observation. First, what is there in the cells of a person's body

Words to Know

DNA (deoxyribonucleic acid): Molecules that make up chromosomes and on which genes are located.

Dominant gene: The state or genetic trait that will always express itself when present as part of a pair of genes in a chromosome.

Gene: A section of a DNA molecule that carries instructions for the formation, functioning, and transmission of specific traits from one generation to another.

Heredity: The transmission of characteristics from parents to offspring.

Nucleotide: A group of atoms present in a DNA molecule.

Proteins: Large molecules that are essential to the structure and functioning of all living cells.

Recessive gene: The state or genetic trait that can express itself only when two genes, one from both parents, are present and act as a kind of code for creating the trait, but will not express itself when paired with a dominant gene.

Triad: Also known as codon; group of three nucleotides that carries a specific message for a cell.

that directs the body to become tall rather than short. Second, how are the directions for "tallness" transmitted from parent to offspring, from one generation to the next?

The history of genetics

Humans have known about hereditary characteristics for thousands of years. That knowledge has been used for the improvement of domestic plants and animals. Until the late nineteenth century, however, that knowledge had been gained by trial-and-error experiments. The modern science of genetics began with the pioneering work of the Austrian monk and botanist Gregor Mendel (1822–1884).

Mendel studied the genetic characteristics of pea plants. He was interested in finding out how certain traits, such as flower color and plant height, were passed on from generation to generation. During his lifetime, he studied dozens of generations of plants of all sizes, shapes, and colors. As a result of his research, Mendel was able to state a few basic laws describing the way genetic traits are inherited. He also came to the conclusion that there must be a specific biological unit responsible for the transmission of genetic traits. He called that unit a factor. Mendel's "factors" were later given the name of genes.

Without question, Mendel was the father of the modern science of genetics. One of the great ironies of history, however, was that his discoveries were lost for more than three decades. Then, in the early 1900s, Mendel's research was rediscovered almost simultaneously by three different biologists, the Dutch botanist Hugo de Vries (1848–1935), the German botanist Karl F. J. Correns (1864–1933), and the Austrian botanist Erich Tschermak von Seysenegg (1871–1962).

Although interest in genetics grew rapidly after 1900, a fundamental problem remained. Geneticists based all of their laws, theories, and experiments on the concept of the gene. But no one had any idea as to what was a gene. It seemed clear that the gene was probably some kind of chemical compound, or some combination of compounds. But no one had been able to determine exactly what kind of compound or compounds it was.

The answer to that question came in 1953. The American biologist James Watson (1928–) and the English chemist Francis Crick (1916–) collaborated to discover that a gene was a section of a very large and complex molecule found in the nuclei of all cells, the deoxyribonucleic acid (DNA) molecule.

The chemistry of genes

Imagine a very long chain of beads strung together to form a strand containing hundreds of thousands of beads. The strand contains beads of only four colors: red, yellow, blue, and green. That strand of beads can be compared to half of a DNA molecule. The other half of the molecule is a second strand almost identical to the first strand.

Watson and Crick showed that the sequence in which various colors of beads occur is significant. A DNA molecule in which the beads are arranged in the sequence blue-yellow-yellow-red-red-blue-blue-blue-, and so on, has meaning for a cell. The sequence tells the "chemical machinery" of the cell to make a certain kind of protein, such as the protein responsible for red hair or blue eyes. Another sequence of colors, for example, red-red-yellow-green-blue-green-red-, and so on, might be the "code" for making blonde hair or green eyes.

The components of a DNA molecule are not, of course, colored beads. They are certain groups of atoms known as nucleotides. Each nucleotide in a DNA molecule is comparable to one of the colored beads in the analogy above. Just as there are only four colors of beads in the above analogy, so there are only four different nucleotides in DNA molecules. Those nucleotides might be represented by the symbols A, C, G, and T (corresponding to bead colors of red, blue, green, and yellow). A DNA molecule, then, is a very long chain of nucleotides with a structure something like the following:

-C-T-A-T-C-G-A-C-T-T-G-A-C-T-T-T-G-C-C-A-C-A-A-C- . . .

The dots at the end of the chain indicate that the chain actually goes on much, much longer.

Watson and Crick said that each set of three nucleotides—they called them triads or codons—carried a specific message that cells could understand. Those messages told a cell to "make red hair," or "make blue eyes," or "help a person to grow tall," or "give a person musical talent," or any one of thousands of other traits that each human possesses.

Francis Crick (right) and James Watson display their model of DNA's structure.

This discovery answered the first question that geneticists had about heredity: how cells know which traits they are "supposed" to make and what functions they are "supposed" to carry out. The same discovery also answered the second question puzzling geneticists: how do these traits get passed down from generation to generation?

The answer to that question is that DNA molecules have the ability to make copies of themselves. When a cell divides (reproduces), so do the DNA molecules it contains. In most cases, two exactly identical molecules are produced from a single parent molecule.

When an egg cell (female reproductive cell) and a sperm cell (male reproductive cell) unite during fertilization, each cell provides DNA to the fertilized egg. The DNA from both parents combines to form DNA for the offspring. Whatever nucleotide sequences the mother and father had in their own cells, they pass on to their child.

Dominant and recessive traits

One fundamental question remains in the above example: suppose that a child is born to a father with red hair and a mother with blonde hair. What color hair will the child have?

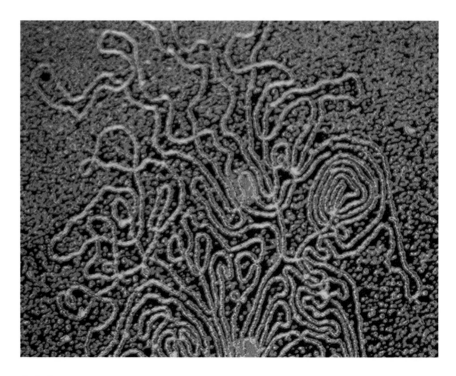

Strands of DNA. *(Reproduced by permission of The Stock Market.)*

Mendel worked with this question long before Watson and Crick discovered the nature of DNA. He found that for any one genetic trait, there were always two possible conditions. A flower might be red or white; a plant might be tall or short; a pea pod might be smooth or wrinkled; and so on. Mendel also discovered that one of these two conditions was more likely to "win out" over the other. He called the "winner" the dominant trait and the loser the recessive trait.

If a pea plant inherits a "tall" gene for height from both parent plants, the offspring is most like to be tall. If the pea plants inherits a "short" gene for height from both parent plants, the offspring is most likely to be short. But if the pea plant inherits a "tall" gene from one parent and a "short" gene from the second parent, the offspring is most likely to be tall.

An important part of Mendel's work was finding out what the mathematical chances of various kinds of combinations might be. For example, he showed how to calculate the probabilities that would result when a "tall" parent pea plant was crossed with a "short" parent pea plant in the first, second, and succeeding generations.

The future of genetics

One can apply the principles of genetics in a great many situations without knowing anything about the structure of DNA molecules. However, the Watson-Crick discovery made possible a revolutionary change in the basic nature of genetics. As long as scientists had no idea as to what a gene was, there was not much they could do to make changes in the genes of a plant, animal, or human. But Watson and Crick showed that genes are nothing other than chemical compounds. If someone can make changes in chemical compounds in a laboratory, that person can also make changes in a DNA molecule. The problems faced are a good deal more difficult since DNA molecules are far more complex than most molecules that chemists work with. But the basic principles involved are the same.

Scientists are exploring a variety of ways in which genes can be modified to produce cells that can do things they could not do before. For example, it is possible to create the gene for the hormone (chemical messenger) known as insulin in a chemical laboratory. The work is fairly difficult, but by no means impossible. It simply requires that the correct atoms be assembled in the correct sequence. That artificial gene can then be inserted into the DNA of other organisms, such as bacteria. When the artificial gene becomes part of the bacterial DNA, it begins to function just like all the other genes in the bacteria's DNA. The bacteria begins to function as an "insulin factory," making a vitally important compound that it could never make before.

One of the most exciting recent developments in genetics is the initiation of the Human Genome Project, which officially began on October 1, 1990. This project is designed to provide a complete genetic road map outlining the location and function of the approximately 50,000 genes in human deoxyribonucleic acid (DNA) and to determine the sequences of the 3,000,000,000 base pairs that make up human DNA. As a result, genetic researchers will have easy access to specific genes to study how the human body works and to develop therapies for diseases. Gene maps for other species of animals also are being developed.

There appears to be virtually no technical limit to the things that scientists can do with genes. But with the promise of genetic research, many ethical and philosophical questions arise. One question is, of course, whether there are social or ethical limits to the kinds of changes scientists ought to be allowed to make in the genes of plants, animals, and humans. With research focusing on the ability to manipulate genes, there is the fear that the results will not always be beneficial. For the most part, the benefits for medicine and agriculture seem to far outweigh the possible abuses, and genetic research continues.

[*See also* **Chromosome; Human Genome Project; Nucleic acid**]

Geologic map

Geologic maps display the arrangement of geologic features of a particular area. These features can include such things as types of rocks, faults, minerals, and groundwater. From studying a geologic map the user can better understand possible dangers like the potential for floods or earthquakes, and help locate important deposits of energy resources, such as water, oil, natural gas, and minerals. Through the use of letters, colors, lines, and symbols, geologic maps help the user gain a better understanding of Earth's makeup.

Elements of geologic maps

Geologic maps use color to represent various types of geologic features or units (a particular type of rock with a known age range). Geologic units are indicated by colors that can range from yellows and reds to purples and browns. Not only are geologic units assigned a color but

Words to Know

Bed: Mass of rock that extends under a large area and is bounded by different material.

Fault: A crack running through rock that is the result of tectonic forces.

Fold: A bend in a layer of rock.

Plates: Large regions of Earth's surface, composed of the crust and uppermost mantle, which move about, forming many of Earth's major geologic surface features.

also a set of letters. The set is usually composed of an initial capital letter followed by one or two lowercased letters. The capital letter represents the age of the geologic unit. The lower-cased letters indicate the geologic unit's name or the type of rock of which it is comprised.

Contact and fault lines. When two geologic units are located next to each other, the place where they meet is called a contact. The two main types of contacts are depositional contacts and faults. Depositional contacts are created when geologic units are composed under, over, or next to each other. The place where they meet is called a depositional contact and is indicated by a thin line. Geologic units can be moved over time by faults. Faults are cracks or fractures in Earth's crust (outer portion of Earth's surface) caused by the movement of land masses, called plates, on either side of the fault line. When plates move suddenly, the result is an earthquake. A fault line (a thick line with the same geologic unit on both sides of the line) indicates geologic units that have been moved by faults after they have been formed. Fault lines are especially important for geologic maps of a state such as California, where faults are known to be active.

Fold lines. Over time, geologic units can be reshaped by Earth's movements into wavelike shapes called folds. (A fold is a bend in a geologic unit that forms due to a change in pressure). Wavelike folds are composed of layers of Earth's crust that bend and buckle under enormous pressure as the crust hardens, compresses, and shortens. Folds may be softly rolling or severe and steep, depending on the amount of pressure and density of the crust. Folding may be massive, creating mile upon mile of mountains like the Appalachian chain, which traverses the eastern United States from

New York to Georgia. A fold axis (a line that follows through the crest, or peak, of a fold) is represented on a geologic map by a line thicker than a depositional contact line.

Lines on a geologic map can be adjusted according to known or unknown locations. When a contact line is indicated but the location is not quite certain, the line will appear as dashed. As the dashes that make up a line become shorter, the more uncertain the location is to establish. This could be due to man-made construction or natural growth of vegetation. If the line appears dotted, the location is very uncertain. Other, more specialized symbols are often used as well on geologic maps to help the user understand the makeup of Earth below.

Strike and dip lines. Over millions and millions of years, rocks form into layers that are called beds. These beds can reach significant heights, such as the walls of the Grand Canyon in Arizona. Sometimes these beds do not stand straight up due to the shifting of Earth's plates (large sections of the Earth's crust and upper mantle, the portion just below the

A geologic map. *(Reproduced by permission of The Gale Group.)*

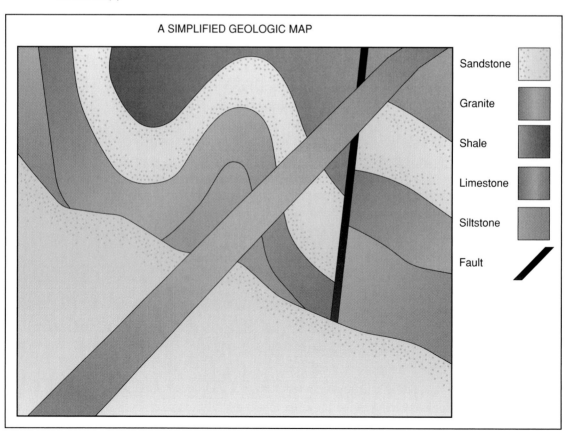

A SIMPLIFIED GEOLOGIC MAP

Sandstone

Granite

Shale

Limestone

Siltstone

Fault

crust). The result is that the bed is tilted. To identify such a bed on a geologic map, a strike and dip symbol is used. The strike and dip symbol is composed of three elements: a long line, a short line, and a number. The strike line is represented by the long line and indicates what part of the bed is still horizontal. The next line, the short line, is called the dip line and indicates which way the bed is tilted. The number, called the dip, follows next and indicates in degrees how much the bed is tilted. The higher the number, the more sharply the bed is tilted.

Map key. To help the user understand a geologic map, a map key is always provided. A map key is a table that displays all the colors and symbols used on a map. Starting with the most recently composed geologic unit and preceding to the oldest, a description of the type of rocks and their age are listed next to the color that represents them on the map. Following the list of geologic units comes another list of symbols, such as different types of lines, and then the strike and dip marks. If necessary, a map key also contains other important information, such as the locations of fossils, deposits of precious metals (such as gold, silver, and platinum, which have historically been valued for their beauty and rarity), and faults.

The future of geologic information

In 1992, the U.S. Congress passed the National Geologic Mapping Act (Public Law 102-285). Part of the act states: "Federal agencies, state and local governments, private industry, and the general public depend on the information provided by geologic maps to determine the extent of potential environmental damage before embarking on projects that could lead to preventable, costly environmental problems or litigation." The act also directs that the U.S. Geological Survey establish a geologic database that involves public and private institutions to help promote a better understanding of Earth and how to protect it.

Two years later, U.S. President Bill Clinton (1946–) signed an executive order for the National Spatial Data Infrastructure (NSDI). This order is particularly important because it specifically provides for the establishment of the National Geospatial Data Clearinghouse. This clearinghouse will allow users to search for geologic information.

The sharing of geologic information is key to achieving a better understanding of Earth. By studying geologic maps, users can identify such potential natural hazard areas for floods, earthquakes, volcanoes, and landslides. These maps can also provide data on important deposits of energy resources such as oil, natural gas, and coal.

[*See also* **Cartography; Fault; Geology; Plate tectonics**]

Geologic time

Geologic time describes the immense span of time—billions of years—revealed in the complex rock surface of Earth. Geologists have devised a geologic time scale that divides Earth's history into units of time. These units are eras, periods, and epochs. A unit is defined in terms of the fossils or rock types found in it that makes it different from the other units. Eras, the four largest time blocks in the scale, are named to indicate the fossils they contain: Precambrian (before ancient life), Paleozoic (ancient life), Mesozoic (middle life), and Cenozoic (recent life). The last three eras are then subdivided into 11 periods. The two most recent periods are further subdivided into seven epochs.

History of the concept of geologic time

Before the eighteenth century, ideas about time and the history of Earth came mostly from religious theories. Many people believed Earth was only a few thousand years old. They also believed that all the physical features of Earth—mountains, valleys, oceans, rivers, continents—were the same as they had always been. Everything that existed on Earth was the same as it had been in the beginning.

In the eighteenth century, geologists began to theorize that Earth's lifetime was immense. However, since they lacked sophisticated scientific measuring devices, they could only offer educated guesses. They compared the rock record from different parts of the world and estimated how long it would take natural processes to form all the rocks on Earth.

Relative dating

Since that time, geologists have learned to study the strata, or the thousands of layers of sedimentary rock that make up the Earth's crust. Over the course of history, the natural weathering of Earth's surface created sediments (rock debris) that settled in layers on the surface. As the layers built up, the underlying layers were compressed together to form sedimentary rock. A basic geological assumption is that lower layers of rock almost always formed before higher layers.

The fossils of changing lifeforms found in the different strata also help geologists determine the long history of Earth. Determining the age of strata by looking at the fossils, position, grain size, minerals, color, and other physical properties contained within them is known as relative dating.

Geologists easily identify rocks containing fossils of primitive lifeforms as being older than rocks containing fossils that are more evolved

Words to Know

Half-life: The time it takes for one-half of the population of a radioactive element to decay.

Radioactive decay: The predictable manner in which a population of atoms of a radioactive element spontaneously fall apart.

Radiometric dating: Use of naturally occurring radioactive elements and their decay products to determine the absolute age of the rocks containing those elements.

Stratigraphy: The branch of geology that catalogues Earth's successions of rock layers.

or advanced. However, the method of relative dating is exactly that, relative. It is not absolute. In addition, complex lifeforms have existed on Earth for only the last 600 million years. Therefore, their fossils represent less than 15 percent of Earth's history.

Absolute dating

A more specific and far-reaching method to assign dates to layers of rocks and events that have occurred in Earth's history is absolute dating. This method employs the natural process of radioactive decay.

Every rock and mineral exists in the world as a mixture of elements. Every element exists as a population of atoms. At the center of an atom is the positively charged nucleus made up of protons and neutrons. Over time, the nucleus of every radioactive element (such as radium and uranium) spontaneously disintegrates, transforming itself into the nucleus of an atom of a different element. In the process of disintegration, the atom gives off radiation (energy emitted in the form of waves). Hence the term radioactive decay.

The nucleus of an atom will continue to decay if it is radioactive. The last radioactive element in a series of these transformations will decay into a stable element, such as lead.

Half-life is a measurement of the time it takes for one-half of a radioactive element to decay. An important feature of the radioactive decay process is that each element decays at its own rate. The half-life of a

Geologic Time Scale

Era	Period	Epoch	Number of Years Ago (approximate; in millions)	
Cenozoic	Quaternary	Holocene	10,000 years to present	
		Pleistocene	2	Modern humans develop
	Tertiary	Pliocene	13	
		Miocene	25	
		Oligocene	36	First primitive apes
		Eocene	58	
		Paleocene	65	Dinosaurs become extinct
Mesozoic	Cretaceous		136	First birds, then first flowering plants
	Jurassic		190	
	Triassic		225	First dinosaurs, then first mammals
Paleozoic	Permian		280	First coniferous trees
	Carboniferous		345	First amphibians and insects, then first reptiles
	Devonian		405	First land plants
	Silurian		425	
	Ordovician		500	First freshwater fishes
	Cambrian		600	First mollusks
Precambrian			3,980	Bacteria and blue-green algae appear, then worms, jellyfish, and sponges

particular element, therefore, is constant and is not affected by any physical conditions (temperature, pressure, etc.) that occur around it. Because of this stable process, scientists are able to estimate when a particular element was formed by measuring the amount of original and transformed atoms in that element. This is known as radiometric or isotope dating.

Determining the age of Earth

The age of the whole Earth is deduced from the ages of other materials in the solar system, namely, meteorites. Meteorites are pieces formed from the cloud of dust and debris left behind after the beginning of the solar system. The meteorites that fall to Earth today have orbited the Sun since that time, unchanged and undisturbed by the processes that have destroyed Earth's first rocks. Radiometric ages for these meteorites fall between 4.45 and 4.55 billion years old.

[*See also* **Dating techniques; Fossil and fossilization; Paleontology; Radioactivity; Rocks**]

Geology

Geology is the scientific study of Earth. Geologists study the planet—its formation, its internal structure, its materials, its chemical and physical processes, and its history. Mountains, valleys, plains, sea floors, minerals, rocks, fossils, and the processes that create and destroy each of these are all the domain of the geologist. Geology is divided into two broad categories of study: physical geology and historical geology.

Physical geology is concerned with the processes occurring on or below the surface of Earth and the materials on which they operate. These processes include volcanic eruptions, landslides, earthquakes, and floods. Materials include rocks, air, seawater, soils, and sediment. Physical geology further divides into more specific branches, each of which deals with its own part of Earth's materials, landforms, and processes. Mineralogy and petrology investigate the composition and origin of minerals and rocks. Volcanologists check lava, rocks, and gases on live, dormant, and extinct volcanoes. Seismologists set up instruments to monitor and predict earthquakes and volcanic eruptions.

Historical geology is concerned with the chronology of events, both physical and biological, that have taken place in Earth's history. Paleontologists study fossils (remains of ancient life) for evidence of the evolution of life on Earth. Fossils not only relate evolution, but also speak of the environment in which the organism lived. Corals in rocks at the top of the Grand Canyon in Arizona, for example, show a shallow sea flooded the area around 290 million years ago. In addition, by determining the ages and types of rocks around the world, geologists piece together continental and oceanic history over the past few billion years. Plate tectonics (the study of the movement of the sections of Earth's crust) adds to the story with details of the changing configuration of the continents and oceans.

Many other sciences also contribute to geology. The study of the chemistry of rocks, minerals, and volcanic gases is known as geochemistry. The physics of Earth is known as geophysics. Paleobotanists study fossil plants. Paleozoologists reconstruct fossil animals, while paleoclimatologists reconstruct ancient climates.

Environmental geologists attempt to minimize both the human impact on Earth and the impact of natural disasters on human kind. Hydrology and hydrogeology, two subdisciplines of environmental geology, deal specifically with water resources. Hydrologists study surface water whereas hydrogeologists study ground water. Both disciplines try to reduce the impact of pollution on these resources. Economic geologists focus on finding the minerals and fossil fuels (oil, natural gas, coal) needed to maintain or improve global standards of living.

[*See also* **Geologic map**]

A physical geologist measuring the height of a lava fountain at Hawaii's Volcanoes National Park. *(Reproduced by permission of United States Geological Survey Photographic Library.)*

Geometry

The term geometry is derived from the Greek word *geometria,* meaning "to measure the Earth." In its most basic sense, then, geometry was a branch of mathematics originally developed and used to measure common features of Earth. Most people today know what those features are: lines, circles, angles, triangles, squares, trapezoids, spheres, cones, cylinders, and the like.

Humans have probably used concepts from geometry as long as civilization has existed. But the subject did not become a real science until about the sixth century B.C. At that point, Greek philosophers began to express the principles of geometry in formal terms. The one person whose name is most closely associated with the development of geometry is Euclid (c. 325–270 B.C.), who wrote a book called *Elements.* This work was the standard textbook in the field for more than 2,000 years, and the basic ideas of geometry are still referred to as Euclidean geometry.

Elements of geometry

Statements.   Statements in geometry take one of two forms: axioms and propositions. An axiom is a statement that mathematicians accept as being true without demanding proof. An axiom is also called a postulate. Actually, mathematicians prefer not to accept any statement without proof. But one has to start somewhere, and Euclid began by listing certain statements as axioms because they seemed so obvious to him that he couldn't see how anyone would disagree.

One axiom is that a single straight line, and only one, can be drawn through two points. Another axiom is that two parallel lines (lines running next to each other like train tracks) will never meet, no matter how far they are extended into space. Indeed, mathematicians accepted these statements as true without trying to prove them for 2,000 years. Statements such as these form the basis of Euclidean geometry.

However, the vast majority of statements in geometry are not axioms but propositions. A proposition is a statement that can be proved or disproved. In fact, it is not too much of a stretch to say that geometry is a branch of mathematics committed to proving propositions.

Proofs.   A proof in geometry requires a series of steps. That series may consist of only one step, or it may contain hundreds or thousands of steps. In every case, the proof begins with an axiom or with some proposition that has already been proved. The mathematician then proceeds from the

Plane

A plane is a geometric figure with only two dimensions: width and length. It has no thickness. The flatness of a plane can be expressed mathematically by thinking about a straight line drawn on the plane's surface. Such a line will lie entirely within the plane with none of its points outside of the plane.

A plane extends forever in both directions. Planes encountered in everyday life (such as a flat piece of paper with certain definite dimensions) and in mathematics often have a specific size. But such planes are only certain segments of the infinite plane itself.

known fact by a series of logical steps to show that the given proposition is true (or not true).

Constructions. A fundamental part of geometric proofs involves constructions. A construction in geometry is a drawing that can be made with the simplest of tools. Euclid permitted the use of a straight edge and a compass only. An example of a straight edge would be a meter stick that contained no markings on it. A compass is permitted in order to determine the size of angles used in a construction.

Many propositions in geometry can be proved by making certain kinds of constructions. For example, Euclid's first proposition was to show that, given a line segment AB, one can construct an equilateral triangle ABC. (An equilateral triangle is one with three equal angles.)

Plane and solid geometry

Euclidean geometry dealt originally with two general kinds of figures: those that can be represented in two dimensions (plane geometry) and those that can be represented in three dimensions (solid geometry). The simplest geometric figure of all is the point. A point is a figure with no dimensions at all. The points we draw on a piece of paper while studying geometry do have a dimension, of course, but that condition is due to the fact that the point must be made with a pencil, whose tip has real dimensions. From a mathematical standpoint, however, the point has no measurable size.

Perhaps the next simplest geometric figure is a line. A line is a series of points. It has dimensions in one direction (length) but in no other. A line can also be defined as the shortest distance between two points. Lines are used to construct all other figures in plane geometry, including angles, triangles, squares, trapezoids, circles, and so on. Since a line has no beginning or end, most of the "lines" one deals with in geometry are actually line segments—portions of a line that do have a limited length.

In general, lines can have one of three relationships to each other. They can be parallel, perpendicular, or at an angle to each other. According to Euclidean geometry, two lines are parallel to each other if they never meet, no matter how far they are extended. Perpendicular lines are lines that form an angle of 90 degrees (a right angle, as in a square or a T) to each other. And two lines that cross each other at any angle other than 90 degrees are simply said to form an angle with each other.

Closed figures. Lines also form closed figures, such as circles, triangles, and quadrilaterals. A circle is a closed figure in which every part of the figure is equidistant (at an equal distance) from some given point called the center of the circle. A triangle is a closed figure consisting of three lines. Triangles are classified according to the sizes of the angles formed by the three lines. A quadrilateral is a figure with four sides. Some common quadrilaterals are the square (in which all four sides are equal), the trapezoid (which has two parallel sides), the parallelogram (which has two pairs of parallel sides), the rhombus (a parallelogram with four equal sides), and the rectangle (a parallelogram with four right- or 90-degree angles).

Solid figures. The basic figures in solid geometry can be visualized as plane figures being rotated through space. Imagine that a circle is caused to rotate around its center. The figure produced is a sphere. Or imagine that a right triangle is rotated around its right angle. The figure produced is a cone.

Area and volume

The fundamental principles of geometry involve statements about the properties of points, lines, and other figures. But one can go beyond those fundamental principles to express certain measurements about such figures. The most common measurements are the length of a line, the area of a plane figure, or the volume of a solid figure. In the real world, length can be determined using a meter stick or yard stick. However, the field of analytic geometry provides a way to determine the length of a line by using principles adapted from geometry.

▼ Words to Know

Axiom: A mathematical statement accepted as true without being proved.

Construction: A geometric drawing that can be made with simple tools, such as a straight edge and a compass.

Euclidean geometry: A type of geometry based on certain axioms originally stated by Greek mathematician Euclid.

Line: A collection of points with one dimension only—that of length.

Line segment: A portion of a line.

Non-Euclidean geometry: A type of geometry based on axioms other than those first proposed by Euclid.

Plane geometry: The study of geometric figures that can be represented in two dimensions only.

Point: A figure with no dimensions.

Proposition: A mathematical statement that can be proved or disproved.

Proof: A mathematical statement that has been demonstrated logically to be correct.

Solid geometry: The study of geometric figures that can be represented in three dimensions.

Mathematical formulas are available for determining the area of any figures in geometry, such as rectangles, squares, various kinds of triangles, and circles. For example, the area of a rectangle is given by the formula $A = l \cdot h$, where l is the length of the rectangle and h is its height. One can find the areas of portions of solid figures as well. For example, the base of a cone is a circle. The area of the base, then, is $A = \pi \cdot r^2$, where π is a constant whose value is approximately 3.1416 and r is the radius of the base. (Pi [π] is the ratio of the circumference of a circle to its diameter, and it is always the same, no matter the size of the circle. The circumference of a circle is its total length around; its diameter is the length of a line segment that passes through the center of the circle from one side to the other. A radius is a line from the center to any point on the circle.)

Formulas for the volume of geometric figures also are available. For example, the volume of a cube (a three-dimensional square) is given by the formula $V = s^3$, where s is equal to the length of one side of the cube.

Other geometries

With the growth of the modern science of mathematics, scholars began to ask whether Euclid's initial axioms were necessarily true. That is, would it be possible to imagine a world in which more than one straight line could be drawn through two points. Such ideas often sound bizarre at first. For example, can you imagine two parallel lines that do eventually meet at some point far in the distance? If so, what does the term parallel really mean?

Yet, such ideas have turned out to be very productive for the study of certain special kinds of spaces. They have been given the name non-Euclidean geometries and are used to study certain kinds of mathematical, scientific, and technical problems.

Gerontology

Gerontology is a branch of sociology that studies aging and the problems—psychological, economic, and social—that arise in old age. Gerontology includes the field of geriatrics, the medical study of the biological process of aging and the treatment of illnesses of old age.

Since the days of the ancient Greeks, speculation about aging has gone hand in hand with the development of medicine as a science. During the 1800s, researchers began to study populations and social patterns of aging in a systematic fashion. During the 1930s, the International Association of Gerontology was organized. Over the next decade, governmental bodies sponsored conferences on aging, and by 1945 the Gerontological Society of America, Inc., was established in Washington, D.C.

In the United States in the late twentieth century, the median age of the total population has increased. On average there are more and more older people than younger ones in the country. Because of this increase, research in the field of gerontology has broadened.

The health and economic status among the elderly vary widely. Gerontologists have been researching the increased costs of health care paid by communities and the federal government for the elderly. Gerontologists also have studied how the aging of a particular member of a family affects the entire family, focusing on issues such as the interrelationships of different generations within a family or the impact of death on those different generations.

[*See also* **Aging and death**]

Glacier

Glaciers are flowing masses of ice, created by years of snowfall and cold temperatures. Approximately one-tenth of Earth is covered by glaciers, including Antarctica and parts of Greenland, Iceland, Canada, Russia, and Alaska. Mountainous regions on every continent except Australia also contain glaciers. Glaciers have enormous powers to reshape the face of Earth. Even today, glaciers are altering how our planet looks, and they hold clues to its past and future.

How glaciers form

Glaciers are created in areas where the air temperature never gets warm enough to completely melt snow. After a snowfall, some or most of the snow may melt when it comes into contact with warmer ground temperatures. As the air temperature drops, the melted snow refreezes, turning into small ice granules called firn or névé (pronounced nay-VAY). As additional layers of snow accumulate on top, the firn underneath is compacted. When the accumulation reaches about 150 feet (46 meters) deep, the weight and pressure cause the lower layers to recrystallize into solid ice. As years pass, snow accumulates and the slab of ice grows steadily thicker. Eventually the mound of ice becomes too massive to sit still, and gravity pulls the ice downhill. Once the ice begins to move, it is considered a glacier.

Types of glaciers

Glaciers that flow down a valley from high mountainous regions usually follow paths originally formed by rivers of snowmelt in the spring and summer. These valley or mountain glaciers end in a valley or ocean, and tend to increase the sharpness and steepness of the surrounding mountains along the way. In the Alps, a mountain system in south-central Europe, there are more than 1,200 valley glaciers.

Piedmont glaciers are large, gently sloping ice mounds. Also known as lakes of ice, piedmont glaciers form when a valley glacier reaches the lowlands or plain at the foot of a mountain and spreads out. These are common in Alaska, Greenland, Iceland, and Antarctica.

Glaciers that form in small valleys on the sides of mountains are called ice caps. Found in Norway, Iceland, Greenland, and Antarctica, ice caps usually do not move out of their basinlike area.

The largest form of glacier is called a continental glacier, a huge ice sheet that moves slowly outward from its center. Ice sheets may cover hun-

Words to Know

Continental glacier: The largest form of and slowest moving glacier, covering large expanses of a continent.

Glacial till: Rock and soil scoured from Earth and transported by a glacier, then deposited along its sides or at its end.

Greenhouse effect: The warming of Earth's atmosphere due to water vapor, carbon dioxide, and other gases in the atmosphere that trap heat radiated from Earth's surface.

Ice age: Period of glacial advance.

Ice caps: Smaller glaciers that form in basinlike depressions in a mountain.

Kettle lakes: Bowl-shaped lakes created by large ice blocks, which formed depressions in Earth's surface.

Meltwater: Melted ice in the glacier's bottom layer, caused by heat that develops as a result of friction with Earth's surface.

Moraines: Large deposits of glacial till that form hills.

Piedmont glacier: Large, gently sloping glaciers found at the foot of mountains, which are fed by alpine glaciers.

Surging: A sudden increase in a glacier's movement as a result of meltwater underneath decreasing its friction.

Valley glacier: Glacier that forms at a high elevation in a mountain region and flows downhill through valleys originally created by rivers.

dreds of thousands of square miles, and are so heavy that they cause the rock underneath to compress into Earth. The largest continental glacier is found on Antarctica, where the ice is more than 2.5 miles (4 kilometers) thick at its center, and hides entire mountain ranges beneath its surface. It extends more than 5 million square miles (12.9 million square kilometers). The Antarctic ice sheet accounts for 90 percent of all the ice in the world, and contains more water than all of Earth's rivers and lakes put together.

Glaciers' effects

Most glaciers that exist today are remnants of the last glacial period from 1,800,000 to 11,000 years ago. As glaciers advance and retreat, they plow through rock, soil, and vegetation like a huge bulldozer, altering everything they come into contact with. Ice acts like an adhesive, scooping up rocks and soil that add to the glacier's tremendous powers of erosion.

Thus, a river valley that was once V-shaped becomes U-shaped; the rocks and soil carried with the glacier, known as glacial till, are deposited in huge mounds along the sides and at the end of the glacier, creating entirely new hills, or moraines. Chunks of ice buried in this till create large depressions that later became what are known as kettle lakes.

Glaciers also scour the land to great depths, creating larger lakes such as the North American Great Lakes. During the last ice age, Earth's surface was depressed due to the weight of the glaciers. As the glaciers retreated, Earth's crust rose upward like a sponge. This crustal rebounding, as it is called, is still occurring at slow rates in parts of North America and Europe.

Muir Inlet, a fiord in Glacier Bay National Park in Alaska, and the glacier creating it. *(Reproduced by permission of JLM Visuals.)*

Most glaciers move fairly slowly, only inches to a few feet per day. When large amounts of ice melt under the glacier as a result of friction with Earth's surface, the meltwater acts like grease to rapidly increase its movement. This sudden increase in speed is called surging.

Clues to Earth's past and future

While the effects of glaciers tell us where they have occurred in the past, present glaciers are providing clues as to variations in climate over time and potential changes in the future. Scientists continue to debate the reasons why ice ages occur, but there seems to be agreement that glaciers increase on the planet when Earth rotates farther away from the Sun. When Earth rotates closer to the Sun, glaciers retreat.

The U.S. National Academy of Sciences has predicted that if global temperatures rise from 1.5 to 5°F (0.75 to 2.5°C) over the twenty-first century as a result of the greenhouse effect, significant portions of Earth's glaciers could melt. (The greenhouse effect is the warming of Earth's atmosphere due to water vapor, carbon dioxide, and other gases in the atmosphere that trap heat radiated from Earth's surface.) Because glaciers hold 75 percent of the world's freshwater supply, such a meltdown would result in massive flooding of every continent's coastlines, drastically altering the shapes of every continent on Earth.

Ice core samples taken from Antarctic ice also have provided evidence of Earth's climate over the last 160,000 years. Data has shown a direct link between warming and cooling trends and the amount of two greenhouse gases, carbon dioxide and methane, in the atmosphere. These same cores show significant increases in both gases in the past 200 years.

Scientific reports issued at the beginning of the twenty-first century indicate that mountain glaciers from Montana to Mount Everest to the Swiss Alps were in a stage of retreat. In the Alps, scientists have estimated that by 2025 glaciers will have lost 90 percent of the ice that was there a century ago. Glacier melting, however, is generally quickest in and near the tropics. Ancient glaciers in the Andes have recently melted at an extraordinary rate. Between 1998 and 2000, one Peruvian glacier pulled back 508 feet (155 meters) a year. And Mount Kilimanjaro in the African country of Tanzania has lost 82 percent of the icecap it had when it was first carefully surveyed in 1912. At the current rate, scientists believe the icecap will disappear before 2015. Scientists theorize that all of these factors indicate that a global warming trend is taking place and that it is at least partly caused by gases released by human activities.

[*See also* **Antarctica; Greenhouse effect; Ice ages; Icebergs**]

Glass

Glass is a hard, brittle substance that is usually transparent or translucent. It is made by melting together sand (silicon dioxide), soda (sodium carbonate), limestone (calcium carbonate), and other ingredients. The simplest form of glass (containing only sand, soda, and lime) is known today as plate or window glass.

Scholars believe that the first humans to make glass may have been Phoenician sailors living around 5000 B.C. Examples of glass used for

A glassblower cutting the blow pipe off the globe he just created. *(Reproduced by permission of Photo Researchers, Inc.)*

Some Special Kinds of Glass and Their Properties and Uses

Type of Glass	Composition, Properties, and Uses
Ceramic glass	Contains titanium oxide; heat and shock resistant; used in range and stove tops, architectural panels, and telescope mirrors.
Enamel glass	Contains lead and borax; resistant to most chemicals; used in bottles, tumblers, glass signs, architectural objects.
Fiberglass	Formed by forcing melted glass through small openings; used in the manufacture of insulation, fabrics, tire cords, and light transmission (optical fibers).
Heat-resistant glass	Contains about 5% borax; trade names include Pyrex® and Vicor®; resistant to shock and sudden changes in temperature; used in laboratory glassware and kitchen utensils.
Laminated glass	Consists of layers of glass and plastic to provide strength and make the final product shatterproof; used in automobile windows.
Optical glass	Contains either lime (crown glass) or lead (flint glass); used for lenses in cameras, microscopes, eyeglasses, and other applications where refraction of light is important.
Photochromic glass	Contains silver halide or borax; changes color when exposed to light; used in eyeglasses that double as sunglasses.

weapons, ornaments, and money from Egypt and Mesopotamia—dating to about 1550 B.C.—still survive.

Humans may well have learned about glass-making by witnessing the natural formation of glass by lightning bolts. When lightning strikes areas where sand, soda, and limestone occur naturally, it can fuse these materials to produce a natural form of glass known as obsidian.

The history of glass-making is a long and fascinating one. Artisans in many parts of the world discovered ways to make colored glass and glass with many special properties. Today, a very large variety of glassy materials exists with many different properties and many applications.

Colored glass

Colored glass is made by adding metallic compounds to the basic sand/soda/lime mixture. For instance, red glass is made by adding certain copper oxides or finely divided gold; yellow glass with compounds of uranium and iron; green glass with certain copper oxides or compounds of uranium and iron; blue with copper oxide, cobalt oxide, or finely divided gold; purple with certain manganese oxides and finely divided gold; milky white with calcium fluoride; and opaque with tin oxide.

Originally, glass was used primarily for decorative objects such as beads, ornaments, and stained glass windows. Eventually, though, artisans and chemists found that the properties of glass could be changed dramatically by adding various substances to the basic sand/soda/lime mixture. Those properties also could be altered by changing the way glass is cooled, or annealed.

For example, plate glass is made first by melting together the basic components—sand, soda, and lime. The liquid mixture is then maintained at its melting point for a long period of time, at least three days. Next, the mixture is allowed to cool down very slowly to room temperature. This process assures that strains within the glass are relieved, making the final product less brittle. Tempered glass is cooled even more slowly, giving it very high strength.

Global climate

Global climate is the term used to describe the sum total of all weather patterns formed over all parts of the planet. In contrast to the term weather, which applies to relatively short-term phenomena such as storms, global climate is used to describe patterns that extend over much longer periods of time, at least a few decades.

Global climatic zones

Ten distinct climatic zones exist on the planet: tropical, subtropical, arid, semi-arid, mediterranean, temperate, northern temperate, mountain, polar, and coastal. The specific designation of each climate zone depends on two major factors: the average temperature and the amount of precipitation received in the zone. For example, temperate zones have fairly uniform rainfall patterns and four different seasons, while tropical zones have high rainfall and temperature and a short dry season. Each of the climatic

Words to Know

Global warming: The rise in Earth's temperature that is attributed to the buildup of carbon dioxide and other pollutants in the atmosphere.

Greenhouse effect: The warming of Earth's atmosphere due to water vapor, carbon dioxide, and other gases in the atmosphere that trap heat radiated from Earth's surface.

Radiation: Energy emitted in the form of waves or particles.

Wavelength: The distance between one peak of a wave of light, heat, or energy and the next corresponding peak.

zones on Earth is inhabited by particular kinds of plants and animals that have adapted to the conditions that exist there.

Factors affecting normal global climate

A number of factors account for Earth's climatic pattern. Among these factors are the amount of solar energy that reaches Earth's surface, the shape and orientation of Earth's orbit around the Sun, and the composition of Earth's atmosphere.

Solar energy. The driving force behind almost all climatic changes on Earth is the Sun. Sunlight that reaches Earth's atmosphere experiences different fates. About 30 percent of the solar radiation reaching the atmosphere is reflected back into space, another 20 percent is absorbed by the atmosphere, and the rest (about 50 percent) is absorbed by Earth's surface.

Earth's orbit. The fact that weather conditions vary on different parts of the planet and that they change throughout the year is a consequence of two features of Earth's orbit around the Sun. First, Earth follows an oval-shaped path, called an ellipse, around the Sun. Because of this, Earth comes closer to the Sun at certain times of the year, absorbing more solar energy. Second, Earth's axis is tilted at an angle of 23.5 degrees in relation to the plane of the Sun. Because of this tilt, different parts of the planet are tilted toward the Sun at different times of the year. Summer occurs in the northern hemisphere in the middle of the year not because the planet is closer to the Sun (it is not), but because the hemisphere is tilted closer to the Sun.

The atmosphere. Earth's climate is strongly affected by the way heat is absorbed in the atmosphere. Sunlight consists largely of radiation with relatively short wavelengths, radiation that is not absorbed by most atmospheric gases. Once that radiation has been absorbed by Earth's surface, however, it is reradiated to the atmosphere in a form that consists of longer wavelengths. These forms of radiation are more readily absorbed by atmospheric gases, especially water vapor and carbon dioxide. As these gases absorb reradiated energy, the temperature of the atmosphere increases, a phenomenon known as the greenhouse effect.

Global climate changes

Changes in global climate have occurred over the course of Earth's history. Volcanic eruptions, more prevalent in the past than today, spewed huge quantities of dust and ash into the atmosphere, reducing the amount of solar radiation reaching Earth and lowering global temperatures. These conditions may have lasted for months or even years.

The movement of landmasses across the planet's face may have had significant climatic effects. The breaking apart of ancient continents probably had a measurable effect on heat exchange between Earth's land surface, ocean waters, and the atmosphere. The creation of major landforms such as mountains had a large effect on the formation and pattern of winds, clouds, and precipitation.

Glacial periods—ice ages—are incidents of large-scale climatic changes on Earth over very long periods of time. In the 1930s, Serbian mathematician Milutin Milankovitch proposed a theory to explain such changes. The Milankovitch theory states that three periodic changes in Earth's orbit around the Sun affect the amount of sunlight reaching Earth at different latitudes, leading to ice ages. First, Earth's axis wobbles like a gyroscope, tracing a complete circle every 23,000 years or so. Second, at the same time while wobbling, the axis tilts between 22 and 24.5 degrees every 41,000 years. Third, Earth's elliptical orbit pulses, moving outward or inward every 100,000 and 433,000 years.

Oscillations (back-and-forth changes) in ocean current temperatures seem to lead to decades-long changes in global climate (the oceans and the atmosphere are linked by their mutual transfer of heat and moisture). Scientists have long known of the existence of a huge, powerful current in the Atlantic Ocean that carries water from the area around Florida northeast to the coast of Ireland, then heads westward where it cools and sinks near the Labrador Peninsula of Canada (there is a similar one in the Pacific). This pipeline of water alternates between warm and cool currents every 20 years or so. When the currents are warm, Northern Europe and Asia experience mild winters. When the currents are cooler, Northern Europe is much colder and drier, while the Mediterranean region, Africa, and the Middle East are warm and wet.

Human effects. During the twentieth century, humans have burned very large quantities of fossil fuels (coal, oil, and natural gas) to operate factories, heat homes and offices, run automobiles, and perform similar tasks. Since carbon dioxide is always produced during the combustion (burning) of a fossil fuel, these activities have contributed to the concentration of that gas in the atmosphere.

Strong evidence now supports the contention that these activities have significantly raised the level of carbon dioxide in Earth's atmosphere. Many scientists now believe that this change means that higher concentrations of carbon dioxide will inevitably lead to a greater retention of heat in the atmosphere and, hence, a higher annual average global temperature. This phenomenon has been called global warming.

If global warming should occur, a number of terrestrial (land) changes may follow. For example, portions of the polar ice cap may melt, increasing the volume of water in the oceans and flooding coastal cities. In addition, regional weather patterns may undergo significant changes.

[*See also* **Atmospheric circulation; Greenhouse effect**]

Graphs and graphing

A graph is a pictorial representation of a set of data. These data can be of two distinct types: continuous or discontinuous. An example of continuous data would be temperature readings taken during a single day. A person may choose to observe and record the temperature once every hour, once every half hour, or on some other schedule. But temperature is a continuous phenomenon. One can read a temperature at any instant of any day.

Other data are discontinuous. Suppose you want to record the number of children in a class who are right-handed or left-handed. Children can be either right-handed or left-handed. Of course, some children might be ambidextrous, that is, capable of using either hand. However, those three choices are the only possibilities. They constitute three distinct categories and are regarded, therefore, as discontinuous data.

Words to Know

Continuous data: A collection of facts that have an infinite number of values.

Data: Factual information, often expressed in numerical terms.

Discontinuous data: A collection of facts that have only a certain number of values.

Function: A relationship between two variables such that for a given value of either there is one discrete value for the second variable.

Variable: A number that can take on a variety of numerical values.

Representations of discontinuous data

Bar graphs. Graphs that depict discontinuous data are common in the daily newspaper. Those graphs usually take one of three forms: bar graphs, picture graphs, or circle (pie) graphs. In a bar graph, the distinct categories to be represented are shown on the horizontal axis. For example, three regions might be marked off for "right-handed students," "left-handed students," and "ambidextrous students." The number of cases belonging to each category, then, are displayed on the vertical axis. If the number of students in each category were 17, 19, and 1, for example, one would draw a bar extending 17 units above the right-handed students category and a second bar extending 19 units above the left-handed category. A third bar—extending 1 unit above the ambidextrous category—would complete the graph.

Picture graphs. A picture graph is similar to a bar graph except some type of pictorial symbol is used to represent the variable being counted. The graph described above could be redrawn using 17 student figures for the right-handed category, 19 student figures for the left-handed category, and 1 student figure for the ambidextrous category.

Representing divisions of a whole. Circle, or pie, graphs are generally used to show how some whole quantity is subdivided among various categories. For example, the state government might want to show that 35 percent of its annual income comes from income taxes, 40 percent from sales taxes, 10 percent from interest, and 15 percent from miscellaneous categories. One way to do that is to make a large circle and then divide the circle up into four parts. The sizes of the four parts would correspond to the way income is split up by the state. One part of the graph would be a wedge whose central angle is 126 degrees ($35\% \times 360°$ = 126°). This wedge represents income from income taxes. Another part of the graph—this one representing sales tax—would have a wedge whose central angle is 144 degrees ($40\% \times 360° = 144°$). The other two wedges would have central angles with 54 and 36 degrees, representing interest and miscellaneous income.

Graphing functions

The most common type of graph used in science is the line graph. A line graph is a graph that shows how two variables are related to each other. Line graphs are used only for continuous data.

For example, it *is* possible to measure the temperature at every moment of the day and night. One can attach a temperature sensor to a pen that draws a line on a graph paper attached to a rotating drum. As time passes, the drum rotates, and the temperature is recorded as a continuous line.

This graph means that for every moment of time, there is a corresponding temperature. This type of relationship is known in mathematics as a function. The two quantities described in the function are the independent variable and the dependent variable. In the example above, the independent variable is time, and the dependent variable is temperature.

In drawing graphs of functions, the independent variable is commonly graphed on the horizontal axis, and the dependent variable is graphed on the vertical axis. The shape of the line produced in graphing a function depends on the kind of relationship between the two variables. The simplest relationship is a linear relationship. In a linear relationship, a change in one variable produces a comparable change in the second. For example, in the equation $y = 3x$, when x is doubled, it also doubles y.

Many relationships are more complex than those that can be expressed as a linear relationship. For example, plants and animals tend to grow for at least part of their lives according to an exponential pattern. An equation that represents an exponential relationship is $y = 2^x$. As x gets larger, y also gets larger, but at a much faster rate. When $x = 1$, $y = 2$; when $x = 2$, $y = 4$; when $x = 3$, $y = 9$, and so on. The graph for this relationship is a curve that rises very rapidly.

Gravity and gravitation

Gravity is the force of attraction between any two objects in the universe. That force depends on two factors: the mass of each object and the distance between them.

Historical background

The story behind English physicist Isaac Newton's (1642–1727) discovery of the gravitational force is one of the most fascinating in all of science. It begins in ancient Greece in the period from the sixth to the third century B.C. During that time, a number of Greek philosophers attempted to explain common observations from the natural world—such as the fact that most objects fall to the ground if they are not held up in some way.

Aristotle. Among the explanations developed for this tendency was one offered by Greek philosopher Aristotle (384–322 B.C.). Aristotle developed a grand scheme of natural philosophy stating that all objects "belonged" in one place or another. Heat belonged in the atmosphere because it originally came from the Sun (as Aristotle taught). For that reason, heat rises. Objects fall toward Earth's surface, Aristotle said, because that's where "earthy" objects belong. Aristotle's philosophy was an attempt to explain why objects fall.

Galileo and Newton. Aristotle's philosophy dominated the thinking of European scholars for nearly 2,000 years. Then, in the sixteenth century, Italian physicist Galileo Galilei (1564–1642) suggested another way of answering questions in science. Scientists should not trouble themselves trying to understand why things happen in the natural world, Galileo said. Instead, they should focus simply on describing how things occur. Galileo also taught that the way to find out about the natural world is not just to think logically about it but to perform experiments that produce measurable results.

One of the most famous experiments attributed to Galileo was the one he conducted at the Leaning Tower of Pisa. He is said to have dropped two balls from the top of the tower and discovered that they both took the same time to reach the ground. Galileo's greatest achievements were not in defining the true nature of gravity, then, but in setting the stage for the work of Isaac Newton, who was born the year Galileo died.

Newton's accomplishments in the field of gravity also are associated with a famous story. Legend has it that Newton was hit on the head by an apple falling from a tree. That event got him wondering about the force

▼ Words to Know

Mass: A measure of the amount of matter in a body.

Orbit: The path followed by a body (such as a planet) in its travel around another body (such as the Sun).

Proportionality constant: A number inserted into an equation to make both sides equal.

Weight: The gravitational attraction of Earth on an object.

between two objects on Earth (the apple and the ground) and the force between two objects in the universe (the force between a planet and the Sun).

Gravity on Earth and in the heavens.   The connection between gravitational forces on Earth and in the heavens is a very important one. Measuring the force of gravity on Earth is very difficult for one simple reason. Suppose we want to measure what happens when an object falls on Earth. In terms of gravity, what actually happens is that the object and the planet Earth are attracted toward each other. The object moves downward toward Earth, and Earth moves upward toward the object. The problem is that Earth is so much larger than the object that it's impossible to see any movement on the part of the planet.

The situation is quite different in the heavens. The reason planets travel in an orbit around the Sun, Newton said, is that they are responding to two forces. One force is caused simply by their motion through the skies. Just imagine that at some time in the past, someone grabbed hold of Mars and threw it past the Sun. Mars would be traveling through space, then, because of the initial velocity that was given to it.

But Mars does not travel in a straight line. It moves in a circle (or nearly a circle) around the Sun. What changes Mars's motion from a straight line to a curve, Newton asked? The answer he proposed was gravity. The gravitational force between the Sun and Mars causes the planet to move out of a straight line and towards the Sun. The combination of the straight line motion and the gravitational force, then, accounts for the shape of Mars's orbit.

But a huge point in Newton's favor was that he already knew all the main points about Mars and its orbit around the Sun. He had a good idea as to how fast the planet was traveling, its mass, the mass of the Sun, and the size of its orbit. Furthermore, the difference in size between Mars and the Sun was great—but not nearly as great as the difference between an apple and Earth.

So Newton derived his idea of the gravitational force by studying the orbit of the planets. He applied that idea to what he knew about the planets and found that he was able to predict almost perfectly the orbits followed by the planets.

Cavendish's findings. Proving the gravitational law on Earth was somewhat more difficult. Probably the most important experiment conducted for this purpose was one carried out by English chemist and physicist Henry Cavendish (1731–1810) in 1798. Cavendish suspended a light rod horizontally from a silk thread. At each end of the rod he hung a lead ball. Then he brought a third lead ball close to one of the two lead balls suspended from the rod. He was able to notice that the two lead balls attracted each other. As they did so, they caused the metal rod to pivot slightly on its silk thread. The amount by which the rod pivoted, Cavendish found out, depended on how closely the lead balls were brought next to each other and how much the two balls weighed (what their masses were). Cavendish's results turned out to confirm Newton's predictions exactly.

These astronauts float in space because gravity is not acting on them. *(Reproduced by permission of National Aeronautics and Space Administration.)*

Einsteinian gravity.   Newton's description of gravitational forces proved to be satisfactory for almost two and a half centuries. Then, observations began to appear in which his gravitational law turned out to be not exactly correct. The differences between predictions based on Newton's law and actual observations were small—too small to have been noticed for many years. But scientists eventually realized that Newton's law was not entirely and always correct.

In the early 1900s, German-born American physicist Albert Einstein (1879–1955) proposed a solution for problems with Newton's law. Interestingly enough, Einstein did not suggest modifications in Newton's law to make it more accurate. Instead, he proposed an entirely new way to think about gravity.

The way to think about gravitational forces, Einstein said, is to imagine that space has shape. Imagine, for example, a thin sheet of rubber stretched very tightly in all directions. Then imagine that the rubber sheet has indentations in it, similar to the depressions caused by pushing in on the sheet with your thumb. Finally, imagine that this dented rubber sheet represents space.

Using this model, Einstein suggested that gravity is nothing other than the effect produced when an object moving through space approaches one of these indentations. If a planet were moving through space and came close to an indentation, for example, it would tend to roll inward toward the dent. The effect to an outside observer would be exactly the same as if the planet were experiencing a gravitational force of attraction to the center of the dent.

Finally, Einstein said, these dents in space are caused by the presence of objects, such as stars and planets. The larger the object, the deeper the dent. Again, the effect observed is the same as it would be with Newtonian gravity. An object traveling through space will be pulled out of its orbit more by a deep dent (a heavy object) than it will be by a shallow dent (a lighter object).

So what's the point of thinking about gravity in Einstein's terms rather than Newton's? The answer is that the mathematics used by Einstein does everything that Newton's law of gravitation does *plus* it solves all of the problems that Newtonian gravity cannot explain.

Fundamental forces

Physicists now believe that all forces in the universe can be reduced to one of four fundamental forces: gravitation, electromagnetism, and the strong and weak force. The strong and weak force are forces discovered in the twentieth century; they are responsible for the way atoms and particles smaller than the atom interact with each other. Electromagnetic forces affect charged or magnetic particles. And the gravitational force affects all bodies of any size whatsoever. Of the four forces, the gravitational force is by far the weakest and probably least understood.

One of the great efforts among physicists during the twentieth century was the attempt to show how all four fundamental forces are really different symptoms of a single force. They have been successful in doing so for the electromagnetic and weak forces, which are now recognized as two forms of a single force. The attempts to unify the remaining forces, including gravitation, however, have been unsuccessful so far.

[*See also* **Celestial mechanics**]

Greenhouse effect

The greenhouse effect is a natural phenomenon that is responsible for the relatively high temperature maintained on Earth's surface and in its atmosphere. The name comes from the process by which greenhouses are thought to collect and hold heat.

The greenhouse mechanism

A greenhouse is a building in which plants are grown and kept. It usually consists of a large expanse of window glass facing in a generally southerly direction. Sunlight that strikes the windows of the greenhouse passes through those windows and strikes the ground inside the greenhouse. This process is possible because glass is transparent to sunlight, that is, it allows sunlight to pass through.

Sunlight that strikes the ground inside a greenhouse either may be reflected or absorbed by the ground. Sunlight that is absorbed by the ground may later be re-emitted in the form of heat waves. When it bounces back towards the windows of the greenhouse, it is not able to pass back through the windows. In either instance, the sunlight undergoes a change in form once it enters the through the windows. The windows are not transparent, but are opaque, to the reflected and reradiated energy. The energy trapped inside the greenhouse is then used to raise the temperature inside the greenhouse. It is this effect that makes it possible for a greenhouse to stay warm even though the outside temperature is quite cold.

⍙ Words to Know

Atmospheric window: A range in the wavelength of radiations, from about 350 to 750 nanometers, that can pass through Earth's atmosphere without being absorbed.

Equilibrium: A process in which the rates at which various changes take place balance each other, resulting in no overall change.

Frequency: The number of waves that pass a given point every second.

Infrared radiation: Another name for heat; a form of radiation with wavelengths in the range from about 700 nanometers to 1 millimeter.

Nanometer: One-billionth of a meter.

Radiation: Energy emitted in the form of waves or particles.

Visible light: A form of radiation with wavelengths in the range from about 400 to about 750 nanometers.

Wavelength: The distance between any two successive crests or troughs in a wave.

The greenhouse effect in Earth's atmosphere

An effect similar to the one just described also occurs in Earth's atmosphere. The atmosphere does not have a glass window, of course, although the gases that make up the atmosphere act something like a window.

Imagine a burst of solar energy reaching the outer edges of Earth's atmosphere. That solar energy consists of many different kinds of radiation, such as visible light, ultraviolet radiation, infrared radiation, X rays, gamma rays, radio waves, and microwaves. These forms of radiation are different from each other in that they all travel with different wavelengths and different frequencies. (The wavelength of a wave is the distance between any two successive crests or troughs [pronounced trawfs] in the wave. The frequency of the radiation is the number of waves that pass a given point every second.) For example, X rays have very short wavelengths and very large frequencies. In contrast, radio waves have very long wavelengths and very small frequencies. The important point, however, is that all forms of radiation, whatever their wavelength and frequency, travel together in a burst of solar energy.

The energy that reaches Earth's atmosphere can experience one of three fates, depending on the kind of radiation and the kind of gases present in the atmosphere. First, about one-third of all the solar energy that reaches Earth's atmosphere is reflected back into space. As far as Earth is concerned, that energy is simply lost to space.

Another one-third of the solar energy is absorbed by gases in Earth's atmosphere. Various gases absorb various types of radiation. Oxygen and ozone, for example, tend to absorb radiation with short wavelengths, such as ultraviolet light. In contrast, carbon dioxide and water absorb radiation with longer wavelengths, such as infrared radiation. When these gases absorb various types of radiation, they convert the energy of sunlight into heat. This phenomenon accounts for some of the heat stored in Earth's atmosphere.

Yet another one-third of the solar energy reaching our atmosphere is able to pass through the atmosphere and strike Earth's surface. This process is similar to the way sunlight is transmitted through windows in a greenhouse. The solar energy that passes through Earth's atmosphere does so because there are very few gases that absorb visible radiation.

Scientists sometimes refer to a "window" in Earth's atmosphere (somewhat similar to a greenhouse window) through which radiation can pass. That atmospheric window is not an object, like a piece of glass, but a range in radiation across which atmospheric gases are transparent. That range is from about 350 to 750 nanometers (a nanometer is one-billionth of a meter). For comparison, the wavelengths of visible light range from about 400 nanometers (for blue light) to 750 nanometers (for red light).

Reflection and absorption. The solar energy that reaches Earth's surface also can experience a number of fates. It can cause ice to melt and water to evaporate; it can be used to convert carbon dioxide and water to carbohydrates in plants (photosynthesis); it can heat parcels of air and water, causing winds, waves, and currents; and it can heat Earth's surface. The last of these fates is the most important. About one-half of all the solar energy that passes through the atmosphere is absorbed by soil, rocks, sand, dirt, and other natural and human-made objects.

All of which is to tell you something you already know. If you put your hand on a patch of dark soil at the end of a sunny day, the soil feels warm. In fact, if you place your hand just above the soil, you can feel heat being given off by the soil. The reason is that objects that are heated by sunlight behave in the same way as the ground in a greenhouse. Those objects give back energy picked up from sunlight, but in a different form. Instead of reradiating the energy in the form of visible light, the objects give the energy back off in the form of heat.

But what happens when heat reradiated from Earth's surface travels back upwards into the atmosphere. Heat is a form of infrared radiation. As pointed out previously, carbon dioxide and water are both good absorbers of infrared radiation. So the very gases that allowed visible light to pass through the atmosphere are now able to absorb (trap) the infrared radiation (heat) reradiated from Earth's surface.

The sum total of all these reactions is that energy from the Sun is captured by both Earth's surface and the gases in the atmosphere. As a result, the planet's annual average temperature is about 55°F (30°C) higher than it would be without an atmosphere.

Human activities and the greenhouse effect

Natural phenomena, such as the greenhouse effect, reach a natural state of equilibrium over many hundreds or thousands of years. (A state of equilibrium is a process in which the rates at which various changes take place balance each other.) Two factors that affect the greenhouse effect are the shape of Earth's orbit and its tilt with regard to the Sun. Both of these factors change slowly over hundreds of thousands of years. When they do, they alter the effects produced by the greenhouse effect. For example, suppose that Earth's orbit changes so that our planet begins to move closer to the Sun. In that case, more solar energy will reach the outer atmosphere and, eventually, the planet's annual average temperature will probably increase.

In recent years, scientists have been exploring the possibility that various human activities also may influence the greenhouse effect. The most important of these activities is thought to be the combustion (burning) of fossil fuels, such as coal, oil, and natural gas.

No one needs to be reminded today of the important role of fossil fuels in our society. We use them for heating homes and offices; for powering our cars, trucks, railroads, airplanes, and other forms of transportation; and for operating industrial processes. But the combustion of any fossil fuel always results in the release of carbon dioxide and water into the atmosphere. By some estimates, the release of carbon dioxide into the atmosphere from fossil fuel combustion reached almost 2.5 billion tons (2.3 billion metric tons) in 1999.

The result of this human activity is that Earth's atmosphere contains a higher concentration of carbon dioxide today than it did a century ago. The most reliable scientific data show that the concentration of carbon dioxide in the atmosphere has increased from about 320 parts per million in 1960 to nearly 360 parts per million today.

Effects of increasing concentrations of carbon dioxide

Many scientists are concerned about the increasing levels of carbon dioxide in Earth's atmosphere. With more carbon dioxide in the atmosphere, they say, more heat will be trapped. Earth's annual average temperature will begin to rise. In early 2001, in a striking report released by the Intergovernmental Panel on Climate Change (a United Nations-sponsored panel of hundreds of scientists), scientists concluded that if greenhouse emissions are not curtailed, the average global surface temperature could rise by nearly 11°F (6°C) over the next 100 years. The scientists also stated that man-made pollution has "contributed substantially" to global warming and that Earth is likely to get a lot hotter than previously predicted.

Such a rise in temperature could have disastrous effects on the world. One result might be the melting of Earth's ice caps at the North and South Poles, with a resulting increase in the volume of the ocean's water. Were that to happen, many of the world's largest cities—those located along the edge of the oceans—might be flooded. Some experts predict dramatic changes in climate that could turn currently productive croplands into deserts, and deserts into productive agricultural regions. Half of all Alpine glaciers would disappear. Coral reefs would be destroyed, and vulnerable plant and animal species would be pushed to extinction.

In 1997, in Kyoto, Japan, representatives from more than 170 nations met to try to agree to decisive actions to reduce their emissions of

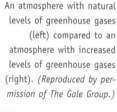

An atmosphere with natural levels of greenhouse gases (left) compared to an atmosphere with increased levels of greenhouse gases (right). *(Reproduced by permission of The Gale Group.)*

greenhouse gases. A treaty, called the Kyoto Protocol, was drafted at the meeting that proposed that 38 industrial nations cut their greenhouse-gas emissions by 2012 to 5.2 percent below levels in 1990 (the United States is the biggest producer of greenhouse gases, producing about 25 percent of the gases associated with global warming; Japan and Russia are the next biggest producers). More than 150 nations signed the treaty, but no industrialized country ratified it, and the treaty cannot take effect until a substantial number of industrial nations ratify it.

In November 2000, in The Hague, Netherlands, officials from around the world met to write the detailed rules for carrying out the Kyoto Protocol. Unfortunately, after less than two weeks, the talks collapsed in disarray with no deal reached to stop global warming. The main reason for the collapse was the argument between the United States and European countries over ways to clean up Earth's atmosphere. Officials attending the meeting did agree to meet once more to tackle the issue of global warming.

Differences of opinion.   As with many environmental issues, experts tend to disagree about one or more aspects of anticipated climate change. Some authorities are not convinced that the addition of carbon dioxide to the atmosphere will have any significant long-term effects on Earth's average annual temperature. Others concede that Earth's temperature may increase, but that the changes predicted are unlikely to occur. They point out that other factors—such as the formation of clouds—might counteract the presence of additional carbon dioxide in the atmosphere. They warn that nations should not act too quickly to reduce the combustion of fossil fuels since that will cause serious economic problems in many parts of the world. They suggest, instead, that we wait for a while to see if greenhouse factors really are beginning to change.

The problem with that suggestion, of course, is that it is possible to wait too long. Suppose that fossil fuel combustion is causing significant changes in the climate. It might take a half century or more to be certain of the relationship between fossil fuel combustion and warmer planetary temperatures. But at that point, it also might be too late to resolve the problem very easily. The carbon dioxide would have been already released to the atmosphere, and climate changes would have already begun to occur. As evidenced by the collapse of climate talks and the failure to ratify the Kyoto Protocol, there is no general consensus among scientists, politicians, businesspeople, and the general public as to what, if anything should be done about the potential for climate change on our planet.

The battle between industry and environmentalists over the issue of global warming continues with no clear vision for the future. In March

2001, U.S. President George W. Bush all but put an end to the possibility that the United States would follow through with the Kyoto Protocol when he said his administration would not seek to curb the emissions of carbon dioxide from power plants. This was a sharp reversal from his position during the presidential campaign in 2000. Ignoring recently published scientific reports, Bush stated that he made his decision "given the incomplete state of scientific knowledge of the causes of, and solutions to, global climate change."

[*See also* **Carbon cycle; Carbon dioxide; Forests; Ozone; Pollution**]

Gynecology

Gynecology is the specialized field of medicine dealing with the health of a woman's genital system. The genital system consists of the reproductive organs, including the uterus (the womb; the organ in which a fetus develops), cervix (the opening between the uterus and the vagina), ovaries (organs that produce eggs and sex hormones), fallopian tubes (organs that carry eggs from the ovaries to the uterus), vagina (the muscu-

Instruments used in a typical gynecological exam. The speculum (center) is used to examine the vagina during cervical smear tests or other procedures. At the lower right is a pile of spatulas used to collect specimens from the vagina or cervix. *(Reproduced by permission of Custom Medical Stock Photo, Inc.)*

Words to Know

In vitro fertilization: A process by which a woman's eggs are fertilized outside her body and then re-implanted back into it.

Menarche: The age at which a woman begins to menstruate.

Menopause: The period in a woman's life during which she ceases menstruating.

Menstruation: The monthly cycle in nonpregnant women during which the uterus sheds its lining when fertilization of an egg does not take place. It is often accompanied by a small discharge of blood.

Pap test: A test that can be used to detect the early stages of uterine cancer.

lar tube that extends from the uterus to outside the body), as well as their supporting structures.

Significant changes occur in a woman's reproductive organs when she reaches menarche (pronounced me-NAR-key). Menarche is the age at which a woman begins to menstruate. (Menstruation is the monthly cycle in nonpregnant women during which the uterus sheds its lining when fertilization of an egg does not take place.) Other changes occur again during any pregnancy that occurs in her life. A third important period of change occurs during menopause, at which time a woman ceases menstruating. A primary goal of the gynecologist is to guide women through these changes in their lives and to ensure that they retain their health throughout each stage.

Testing

The gynecologist uses a variety of tests to determine the health of a woman's reproductive organs. One such test is known as the Pap test, named after the Greek American physician George Papanicolaou (1883–1962) who developed the test in the mid-twentieth century. The Pap test involves the removal, staining, and study of cells taken from the vagina and cervix. The test can be used to detect the early stages of uterine cancer.

Gynecologists also can investigate the reasons that a woman is unable to become pregnant. Typical problems involve plugged fallopian tubes or a hormonal (chemical) imbalance that prevents an egg from becoming mature, releasing properly from the ovaries, or implanting onto the uterine wall. In each of these cases, steps can be taken to correct or bypass the problem so the woman can bear children.

Gynecology has advanced to the point that a physician can force the ovaries to produce eggs. These eggs can then be removed and fertilized in a dish and then implanted in the uterus. This method is known as in vitro fertilization because fertilization occurs within glass dishes (*vitro* is Latin for "glass") rather than a living body. In addition, the science of gynecology continues to make advances against the diseases and disorders that may deny a woman the ability to have children.

[*See also* **Puberty; Reproductive system**]

A spinning gyroscope is very resistant to any change in its orientation in space, allowing these gyroscopes to be tilted without falling. (*Reproduced by permission of The Stock Market.*)

Gyroscope

A gyroscope is an instrument consisting of a frame supporting a disk or wheel that spins rapidly about an axis. Technically, a gyroscope is any body that spins on a movable axis, including a child's toy top and the planet Earth. A gyroscope maintains a fixed axis of spin in spite of forces of gravity and magnetic fields.

French physicist Jean Bernard Léon Foucault (1819–1868) invented the gyroscope in 1852. Foucault mounted a heavy wheel onto a shaft and spun it rapidly. When he then turned the shaft with his hands, the wheel resisted shifting from the plane in which it was spinning.

The gyroscope follows one of the basic laws of physics, rotational inertia. This law simply states that a body that is set spinning has a tendency to keep spinning.

Foucault's gyroscope demonstrated the rotation of Earth. The spinning wheel, which was not stationary, retained its alignment in space while Earth turned under it. Foucault also found that the force of Earth's rotation caused the gyroscope's axis to move gradually until it was aligned parallel to Earth's axis in a north-south direction.

Unlike traditional magnetic compasses, the gyroscope can indicate true, or geographic, north rather than magnetic north, which varies depending on the location of the compass. Once a gyroscope is set spinning, no amount of tilting or turning will affect the gyroscope. This stability has allowed the gyroscope to replace the magnetic compass on ships and in airplanes.

Where to Learn More

Books

Earth Sciences

Cox, Reg, and Neil Morris. *The Natural World*. Philadelphia, PA: Chelsea House, 2000.

Dasch, E. Julius, editor. *Earth Sciences for Students*. Four volumes. New York: Macmillan Reference, 1999.

Denecke, Edward J., Jr. *Let's Review: Earth Science*. Second edition. Hauppauge, NY: Barron's, 2001.

Engelbert, Phillis. *Dangerous Planet: The Science of Natural Disasters*. Three volumes. Farmington Hills, MI: UXL, 2001.

Gardner, Robert. *Human Evolution*. New York: Franklin Watts, 1999.

Hall, Stephen. *Exploring the Oceans*. Milwaukee, WI: Gareth Stevens, 2000.

Knapp, Brian. *Earth Science: Discovering the Secrets of the Earth*. Eight volumes. Danbury, CT: Grolier Educational, 2000.

Llewellyn, Claire. *Our Planet Earth*. New York: Scholastic Reference, 1997.

Moloney, Norah. *The Young Oxford Book of Archaeology*. New York: Oxford University Press, 1997.

Nardo, Don. *Origin of Species: Darwin's Theory of Evolution*. San Diego, CA: Lucent Books, 2001.

Silverstein, Alvin, Virginia Silverstein, and Laura Silverstein Nunn.*Weather and Climate*. Brookfield, CN: Twenty-First Century Books, 1998.

Williams, Bob, Bob Ashley, Larry Underwood, and Jack Herschbach. *Geography*. Parsippany, NJ: Dale Seymour Publications, 1997.

Life Sciences

Barrett, Paul M. *National Geographic Dinosaurs*. Washington, D.C.: National Geographic Society, 2001.

Fullick, Ann. *The Living World*. Des Plaines, IL: Heinemann Library, 1999.

Gamlin, Linda. *Eyewitness: Evolution*. New York: Dorling Kindersley, 2000.

Greenaway, Theresa. *The Plant Kingdom: A Guide to Plant Classification and Biodiversity*. Austin, TX: Raintree Steck-Vaughn, 2000.

Kidd, J. S., and Renee A Kidd. *Life Lines: The Story of the New Genetics*. New York: Facts on File, 1999.

Kinney, Karin, editor. *Our Environment*. Alexandria, VA: Time-Life Books, 2000.

Where to Learn More

Nagel, Rob. *Body by Design: From the Digestive System to the Skeleton.* Two volumes. Farmington Hills, MI: UXL., 2000.

Parker, Steve. *The Beginner's Guide to Animal Autopsy: A "Hands-in" Approach to Zoology, the World of Creatures and What's Inside Them.* Brookfield, CN: Copper Beech Books, 1997.

Pringle, Laurence. *Global Warming: The Threat of Earth's Changing Climate.* New York: SeaStar Books, 2001.

Riley, Peter. *Plant Life.* New York: Franklin Watts, 1999.

Stanley, Debbie. *Genetic Engineering: The Cloning Debate.* New York: Rosen Publishing Group, 2000.

Whyman, Kate. *The Animal Kingdom: A Guide to Vertebrate Classification and Biodiversity.* Austin, TX: Raintree Steck-Vaughn, 1999.

Physical Sciences

Allen, Jerry, and Georgiana Allen. *The Horse and the Iron Ball: A Journey Through Time, Space, and Technology.* Minneapolis, MN: Lerner Publications, 2000.

Berger, Samantha, *Light.* New York: Scholastic, 1999.

Bonnet, Bob L., and Dan Keen. *Physics.* New York: Sterling Publishing, 1999.

Clark, Stuart. *Discovering the Universe.* Milwaukee, WI: Gareth Stevens, 2000.

Fleisher, Paul, and Tim Seeley. *Matter and Energy: Basic Principles of Matter and Thermodynamics.* Minneapolis, MN: Lerner Publishing, 2001.

Gribbin, John. *Eyewitness: Time and Space.* New York: Dorling Kindersley, 2000.

Holland, Simon. *Space.* New York: Dorling Kindersley, 2001.

Kidd, J. S., and Renee A. Kidd. *Quarks and Sparks: The Story of Nuclear Power.* New York: Facts on File, 1999.

Levine, Shar, and Leslie Johnstone. *The Science of Sound and Music.* New York: Sterling Publishing, 2000

Naeye, Robert. *Signals from Space: The Chandra X-ray Observatory.* Austin, TX: Raintree Steck-Vaughn, 2001.

Newmark, Ann. *Chemistry.* New York: Dorling Kindersley, 1999.

Oxlade, Chris. *Acids and Bases.* Chicago, IL: Heinemann Library, 2001.

Vogt, Gregory L. *Deep Space Astronomy.* Brookfield, CT: Twenty-First Century Books, 1999.

Technology and Engineering Sciences

Baker, Christopher W. *Scientific Visualization: The New Eyes of Science.* Brookfield, CT: Millbrook Press, 2000.

Cobb, Allan B. *Scientifically Engineered Foods: The Debate over What's on Your Plate.* New York: Rosen Publishing Group, 2000.

Cole, Michael D. *Space Launch Disaster: When Liftoff Goes Wrong.* Springfield, NJ: Enslow, 2000.

Deedrick, Tami. *The Internet.* Austin, TX: Raintree Steck-Vaughn, 2001.

DuTemple, Leslie A. *Oil Spills.* San Diego, CA: Lucent Books, 1999.

Gaines, Ann Graham. *Satellite Communication.* Mankata, MN: Smart Apple Media, 2000.

Gardner, Robert, and Dennis Shortelle. *From Talking Drums to the Internet: An Encyclopedia of Communications Technology.* Santa Barbara, CA: ABC-Clio, 1997.

Graham, Ian S. *Radio and Television.* Austin, TX: Raintree Steck-Vaughn, 2000.

Parker, Steve. *Lasers: Now and into the Future.* Englewood Cliffs, NJ: Silver Burdett Press, 1998.

Sachs, Jessica Snyder. *The Encyclopedia of Inventions*. New York: Franklin Watts, 2001.

Wilkinson, Philip. *Building*. New York: Dorling Kindersley, 2000.

Wilson, Anthony. *Communications: How the Future Began*. New York: Larousse Kingfisher Chambers, 1999.

Periodicals

Archaeology. Published by Archaeological Institute of America, 656 Beacon Street, 4th Floor, Boston, Massachusetts 02215. Also online at www.archaeology.org.

Astronomy. Published by Kalmbach Publishing Company, 21027 Crossroads Circle, Brookfield, WI 53186. Also online at www.astronomy.com.

Discover. Published by Walt Disney Magazine, Publishing Group, 500 S. Buena Vista, Burbank, CA 91521. Also online at www.discover.com.

National Geographic. Published by National Geographic Society, 17th & M Streets, NW, Washington, DC 20036. Also online at www.nationalgeographic.com.

New Scientist. Published by New Scientist, 151 Wardour St., London, England W1F 8WE. Also online at www.newscientist.com (includes links to more than 1,600 science sites).

Popular Science. Published by Times Mirror Magazines, Inc., 2 Park Ave., New York, NY 10024. Also online at www.popsci.com.

Science. Published by American Association for the Advancement of Science, 1333 H Street, NW, Washington, DC 20005. Also online at www.sciencemag.org.

Science News. Published by Science Service, Inc., 1719 N Street, NW, Washington, DC 20036. Also online at www.sciencenews.org.

Scientific American. Published by Scientific American, Inc., 415 Madison Ave, New York, NY 10017. Also online at www.sciam.com.

Smithsonian. Published by Smithsonian Institution, Arts & Industries Bldg., 900 Jefferson Dr., Washington, DC 20560. Also online at www.smithsonianmag.com.

Weatherwise. Published by Heldref Publications, 1319 Eighteenth St., NW, Washington, DC 20036. Also online at www.weatherwise.org.

Web Sites

Cyber Anatomy (provides detailed information on eleven body systems and the special senses) *http://library.thinkquest.org/11965/*

The DNA Learning Center (provides in-depth information about genes for students and educators) *http://vector.cshl.org/*

Educational Hotlists at the Franklin Institute (provides extensive links and other resources on science subjects ranging from animals to wind energy) *http://sln.fi.edu/tfi/hotlists/hotlists.html*

ENC Web Links: Science (provides an extensive list of links to sites covering subject areas under earth and space science, physical science, life science, process skills, and the history of science) *http://www.enc.org/weblinks/science/*

ENC Web Links: Math topics (provides an extensive list of links to sites covering subject areas under topics such as advanced mathematics, algebra, geometry, data analysis and probability, applied mathematics, numbers and operations, measurement, and problem solving) *http://www.enc.org/weblinks/math/*

Encyclopaedia Britannica Discovering Dinosaurs Activity Guide *http://dinosaurs.eb.com/dinosaurs/study/*

The Exploratorium: The Museum of Science, Art, and Human Perception *http://www.exploratorium.edu/*

ExploreMath.com (provides highly interactive math activities for students and educators) *http://www.exploremath.com/*

ExploreScience.com (provides highly interactive science activities for students and educators) *http://www.explorescience.com/*

Imagine the Universe! (provides information about the universe for students aged 14 and up) *http://imagine.gsfc.nasa.gov/*

Mad Sci Network (highly searchable site provides extensive science information in addition to a search engine and a library to find science resources on the Internet; also allows students to submit questions to scientists) *http://www.madsci.org/*

The Math Forum (provides math-related information and resources for elementary through graduate-level students) *http://forum.swarthmore.edu/*

NASA Human Spaceflight: International Space Station (NASA homepage for the space station) *http://www.spaceflight.nasa.gov/station/*

NASA's Origins Program (provides up-to-the-minute information on the scientific quest to understand life and its place in the universe) *http://origins.jpl.nasa.gov/*

National Human Genome Research Institute (provides extensive information about the Human Genome Project) *http://www.nhgri.nih.gov:80/index.html*

New Scientist Online Magazine *http://www.newscientist.com/*

The Nine Planets (provides a multimedia tour of the history, mythology, and current scientific knowledge of each of the planets and moons in our solar system) *http://seds.lpl.arizona.edu/nineplanets/nineplanets/nineplanets.html*

The Particle Adventure (provides an interactive tour of quarks, neutrinos, antimatter, extra dimensions, dark matter, accelerators, and particle detectors) *http://particleadventure.org/*

PhysLink: Physics and astronomy online education and reference *http://physlink.com/*

Savage Earth Online (online version of the PBS series exploring earthquakes, volcanoes, tsunamis, and other seismic activity) *http://www.pbs.org/wnet/savageearth/*

Science at NASA (provides breaking information on astronomy, space science, earth science, and biological and physical sciences) *http://science.msfc.nasa.gov/*

Science Learning Network (provides Internet-guided science applications as well as many middle school science links) *http://www.sln.org/*

SciTech Daily Review (provides breaking science news and links to dozens of science and technology publications; also provides links to numerous "interesting" science sites) *http://www.scitechdaily.com/*

Space.com (space news, games, entertainment, and science fiction) *http://www.space.com/index.html*

SpaceDaily.com (provides latest news about space and space travel) *http://www.spacedaily.com/*

SpaceWeather.com (science news and information about the Sun-Earth environment) *http://www.spaceweather.com/*

The Why Files (exploration of the science behind the news; funded by the National Science Foundation) *http://whyfiles.org/*

Index

Italic type indicates volume numbers; **boldface** type indicates entries and their page numbers; (ill.) indicates illustrations.

A

Abacus *1:* **1-2** 1 (ill.)
Abelson, Philip *1:* 24
Abortion *3:* 565
Abrasives *1:* **2-4,** 3 (ill.)
Absolute dating *4:* 616
Absolute zero *3:* 595-596
Abyssal plains *7:* 1411
Acceleration *1:* **4-6**
Acetylsalicylic acid *1:* **6-9,** 8 (ill.)
Acheson, Edward G. *1:* 2
Acid rain *1:* **9-14,** 10 (ill.), 12 (ill.), *6:* 1163, *8:* 1553
Acidifying agents *1:* 66
Acids and bases *1:* **14-16,** *8:* 1495
Acoustics *1:* **17-23,** 17 (ill.), 20 (ill.)
Acquired immunodeficiency syndrome. *See* **AIDS (acquired immunodeficiency syndrome)**
Acrophobia *8:* 1497
Actinides *1:* **23-26,** 24 (ill.)
Acupressure *1:* 121
Acupuncture *1:* 121
Adams, John Couch *7:* 1330
Adaptation *1:* **26-32,** 29 (ill.), 30 (ill.)
Addiction *1:* **32-37,** 35 (ill.), *3:* 478
Addison's disease *5:* 801

Adena burial mounds *7:* 1300
Adenosine triphosphate *7:* 1258
ADHD *2:* 237-238
Adhesives *1:* **37-39,** 38 (ill.)
Adiabatic demagnetization *3:* 597
ADP *7:* 1258
Adrenal glands *5:* 796 (ill.)
Adrenaline *5:* 800
Aerobic respiration *9:* 1673
Aerodynamics *1:* **39-43,** 40 (ill.)
Aerosols *1:* **43-49,** 43 (ill.)
Africa *1:* **49-54,** 50 (ill.), 53 (ill.)
Afterburners *6:* 1146
Agent Orange *1:* **54-59,** 57 (ill.)
Aging and death *1:* **59-62**
Agoraphobia *8:* 1497
Agriculture *1:* **62-65,** 63, 64 (ill.), *3:*582-590, *5:* 902-903, *9:* 1743-744, *7:* 1433 (ill.)
Agrochemicals *1:* **65-69,** 67 (ill.), 68 (ill.)
Agroecosystems *2:* 302
AI. *See* **Artificial intelligence**
AIDS (acquired immunodeficiency syndrome) *1:* **70-74,** 72 (ill.), *8:* 1583, *9:* 1737
Air flow *1:* 40 (ill.)
Air masses and fronts *1:* **80-82,** 80 (ill.)
Air pollution *8:* 1552, 1558
Aircraft *1:* **74-79,** 75 (ill.), 78 (ill.)
Airfoil *1:* 41
Airplanes. *See* **Aircraft**
Airships *1:* 75

Al-jabr wa'l Muqabalah 1: 97

Al-Khwarizmi   *1:* 97

Alchemy   *1:* **82-85**

Alcohol (liquor)   *1:* 32, 85-87

Alcoholism   *1:* **85-88**

Alcohols   *1:* **88-91,** 89 (ill.)

Aldrin, Edwin   *9:* 1779

Ale   *2:* 354

Algae   *1:* **91-97,** 93 (ill.), 94 (ill.)

Algal blooms   *1:* 96

Algebra   *1:* **97-99,** *2:* 333-334

Algorithms   *1:* 190

Alkali metals   *1:* **99-102,** 101 (ill.)

Alkaline earth metals   *1:* **102-106,** 104 (ill.)

Alleles   *7:* 1248

Allergic rhinitis   *1:* 106

Allergy   *1:* **106-110,** 108 (ill.)

Alloy   *1:* **110-111**

Alpha particles   *2:* 233, *8:* 1620, 1632

Alps   *5:* 827, *7:* 1301

Alternating current (AC)   *4:* 741

Alternation of generations   *9:* 1667

Alternative energy sources   *1:* **111-118,** 114 (ill.), 115 (ill.), *6:* 1069

Alternative medicine   *1:* **118-122**

Altimeter   *2:* 266

Aluminum   *1:* 122-124, 125 (ill.)

Aluminum family   *1:* **122-126,** 125 (ill.)

Alzheimer, Alois   *1:* 127

Alzheimer's disease   *1:* 62, **126-130,** 128 (ill.)

Amazon basin   *9:* 1774

American Red Cross   *2:* 330

Ames test   *2:* 408

Amino acid   *1:* **130-131**

Aminoglycosides   *1:* 158

Ammonia   *7:* 1346

Ammonification   *7:* 1343

Amniocentesis   *2:* 322

Amoeba   *1:* **131-134,** 132 (ill.)

Ampere   *3:* 582, *4:* 737

Amère, André   *4:* 737, *6:* 1212

Ampere's law   *4:* 747

Amphibians   *1:* **134-137,** 136 (ill.)

Amphiboles   *1:* 191

Amphineura   *7:* 1289

Amplitude modulation   *8:* 1627

Amundsen, Roald   *1:* 152

Anabolism   *7:* 1255

Anaerobic respiration   *9:* 1676

Anatomy   *1:* **138-141,** 140 (ill.)

Anderson, Carl   *1:* 163, *4:* 773

Andes Mountains   *7:* 1301, *9:* 1775-1776

Andromeda galaxy   *5:* 939 (ill.)

Anemia   *1:* 8, *6:* 1220

Aneroid barometer   *2:* 266

Anesthesia   *1:* **142-145,** 143 (ill.)

Angel Falls   *9:* 1774

Angiosperms   *9:* 1729

Animal behavior   *2:* 272

Animal hormones   *6:* 1053

Animal husbandry   *7:* 1433

Animals   *1:* **145-147,** 146 (ill.), *6:* 1133-1134

Anorexia nervosa   *4:* 712

Antarctic Treaty   *1:* 153

Antarctica   *1:* **147-153,** 148 (ill.), 152 (ill.)

Antennas   *1:* **153-155,** 154 (ill.)

Anthrax   *2:* 287

Antibiotics   *1:* **155-159,** 157 (ill.)

Antibody and antigen   *1:* **159-162,** *2:* 311

Anticyclones, cyclones and   *3:* 608-610

Antidiuretic hormone   *5:* 798

Antigens, antibodies and   *1:* 159-162

Antimatter   *1:* 163

Antimony   *7:* 1348

Antiparticles   *1:* **163-164**

Antiprotons   *1:* 163

Antipsychotic drugs   *8:* 1598

Antiseptics   *1:* **164-166**

Anurans   *1:* 136

Apennines   *5:* 827

Apes   *8:* 1572

Apgar Score   *2:* 322

Aphasia   *9:* 1798, 1799

Apollo 11   *9:* 1779, 1780 (ill.)

Apollo objects   *1:* 202

Appalachian Mountains   *7:* 1356

Appendicular skeleton   *9:* 1741

Aquaculture   *1:* **166-168,** 167 (ill.)

Arabian Peninsula.   *See* **Middle East**

Arabic numbers.   *See* **Hindu-Arabic number system**

Arachnids   *1:* **168-171,** 170 (ill.)

Arachnoid   *2:* 342

Arachnophobia   *8:* 1497

Ararat, Mount   *1:* 197

Archaeoastronomy *1:* **171-173,** 172 (ill.)

Archaeology *1:* **173-177,** 175 (ill.), 176 (ill.), *7:* 1323-1327

Archaeology, oceanic. *See* **Nautical archaeology**

Archaeopteryx lithographica *2:* *312*

Archimedes *2:* 360

Archimedes' Principle *2:* 360

Argon *7:* 1349, 1350

Ariel *10:* 1954

Aristotle *1:* 138, *2:* 291, *5:* 1012, *6:* 1169

Arithmetic *1:* 97, **177-181,** *3:* 534-536

Arkwright, Edmund *6:* 1098

Armstrong, Neil *9:* 1779

Arnold of Villanova *2:* 404

ARPANET *6:* 1124

Arrhenius, Svante *1:* 14, *8:* 1495

Arsenic *7:* 1348

Arthritis *1:* **181-183,** 182 (ill.)

Arthropods *1:* **183-186,** 184 (ill.)

Artificial blood *2:* 330

Artificial fibers *1:* **186-188,** 187 (ill.)

Artificial intelligence *1:* **188-190,** *2:* 244

Asbestos *1:* **191-194,** 192 (ill.), *6:* 1092

Ascorbic acid. *See* **Vitamin C**

Asexual reproduction *9:* 1664 (ill.), 1665

Asia *1:* **194-200,** 195 (ill.), 198 (ill.)

Aspirin. *See* **Acetylsalicylic acid**

Assembly language *3:* 551

Assembly line *7:* 1238

Astatine *6:* 1035

Asterisms *3:* 560

Asteroid belt *1:* 201

Asteroids *1:* **200-204,** 203 (ill.), *9:* 1764

Asthenosphere *8:* 1535, 1536

Asthma *1:* **204-207,** 206 (ill.), *9:* 1681

Aston, William *7:* 1240

Astronomia nova *3:* 425

Astronomy, infrared *6:* 1100-1103

Astronomy, ultraviolet *10:* 1943-1946

Astronomy, x-ray *10:* 2038-2041

Astrophysics *1:* **207-209,** 208 (ill.)

Atherosclerosis *3:* 484

Atmosphere observation *2:* **215-217,** 216 (ill.)

Atmosphere, composition and structure *2:* **211-215,** 214 (ill.)

Atmospheric circulation *2:* **218-221,** 220 (ill.)

Atmospheric optical effects *2:* **221-225,** 223 (ill.)

Atmospheric pressure *2:* **225,** 265, *8:* 1571

Atom *2:* **226-229,** 227 (ill.)

Atomic bomb *7:* 1364, 1381

Atomic clocks *10:* 1895-1896

Atomic mass *2:* 228, **229-232**

Atomic number *4:* 777

Atomic theory *2:* **232-236,** 234 (ill.)

ATP *7:* 1258

Attention-deficit hyperactivity disorder (ADHD) *2:* **237-238**

Audiocassettes. *See* **Magnetic recording/audiocassettes**

Auer metal *6:* 1165

Auroras *2:* 223, 223 (ill.)

Australia *2:* **238-242,** 239 (ill.), 241 (ill.)

Australopithecus afarensis *6:* 1056, 1057 (ill.)

Australopithecus africanus *6:* 1056

Autistic savants. *See* **Savants**

Autoimmune diseases *1:* 162

Automation *2:* **242-245,** 244 (ill.)

Automobiles *2:* **245-251,** 246 (ill.), 249 (ill.)

Autosomal dominant disorders *5:* 966

Auxins *6:* 1051

Avogadro, Amadeo *7:* 1282

Avogadro's number *7:* 1282

Axial skeleton *9:* 1740

Axioms *1:* 179

Axle *6:* 1207

Ayers Rock *2:* 240

AZT *1:* 73

B

B-2 Stealth Bomber *1:* 78 (ill.)

Babbage, Charles *3:* 547

Babbitt, Seward *9:* 1691

Bacitracin *1:* 158

Bacteria *2:* **253-260,** 255 (ill.), 256 (ill.), 259 (ill.)

Bacteriophages *10:* 1974

Baekeland, Leo H.   *8:* 1565
Bakelite   *8:* 1565
Balard, Antoine   *6:* 1034
Baldwin, Frank Stephen   *2:* 371
Ballistics   *2:* **260-261**
Balloons   *1:* 75, *2:* ***261-265**, 263 (ill.),*
   264 (ill.)
Bardeen, John   *10:* 1910
Barite   *6:* 1093
Barium   *1:* 105
Barnard, Christiaan   *6:* 1043, *10:* 1926
Barometer   *2:* **265-267**, 267 (ill.)
Barrier islands   *3:* 500
Bases, acids and 1: 14-16
Basophils   *2:* 329
Bats   *4:* 721
Battery   *2:* **268-270**, 268 (ill.)
Battle fatigue   *9:* 1826
Beaches, coasts and   *3:* 498-500
Becquerel, Henri   *8:* 1630
Bednorz, Georg   *10:* 1851
Behavior (human and animal), study of.
   See **Psychology**
Behavior   *2:* **270-273**, 271 (ill.), 272
   (ill.)
Behaviorism (psychology)   *8:* 1595
Bell Burnell, Jocelyn   *7:* 1340
Bell, Alexander Graham   *10:* 1867 (ill.)
Benthic zone   *7:* 1415
Benz, Karl Friedrich   *2:* 246 (ill.)
Berger, Hans   *9:* 1745
Beriberi   *6:* 1219, *10:* 1982
Bernoulli's principle   *1:* 40, 42, *5:* 884
Beryllium   *1:* 103
Berzelius, Jöns Jakob   *2:* 230
Bessemer converter   *7:* 1445, *10:* 1916
Bessemer, Henry   *10:* 1916
Beta carotene   *10:* 1984
Beta particles   *8:* 1632
Bichat, Xavier   *1:* 141
Big bang theory   *2:* **273-276**, 274 (ill.),
   4: 780
Bigelow, Julian   *3:* 606
Binary number system   *7:* 1397
Binary stars   *2:* **276-278**, 278 (ill.)
Binomial nomenclature   *2:* 337
Biochemistry   *2:* **279-280**
Biodegradable   *2:* **280-281**
Biodiversity   *2:* **281-283**, 282 (ill.)
Bioenergy   *1:* 117, *2:* **284-287**, 284
   (ill.)

Bioenergy fuels   *2:* 286
Biofeedback   *1:* 119
Biological warfare   *2:* **287-290**
Biological Weapons Convention Treaty
   2: 290
Biology   *2:* **290-293**, *7:* 1283-1285
Bioluminescence   *6:* 1198
Biomass energy.   *See* **Bioenergy**
Biomes   *2:* **293-302**, 295 (ill.), 297
   (ill.), 301 (ill.)
Biophysics   *2:* **302-304**
Bioremediation   *7:* 1423
Biosphere 2 Project   *2:* 307-309
Biospheres   *2:* **304-309**, 306 (ill.)
Biot, Jean-Baptiste   *7:* 1262
Biotechnology   *2:* **309-312**, 311 (ill.)
Bipolar disorder   *4:* 633
Birds   *2:* **312-315**, 314 (ill.)
Birth   *2:* **315-319**, 317 (ill.), 318 (ill.)
Birth control.   *See* **Contraception**
Birth defects   *2:* **319-322**, 321 (ill.)
Bismuth   *7:* 1349
Bjerknes, Jacob   *1:* 80, *10:* 2022
Bjerknes, Vilhelm   *1:* 80, *10:* 2022
Black Death   *8:* 1520
Black dwarf   *10:* 2028
Black holes   *2:* **322-326**, 325 (ill.),
   9: 1654
Blanc, Mont   *5:* 827
Bleuler, Eugen   *9:* 1718
Blood   *2:* **326-330**, 328 (ill.), 330,
   3: 483
Blood banks   *2:* 330
Blood pressure   *3:* 483
Blood supply   *2:* **330-333**
Blood vessels   *3:* 482
Blue stars   *9:* 1802
Bode, Johann   *1:* 201
Bode's Law   *1:* 201
Bogs   *10:* 2025
Bohr, Niels   *2:* 235
Bones.   *See* **Skeletal system**
Bones, study of diseases of or injuries to.
   See **Orthopedics**
Boole, George   *2:* 333
Boolean algebra   *2:* **333-334**
Bopp, Thomas   *3:* 529
Borax   *1:* 126, *6:* 1094
Boreal coniferous forests   *2:* 294
Bores, Leo   *8:* 1617
Boron   *1:* 124-126

Boron compounds   *6:* 1094
Bort, Léon Teisserenc de   *10:* 2021
Bosons   *10:* 1831
Botany   *2:* **334-337,** 336 (ill.)
Botulism   *2:* 258, 288
Boundary layer effects   *5:* 885
Bovine growth hormone   *7:* 1434
Boyle, Robert   *4:* 780
Boyle's law   *5:* 960
Braham, R. R.   *10:* 2022
Brahe, Tycho   *3:* 574
Brain   *2:* **337-351,** 339 (ill.), 341 (ill.)
Brain disorders   *2:* 345
Brass   *10:* 1920
Brattain, Walter   *10:* 1910
Breathing   *9:* 1680
Brewing   *2:* **352-354,** 352 (ill.)
Bridges   *2:* **354-358,** 357 (ill.)
Bright nebulae   *7:* 1328
British system of measurement   *10:* 1948
Bromine   *6:* 1034
Bronchitis   *9:* 1681
Bronchodilators   *1:* 205
Brønsted, J. N.   *1:* 15
Brønsted, J. N.   *1:* 15
Bronze   *2:* 401
Bronze Age   *6:* 1036
Brown algae   *1:* 95
Brown dwarf   *2:* **358-359**
Brucellosis   *2:* 288
Bryan, Kirk   *8:* 1457
Bubonic plague   *8:* 1518
Buckminsterfullerene   *2:* 398, 399 (ill.)
Bugs.   *See* **Insects**
Bulimia   *4:* 1714-1716
Buoyancy   *1:* 74, *2:* **360-361,** 360 (ill.)
Burial mounds   *7:* 1298
Burns   *2:* **361-364,** 362 (ill.)
Bushnell, David   *10:* 1834
Butterflies   *2:* **364-367,** 364 (ill.)
Byers, Horace   *10:* 2022

C

C-12   *2:* 231
C-14   *1:* 176, *4:* 617
Cable television   *10:* 1877
Cactus   *4:* 635 (ill.)
CAD/CAM   *2:* **369-370,** 369 (ill.)

Caffeine   *1:* 34
Caisson   *2:* 356
Calcite   *3:* 422
Calcium   *1:* 104 (ill.), 105
Calcium carbonate   *1:* 104 (ill.)
Calculators   *2:* **370-371,** 370 (ill.)
Calculus   *2:* **371-372**
Calderas   *6:* 1161
Calendars   *2:* **372-375,** 374 (ill.)
Callisto   *6:* 1148, 1149
Calories   *2:* **375-376,** *6:* 1045
Calving (icebergs)   *6:* 1078, 1079 (ill.)
Cambium   *10:* 1927
Cambrian period   *8:* 1461
Cameroon, Mount   *1:* 51
Canadian Shield   *7:* 1355
Canals   *2:* **376-379,** 378 (ill.)
Cancer   *2:* **379-382,** 379 (ill.), 381 (ill.), *10:* 1935
Canines   *2:* **382-387,** 383 (ill.), 385 (ill.)
Cannabis sativa   *6:* 1224, 1226 (ill.)
Cannon, W. B.   *8:* 1516
Capacitor   *4:* 749
Carbohydrates   *2:* **387-389,** *7:* 1400
Carbon   *2:* 396
Carbon compounds, study of.   *See* **Organic chemistry**
Carbon cycle   *2:* **389-393,** 391 (ill.)
Carbon dioxide   *2:* **393-395,** 394 (ill.)
Carbon family   *2:* **395-403,** 396 (ill.), 397 (ill.), 399 (ill.)
Carbon monoxide   *2:* **403-406**
Carbon-12   *2:* 231
Carbon-14   *4:* 617
Carboniferous period   *8:* 1462
Carborundum   *1:* 2
Carcinogens   *2:* **406-408**
Carcinomas   *2:* 381
Cardano, Girolamo   *8:* 1576
Cardiac muscle   *7:* 1312
Cardiovascular system   *3:* 480
Caries   *4:* 628
Carlson, Chester   *8:* 1502, 1501 (ill.)
Carnot, Nicholas   *6:* 1118
Carnot, Sadi   *10:* 1885
Carothers, Wallace   *1:* 186
Carpal tunnel syndrome   *2:* **408-410**
Cartography   *2:* **410-412,** 411 (ill.)
Cascade Mountains   *7:* 1358
Caspian Sea   *5:* 823, 824

Cassini division   *9:* 1711
Cassini, Giovanni Domenico   *9:* 1711
Cassini orbiter   *9:* 1712
CAT scans   *2:* 304, *8:* 1640
Catabolism   *7:* 1255
Catalysts and catalysis   *3:* **413-415**
Catastrophism   *3:* **415**
Cathode   *3:* **415-416**
Cathode-ray tube   *3:* **417-420,** 418
   (ill.)
Cats.   *See* **Felines**
Caucasus Mountains   *5:* 823
Cavendish, Henry   *6:* 1069, *7:* 1345
Caves   *3:* **420-423,** 422 (ill.)
Cavities (dental)   *4:* 628
Cayley, George   *1:* 77
CDC   *6:* 1180
CDs.   *See* **Compact disc**
Celestial mechanics   *3:* **423-428,** 427
   (ill.)
Cell wall (plants)   *3:* 436
Cells   *3:* **428-436,** 432 (ill.), 435 (ill.)
Cells, electrochemical   *3:* **436-439**
Cellular metabolism   *7:* 1258
Cellular/digital technology   *3:* **439-441**
Cellulose   *2:* 389, *3:* **442-445,** 442 (ill.)
Celsius temperature scale   *10:* 1882
Celsius, Anders   *10:* 1882
Cenozoic era   *5:* 990, *8:* 1462
Center for Disease Control (CDC)
   6: 1180
Central Asia   *1:* 198
Central Dogma   *7:* 1283
Central Lowlands (North America)
   7: 1356
Centrifuge   *3:* **445-446,** 446 (ill.)
Cephalopoda   *7:* 1289
Cephalosporin   *1:* 158
Cepheid variables   *10:* 1964
Ceramic   *3:* **447-448**
Cerebellum   *2:* 345
Cerebral cortex   *2:* 343
Cerebrum   *2:* 343
Čerenkov effect   *6:* 1189
Cerium   *6:* 1163
Cesium   *1:* 102
Cetaceans   *3:* **448-451,** 450 (ill.), *4:*
   681 (ill.), *7:* 1416 (ill.)
CFCs   *6:* 1032, *7:* 1453-1454, *8:* 1555,
Chadwick, James   *2:* 235, *7:* 1338
Chain, Ernst   *1:* 157

Chamberlain, Owen   *1:* 163
Chancroid   *9:* 1735, 1736
Chandra X-ray Observatory   *10:* 2040
Chandrasekhar, Subrahmanyan
   10: 1854
Chandrasekhar's limit   *10:* 1854
Chao Phraya River   *1:* 200
Chaos theory   *3:* **451-453**
Chaparral   *2:* 296
Chappe, Claude   *10:* 1864
Chappe, Ignace   *10:* 1864
Charles's law   *5:* 961
Charon   *8:* 1541, 1541 (ill.), 1542
Chassis   *2:* 250
Cheetahs   *5:* 861
Chemical bond   *3:* **453-457**
Chemical compounds   *3:* 541-546
Chemical elements   *4:* 774-781
Chemical equations   *5 :* *815-817*
Chemical equilibrium   *5:* 817-820
Chemical warfare   *3:* **457-463,** 459
   (ill.), 461 (ill.)*6:* 1032
Chemiluminescence   *6:* 1198
Chemistry   *3:* **463-469,** 465 (ill.) ,467
   (ill.), *8:* 1603
Chemoreceptors   *8:* 1484
Chemosynthesis   *7:* 1418
Chemotherapy   *2:* 382
Chichén Itzá   *1:* 173
Chicxulub   *1:* 202
Childbed fever   *1:* 164
Chimpanzees   *8:* 1572
Chiropractic   *1:* 120
Chladni, Ernst   *1:* 17
Chlamydia   *9:* 1735, 1736
Chlorination   *6:* 1033
Chlorine   *6:* 1032
Chlorofluorocarbons.   *See* **CFCs**
Chloroform   *1:* 142, 143, 143 (ill.)
Chlorophyll   *1:* 103
Chlorophyta   *1:* 94
Chloroplasts   *3:* 436, *8:* 1506 (ill.)
Chlorpromazine   *10:* 1906
Cholesterol   *3:* **469-471,** 471 (ill.), *6:*
   1042
Chorionic villus sampling   *2:* 322, *4:*
   790
Chromatic aberration   *10:* 1871
Chromatography   *8:* 1604
Chromosomes   *3:* **472-476,** 472 (ill.),
   475 (ill.)

Chromosphere   *10:* 1846
Chrysalis   *2:* 366, *7:* 1261 (ill.)
Chrysophyta   *1:* 93
Chu, Paul Ching-Wu   *10:* 1851
Cigarette smoke   *3:* **476-478,** 477 (ill.)
Cigarettes, addiction to   *1:* 34
Ciliophora   *8:* 1592
Circle   *3:* **478-480,** 479 (ill.)
Circular acceleration   *1:* 5
Circular accelerators   *8:* 1479
Circulatory system   *3:* **480-484,** 482 (ill.)
Classical conditioning   *9:* 1657
Clausius, Rudolf   *10:* 1885
Claustrophobia   *8:* 1497
Climax community   *10:* 1839
Clones and cloning   *3:* **484-490,** 486 (ill.), 489 (ill.)
Clostridium botulinum   *2:* 258
Clostridium tetani   *2:* 258
Clouds   *3:* **490-492,** 491 (ill.)
Coal   *3:* **492-498,** 496 (ill.)
Coast and beach   *3:* **498-500.** 500 (ill.)
Coastal Plain (North America)   *7:* 1356
Cobalt-60   *7:* 1373
COBE (Cosmic Background Explorer)   *2:* 276
COBOL   *3:* 551
Cocaine   *1:* 34, *3:* **501-505,** 503 (ill.)
Cockroaches   *3:* **505-508,** 507 (ill.)
Coelacanth   *3:* **508-511,** 510 (ill.)
Cognition   *3:* **511-515,** 513 (ill.), 514 (ill.)
Cold fronts   *1:* 81, 81 (ill.)
Cold fusion   *7:* 1371
Cold-deciduous forests   *5:* 909
Collins, Francis   *6:* 1064
Collins, Michael   *9:* 1779
Colloids   *3:* **515-517,** 517 (ill.)
Color   *3:* **518-522,** 521 (ill.)
Color blindness   *5:* 971
Colorant   *4:* 686
Colt, Samuel   *7:* 1237
Columbus, Christopher   *1:* 63
Coma   *2:* 345
Combined gas law   *5:* 960
Combustion   *3:* **522-527,** 524 (ill.), *7:* 1441
Comet Hale-Bopp   *3:* 529
Comet Shoemaker-Levy 9   *6:* 1151
Comet, Halley's   *3:* 528

Comets   *3:* **527-531,** 529 (ill.), *6:* 1151, *9:* 1765
Common cold   *10:* 1978
Compact disc   *3:* **531-533,** 532 (ill.)
Comparative genomics   *6:* 1067
Complex numbers   *3:* **534-536,** 534 (ill.), *6:* 1082
Composite materials   *3:* **536-539**
Composting   *3:* **539-541,** 539 (ill.)
Compound, chemical   *3:* **541-546,** 543 (ill.)
Compton Gamma Ray Observatory   *5:* 949
Compulsion   *7:* 1405
Computer Aided Design and Manufacturing.   *See* **CAD/CAM**
Computer languages   *1:* 189, *3:* 551
Computer software   *3:* **549-554,** 553 (ill.)
Computer, analog   *3:* **546-547**
Computer, digital   *3:* **547-549,** 548 (ill.)
Computerized axial tomography.   *See* **CAT scans**
Concave lenses   *6:* 1185
Conditioning   *9:* 1657
Condom   *3:* 563
Conduction   *6:* 1044
Conductivity, electrical.   *See* **Electrical conductivity**
Conservation laws   *3:* **554-558.** 557 (ill.)
Conservation of electric charge   *3:* 556
Conservation of momentum   *7:* 1290
Conservation of parity   *3:* 558
Constellations   *3:* **558-560,** 559 (ill.)
Contact lines   *5:* 987
Continental Divide   *7:* 1357
Continental drift   *8:* 1534
Continental margin   *3:* **560-562**
Continental rise   *3:* 562
Continental shelf   *2:* 300
Continental slope   *3:* 561
Contraception   *3:* **562-566,** 564 (ill.)
Convection   *6:* 1044
Convention on International Trade in Endangered Species   *5:* 795
Convex lenses   *6:* 1185
Cooke, William Fothergill   *10:* 1865
Coordination compounds   *3:* 544
Copernican system   *3:* 574
Copper   *10:* 1919-1921, 1920 (ill.)

Coral   *3:* **566-569,** 567 (ill.), 568 (ill.)
Coral reefs   *2:* 301
Core   *4:* 711
Coriolis effect   *2:* 219, *10:* 2029
Corona   *10:* 1846
Coronary artery disease   *6:* 1042
Coronas   *2:* 225
Correlation   *3:* **569-571**
Corson, D. R.   *6:* 1035
Corti, Alfonso Giacomo Gaspare
    4: 695
Corticosteroids   *1:* 206
Corundum   *6:* 1094
Cosmetic plastic surgery   *8:* 1530
Cosmic Background Explorer (COBE)
    2: 276
Cosmic dust   *6:* 1130
Cosmic microwave background   *2:* 275,
    8: 1637
Cosmic rays   *3:* **571-573,** 573 (ill.)
Cosmology   *1:* 171, *3:* **574-577**
Cotton   *3:* **577-579,** 578 (ill.)
Coulomb   *3:* **579-582**
Coulomb, Charles*3:* 579,   *6:* 1212
Coulomb's law   *4:* 744
Courtois, Bernard   *6:* 1035
Courtship behaviors   *2:* 273
Covalent bonding   *3:* 455
Cowan, Clyde   *10:* 1833
Coxwell, Henry Tracey   *2:* 263
Coyotes   *2:* 385
Craniotomy   *8:* 1528
Creationism   *3:* 577
Crick, Francis   *3:* 473, *4:* 786, *5:* 973,
    980 (ill.), 982, *7:* 1389
Cro-Magnon man   *6:* 1059
Crop rotation   *3:* 589
Crops   *3:* **582-590,** 583 (ill.), 589 (ill.)
Crude oil   *8:* 1492
Crust   *4:* 709
Crustaceans   *3:* **590-593,** 592 (ill.)
Cryobiology   *3:* **593-595**
Cryogenics   *3:* **595-601,** 597 (ill.)
Crystal   *3:* **601-604,** 602 (ill.), 603 (ill.)
Curie, Marie   *7:* 1450
Current electricity   *4:* 742
Currents, ocean   *3:* **604-605**
Cybernetics   *3:* **605-608,** 607 (ill.)
Cyclamate   *3:* **608**
Cyclone and anticyclone   *3:* **608-610,**
    609 (ill.)

Cyclotron   *1:* 163, *8:* 1479, 1480 (ill.)
Cystic fibrosis   *2:* 320
Cytokinin   *6:* 1052
Cytoskeleton   *3:* 434

D

Da Vinci, Leonardo   *2:* 291, *4:* 691, *10:*
    2020
Daddy longlegs   *1:* 171
Dalton, John   *2:* 226, 229, *2:* 232
Dalton's theory   *2:* 232
Dam   *4:* **611-613,** 612 (ill.)
Damselfly   *1:* 184 (ill.)
Danube River   *5:* 824
Dark matter   *4:* **613-616,** 615 (ill.)
Dark nebulae   *6:* 1131, *7:* 1330
Dart, Raymond   *6:* 1056
Darwin, Charles   *1:* 29, *6:* 1051, *8:*
    1510
Dating techniques   *4:* **616-619,** 618
    (ill.)
Davy, Humphry   *1:* 142, chlorine *6:*
    1032, 1087
DDT (dichlorodiphenyltrichloroethane)
    1: 69, *4:* **619-622,** 620 (ill.)
De Bort, Léon Philippe Teisserenc   *2:*
    263
De Candolle, Augustin Pyrame
    8: 1509
De curatorum chirurgia   *8:* 1528
De Forest, Lee   *10:* 1961
De materia medica   *5:* 877
De Soto, Hernando   *7:* 1299
Dead Sea   *1:* 196
Death   *1:* 59-62
Decay   *7:* 1442
Decimal system   *1:* 178
Decomposition   *2:* 392, *9:* 1648
Deimos   *6:* 1229
Dementia   *4:* **622-624,** 623 (ill.)
Democritus   *2:* 226, 232
Dendrochronology.   *See* **Tree-ring
    dating**
Denitrification   *7:* 1343
Density   *4:* **624-626,** 625 (ill.)
Dentistry   *4:* **626-630,** 628 (ill.), 629
    (ill.)
Depression   *4:* **630-634,** 632 (ill.)
Depth perception   *8:* 1483 (ill.), 1484

Dermis   *6:* 1111
Desalination   *7:* 1439, *10:* 2012
Descartes, René   *6:* 1184
The Descent of Man   *6:* 1055
Desert   *2:* 296, *4:* **634-638,** 635 (ill.), 636 (ill.)
Detergents, soaps and   *9:* 1756-1758
Devonian period   *8:* 1461
Dew point   *3:* 490
Dexedrine   *2:* 238
Diabetes mellitus   *4:* **638-640**
Diagnosis   *4:* **640-644,** 643 (ill.)
Dialysis   *4:* **644-646,** *7:* 1439
Diamond   *2:* 396 (ill.), 397
Diencephalon   *2:* 342
Diesel engine   *4:* **646-647,** 647 (ill.)
Diesel, Rudolf   *4:* 646, *10:* 1835
Differential calculus   *2:* 372
Diffraction   *4:* **648-651,** 648 (ill.)
Diffraction gratings   *4:* 650
Diffusion   *4:* **651-653,** 652 (ill.)
Digestion   *7:* 1255
Digestive system   *4:* **653-658,** 657 (ill.)
Digital audio tape   *6:* 1211
Digital technology.   *See* **Cellular/digital technology**
Dingoes   *2:* 385, 385 (ill.)
Dinosaurs   *4:* **658-665,** 660 (ill.), 663 (ill.), 664 (ill.)
Diodes   *4:* **665-666,** *6:* 1176-1179
Dioscorides   *5:* 878
Dioxin   *4:* **667-669**
Dirac, Paul   *1:* 163, *4:* 772
Dirac's hypothesis   *1:* 163
Direct current (DC)   *4:* 741
Dirigible   *1:* 75
Disaccharides   *2:* 388
Disassociation   *7:* 1305
Disease   *4:* **669-675,** 670 (ill.), 673 (ill.), *8:* 1518
Dissection   *10:* 1989
Distillation   *4:* **675-677,** 676 (ill.)
DNA   *1:* 61, *2:* 310, *3:* 434, 473-474, *5:* 972-975, 980 (ill.), 981-984, *7:* 1389-1390
    forensic science   *5:* 900
    human genome project   *6:* 1060-1068
    mutation   *7:* 1314-1316
Döbereiner, Johann Wolfgang   *8:* 1486
Dogs.   *See* **Canines**

Dollard, John   *10:* 1871
Dolly (clone)   *3:* 486
Dolphins   *3:* 448, 449 (ill.)
Domagk, Gerhard   *1:* 156
Domain names (computers)   *6:* 1127
Dopamine   *9:* 1720
Doppler effect   *4:* **677-680,** 679 (ill.), *9:* 1654
Doppler radar   *2:* 220 (ill.), *10:* 2023
Doppler, Christian Johann   *9:* 1654
Down syndrome   *2:* 319
Down, John Langdon Haydon   *9:* 1713
Drake, Edwin L.   *7:* 1419
Drebbel, Cornelius   *10:* 1834
Drew, Richard   *1:* 39
Drift nets   *4:* **680-682,** 681 (ill.)
Drinker, Philip   *8:* 1548
Drought   *4:* **682-684,** 683 (ill.)
Dry cell (battery)   *2:* 269
Dry ice   *2:* 395
Drying (food preservation)   *5:* 890
Dubois, Marie-Eugene   *6:* 1058
Duodenum   *4:* 655
Dura mater   *2:* 342
Dust Bowl   *4:* 682
Dust devils   *10:* 1902
Dust mites   *1:* 107, 108 (ill.)
DVD technology   *4:* **684-686**
Dyes and pigments   *4:* **686-690,** 688 (ill.)
Dynamite   *5:* 845
Dysarthria   *9:* 1798
Dyslexia   *4:* **690-691,** 690 (ill.)
Dysphonia   *9:* 1798
Dysprosium   *6:* 1163

E

E = mc^2 *7:* 1363, 1366, *9:* 1662
Ear   *4:* **693-698,** 696 (ill.)
Earth (planet)   *4:* **698-702,** 699 (ill.)
Earth science   *4:* **707-708**
Earth Summit   *5:* 796
Earth's interior   *4:* **708-711,** 710 (ill.)
Earthquake   *4:* **702-707,** 705 (ill.), 706 (ill.)
Eating disorders   *4:* **711-717,** 713 (ill.)
Ebola virus   *4:* **717-720,** 719 (ill.)
Echolocation   *4:* **720-722**
Eclipse   *4:* **723-725,** 723 (ill.)

Ecological pyramid *5:* 894 (ill.), 896
Ecological system. *See* **Ecosystem**
Ecologists *4:* 728
Ecology *4:* **725-728**
Ecosystem *4:* **728-730,** 729 (ill.)
Edison, Thomas Alva *6:* 1088
EEG (electroencephalogram) *2:* 348, *9:* 1746
Eijkman, Christian *10:* 1981
Einstein, Albert *4:* 691, *7:* 1428, *9:* 1659 (ill.)
   photoelectric effect *6:* 1188, *8:* 1504
   space-time continuum *9:* 1777
   theory of relativity *9:* 1659-1664
Einthoven, William *4:* 751
EKG (electrocardiogram) *4:* 751-755
El Niño *4:* **782-785,** 784 (ill.)
Elasticity *4:* **730-731**
Elbert, Mount *7:* 1357
Elbrus, Mount *5:* 823
Electric arc *4:* **734-737,** 735 (ill.)
Electric charge *4:* 743
Electric circuits *4:* 739, 740 (ill.)
Electric current *4:* 731, 734, **737-741,** 740 (ill.), 746, 748, 761, 767, 771, 773
Electric fields *4:* 743, 759
Electric motor *4:* **747-750,** 747 (ill.)
Electrical conductivity *4:* **731-734,** 735
Electrical force *3:* 579, 581-582, *4:* 744
Electrical resistance *4:* 732, 738, 746
Electricity *4:* **741-747,** 745 (ill.)
Electrocardiogram *4:* **751-755,** 753 (ill.), 754 (ill.)
Electrochemical cells *3:* 416, 436-439
Electrodialysis *4:* 646
Electroluminescence *6:* 1198
Electrolysis *4:* **755-758**
Electrolyte *4:* 755
Electrolytic cell *3:* 438
Electromagnet *6:* 1215
Electromagnetic field *4:* **758-760**
Electromagnetic induction *4:* **760-763,** 762 (ill.)
Electromagnetic radiation *8:* 1619
Electromagnetic spectrum *4:* **763-765,** *4:* 768, *6:* 1100, 1185, *8:* 1633, *9:* 1795
Electromagnetic waves *7:* 1268
Electromagnetism *4:* **766-768,** 766 (ill.)

Electron *4:* **768-773**
Electron gun *3:* 417
Electronegativity *3:* 455
Electronics *4:* **773-774,** 773 (ill.)
Electrons *4:* **768-773,** *10:* 1832, 1833
Electroplating *4:* 758
Element, chemical *4:* **774-781,** 778 (ill.)
Elementary algebra *1:* 98
Elements *4:* 775, 777, *8:* 1490, *10:* 1913
Embryo and embryonic development *4:* **785-791,** 788 (ill.)
Embryology *4:* 786
Embryonic transfer *4:* 790-791
Emphysema *9:* 1681
Encke division *9:* 1711
Encke, Johann *9:* 1711
Endangered species *5:* **793-796,** 795 (ill.)
Endangered Species Act *5:* 795
Endocrine system *5:* **796-801,** 799 (ill.)
Endoplasmic reticulum *3:* 433
Energy *5:* **801-805**
Energy and mass *9:* 1662
Energy conservation *1:* 117
Energy, alternative sources of *1:* 111-118, *6:* 1069
Engels, Friedrich *6:* 1097
Engineering *5:* **805-807,** 806 (ill.)
Engines *2:* 246, *6:* 1117, 1143, *9:* 1817, *10:* 1835
English units of measurement. *See* **British system of measurement**
ENIAC *3:* 551
Entropy *10:* 1886
Environment
   air pollution *8:* 1552, 1553
   effect of aerosols on *1:* 47,48
   effect of carbon dioxide on *8:* 1554
   effect of use of fossil fuels on *2:* 285, *7:* 1454
   impact of aquaculture on *1:* 168
   industrial chemicals *8:* 1557
   ozone depletion *8:* 1555
   poisons and toxins *8:* 1546
   tropical deforestation *9:* 1744
   water pollution *8:* 1556
Environmental ethics *5:* **807-811,** 809 (ill.), 810 (ill.)

Enzyme   *5:* **812-815,** 812 (ill.), 814 (ill.)

Eosinophils   *2:* 329

Epidemics   *4:* 671

Epidermis   *2:* 362, *6:* 1110

Epilepsy   *2:* 347-349

Equation, chemical   *5:* **815-817**

Equilibrium, chemical   *5:* **817-820**

Equinox   *9:* 1728

Erasistratus   *1:* 138

Erbium   *6:* 1163

Erosion   *3:* 498, *5:* **820-823,** 821 (ill.), *9:* 1762

Erythroblastosis fetalis   *9:* 1685

Erythrocytes   *2:* 327

Escherichia coli   *2:* 258

Esophagitis   *4:* 656

Estrogen   *5:* 801, *8:* 1599, 1600

Estuaries   *2:* 300

Ethanol   *1:* 89-91

Ether   *1:* 142, 143

Ethics   *3:* 489, *5:* 807-811

Ethylene glycol   *1:* 91

Euglenoids   *1:* 92

Euglenophyta   *1:* 92

Eukaryotes   *3:* 429, 432-435

Europa   *6:* 1148, 1149

Europe   *5:* **823-828,** 825 (ill.), 827 (ill.)

Europium   *6:* 1163

Eutrophication   *1:* 96, *5:* **828-831,** 830 (ill.)

Evans, Oliver   *7:* 1237, *9:* 1820

Evaporation   *5:* **831-832**

Everest, Mount   *1:* 194

Evergreen broadleaf forests   *5:* 909

Evergreen tropical rain forest   *2:* 298

Evolution   *1:* 26, 51, *5:* **832-839**

Excretory system   *5:* **839-842**

Exhaust system   *2:* 247

Exoplanets.   *See* **Extrasolar planets**

Exosphere   *2:* 214

Expansion, thermal   *5:* 842-843, *10:* **1883-1884**

Expert systems   *1:* 188

Explosives   *5:* **843-847**

Extrasolar planets   *5:* **847-848,** 846 (ill.)

Extreme Ultraviolet Explorer   *6:* 1123

Exxon   *Valdez* 7: *1424, 1425 (ill.)*

Eye   *5:* **848-853,** 851 (ill.)

Eye surgery   *8:* 1615-1618

F

Fahrenheit temperature scale   *10:* 1882

Fahrenheit, Gabriel Daniel   *10:* 1882

Far East   *1:* 199

Faraday, Michael   *4:* 761, 767, *6:* 1212

Farming.   *See* **Agriculture**

Farnsworth, Philo   *10:* 1875

Farsightedness   *5:* 851

Father of

   acoustics   *1:* 17

   American psychiatry   *9:* 1713

   genetics   *5:* 982

   heavier-than-air craft   *1:* 77

   lunar topography   *7:* 1296

   medicine   *2:* 348

   modern chemistry   *3:* 465

   modern dentistry   *4:* 627

   modern evolutionary theory   *5:* 833

   modern plastic surgery   *8:* 1529

   rigid airships   *1:* 75

   thermochemistry   *3:* 525

Fats   *6:* 1191

Fauchard, Pierre   *4:* 627

Fault   *5:* **855,** 856 (ill.)

Fault lines   *5:* 987

Fear, abnormal or irrational.   *See* **Phobias**

Feldspar   *6:* 1094

Felines   *5:* **855-864,** 861, 862 (ill.)

Fermat, Pierre de   *7:* 1393, *8:* 1576

Fermat's last theorem   *7:* 1393

Fermentation   *5:* **864-867,** *10:* 2043

Fermi, Enrico   *7:* 1365

Ferrell, William   *2:* 218

Fertilization   *5:* **867-870,** 868 (ill.)

Fertilizers   *1:* 66

Fetal alcohol syndrome   *1:* 87

Fiber optics   *5:* **870-872,** 871 (ill.)

Fillings (dental)   *4:* 628

Filovirus   *4:* 717

Filtration   *5:* **872-875**

Fingerprinting   *5:* 900

Fire algae   *1:* 94

First law of motion   *6:* 1170

First law of planetary motion   *7:* 1426

First law of thermodynamics   *10:* 1885

Fish   *5:* **875-878,** 876 (ill.)

Fish farming   *1:* 166

Fishes, age of   *8:* 1461

FitzGerald, George Francis   *9:* 1660

Flash lock   *6:* 1193
Fleas   *8:* 1474, 1474 (ill.)
Fleischmann, Martin   *7:* 1371
Fleming, Alexander   *1:* 156
Fleming, John Ambrose   *10:* 1961
Florey, Howard   *1:* 157
Flower   *5:* 878-862, 881 (ill.)
Flu.   *See* **Influenza**
Fluid dynamics   *5:* 882-886
Flukes   *8:* 1473
Fluorescence   *6:* 1197
Fluorescent light   *5:* 886-888, 888 (ill.)
Fluoridation   *5:* 889-890
Fluoride   *5:* 889
Fluorine   *6:* 1031-1032
Fluorspar   *6:* 1095
Fly shuttle   *6:* 1097
Fold lines   *5:* 987
Food irradiation   *5:* 893
Food preservation   *5:* 890-894
Food pyramid   *7:* 1402, 1402 (ill.)
Food web and food chain   *5:* 894-898, 896 (ill.)
Ford, Henry   *2:* 249 (ill.), *7:* 1237-1238
Forensic science   *5:* 898-901, 899 (ill.), *6:* 1067
Forestry   *5:* 901-907, 905 (ill.), 906 (ill.)
Forests   *2:* 294-295, *5:* 907-914, 909 (ill.), 910 (ill.), 913 (ill.)
Formula, chemical   *5:* 914-917
FORTRAN   *3:* 551
Fossil and fossilization   *5:* 917-921, 919 (ill.), 920 (ill.), *6:* 1055, *7:* 1326 (ill.), *8:* 1458
Fossil fuels   *1:* 112, *2:* 284, 392, *7:* 1319
Fossils, study of.   *See* **Paleontology**
Foxes   *2:* 384
Fractals   *5:* 921-923, 922 (ill.)
Fractions, common   *5:* 923-924
Fracture zones   *7:* 1410
Francium   *1:* 102
Free radicals   *1:* 61
Freezing point   *3:* 490
Frequency   *4:* 763, *5:* 925-926
Frequency modulation   *8:* 1628
Freshwater biomes   *2:* 298
Freud, Sigmund   *8:* 1593, 1594
Friction   *5:* 926-927
Frisch, Otto   *7:* 1362

Fronts   *1:* 80-82
Fry, Arthur   *1:* 39
Fujita Tornado Scale   *10:* 1902
Fujita, T. Theodore   *10:* 1902
Fuller, R. Buckminster   *2:* 398
Fulton, Robert   *10:* 1835
Functions (mathematics)   *5:* 927-930, *8:* 1485
Functional groups   *7:* 1430
Fungi   *5:* 930-934, 932 (ill.)
Fungicides   *1:* 67
Funk, Casimir   *10:* 1982
Fyodorov, Svyatoslav N.   *8:* 1617

G

Gabor, Dennis   *6:* 1049
Gadolinium   *6:* 1163
Gagarin, Yury   *9:* 1778
Gaia hypothesis   *5:* 935-940
Galactic clusters   *9:* 1808
Galaxies, active   *5:* 944
Galaxies   *5:* 941-945, 941 (ill.), 943 (ill.), *9:* 1806-1808
Galen, Claudius   *1:* 139
Galileo Galilei   *1:* 4, *5:* 1012, *6: 1149, 1170, 1184,* 7: *1296,* 10: *1869*
Galileo probe   *6:* 1149
Gall bladder   *3:* 469, *4:* 653, 655
Galle, Johann   *7:* 1330
Gallium   *1:* 126
Gallo, Robert   *10:* 1978
Gallstones   *3:* 469
Galvani, Luigi   *2:* 304, *4:* 751
Gambling   *1:* 36
Game theory   *5:* 945-949
Gamma rays   *4:* 765, *5:* 949-951, *8:* 1632
Gamma-ray burst   *5:* 952-955, 952 (ill.), 954 (ill.)
Ganges Plain   *1:* 197
Ganymede   *6:* 1148, 1149
Garbage.   *See* **Waste management**
Gardening.   *See* **Horticulture**
Gas, natural   *7:* 1319-1321
Gases, electrical conductivity in   *4:* 735
Gases, liquefaction of   *5:* 955-958
Gases, properties of   *5:* 959-962, 959 (ill.)
Gasohol   *1:* 91

Gastropoda   *7:* 1288
Gauss, Carl Friedrich   *6:* 1212
Gay-Lussac, Joseph Louis   *2:* 262
Gay-Lussac's law   *5:* 962
Geiger counter   *8:* 1625
Gell-Mann, Murray   *10:* 1829
Generators   *5:* **962-966,** 964 (ill.)
Genes   *7:* 1248
Genes, mapping.   *See* **Human Genome Project**
Genetic disorders   *5:* **966-973,** 968 (ill.), 968 (ill.)
Genetic engineering   *2:* 310, *5:* **973-980,** 976 (ill.), 979 (ill.)
Genetic fingerprinting   *5:* 900
Genetics   *5:* **980-986,** 983 (ill.)
Geneva Protocol   *2:* 289
Genital herpes   *9:* 1735
Genital warts   *9:* 1735, 1737
Geocentric theory   *3:* 574
Geologic map   *5:* **986-989,** 988 (ill.)
Geologic time   *5:* **990-993**
Geologic time scale   *5:* 988
Geology   *5:* **993-994,** 944 (ill.)
Geometry   *5:* **995-999**
Geothermal energy   *1:* 116
Gerbert of Aurillac   *7:* 1396
Geriatrics   *5:* 999
Germ warfare.   *See* **Biological warfare**
Germanium   *2:* 401
Gerontology   *5:* **999**
Gestalt psychology   *8:* 1595
Gibberellin   *6:* 1051
Gilbert, William   *6:* 1212
Gillies, Harold Delf   *8:* 1529
Gills   *5:* 877
Glacier   *5:* **1000-1003,** 1002 (ill.)
Glaisher, James   *2:* 263
Glass   *5:* **1004-1006,** 1004 (ill.)
Glenn, John   *9:* 1779
Gliders   *1:* 77
Global Biodiversity Strategy   *2:* 283
Global climate   *5:* **1006-1009**
Globular clusters   *9:* 1802, 1808
Glucose   *2:* 388
Gluons   *10:* 1831
Glutamate   *9:* 1720
Glycerol   *1:* 91
Glycogen   *2:* 389
Gobi Desert   *1:* 199
Goddard, Robert H.   *9:* 1695 (ill.)

Goiter   *6:* 1220
Gold   *8:* 1566-1569
Goldberger, Joseph   *6:* 1219
Golden-brown algae   *1:* 93
Golgi body   *3:* 433
Gondwanaland   *1:* 149
Gonorrhea   *9:* 1735, 1736
Gorillas   *8:* 1572
Gould, Stephen Jay   *1:* 32
Graphs and graphing   *5:* **1009-1011**
Grasslands   *2:* 296
Gravitons   *10:* 1831
Gravity and gravitation   *5:* **1012-1016,** 1014 (ill.)
Gray, Elisha   *10:* 1867
Great Barrier Reef   *2:* 240
Great Dividing Range   *2:* 240
Great Lakes   *6:* 1159
Great Plains   *4:* 682, *7:* 1356
Great Red Spot (Jupiter)   *6:* 1149, 1150 (ill.)
Great Rift Valley   *1:* 49, 51
Great White Spot (Saturn)   *9:* 1709
Green algae   *1:* 94
Green flashes   *2:* 224
Greenhouse effect   *2:* 285, 393, *5:* 1003, **1016-1022,** 1020 (ill.). *8:* 1554, *10:* 1965
Gregorian calendar   *2:* 373, 375
Grissom, Virgil   *9:* 1779
Growth hormone   *5:* 797
Growth rings (trees)   *4:* 619
Guiana Highlands   *9:* 1772
Guided imagery   *1:* 119
Gum disease   *4:* 630
Guth, Alan   *2:* 276
Gymnophions   *1:* 137
Gymnosperms   *9:* 1729
Gynecology   *5:* **1022-1024,** 1022 (ill.)
Gyroscope   *5:* **1024-1025,** 1024 (ill.)

H

H.M.S. *Challenger* 7: *1413*
Haber process   *7:* 1346
Haber, Fritz   *7:* 1346
Hadley, George   *2:* 218
Hahn, Otto   *7:* 1361
Hale, Alan   *3:* 529
Hale-Bopp comet   *3:* 529

Hales, Stephen *2:* 337
Half-life *6:* **1027**
Halite *6:* 1096
Hall, Charles M. *1:* 124, *4:* 757
Hall, Chester Moore *10:* 1871
Hall, John *7:* 1237
Halley, Edmond *7:* 1262, *10:* 2020
Halley's comet *3:* 528
Hallucinogens *6:* **1027-1030**
Haloes *2:* 224
Halogens *6:* **1030-1036**
Hand tools *6:* **1036-1037,** 1036 (ill.)
Hard water *9:* 1757
Hargreaves, James *6:* 1098
Harmonices mundi *3:* 425
Harmonics *5:* 925
Hart, William Aaron *7:* 1320
Harvestmen (spider) *1:* 171, 170 (ill.)
Harvey, William *1:* 139, *2:* 292
Hazardous waste *10:* 2006-2007, 2006 (ill.)
HDTV *10:* 1879
Heart *6:* **1037-1043,** 1041 (ill.), 1042 (ill.)
Heart attack *6:* 1043
Heart diseases *3:* 470, *6:* 1040
Heart transplants *10:* 1926
Heart, measure of electrical activity.
    See **Electrocardiogram**
Heartburn *4:* 656
Heat *6:* **1043-1046**
Heat transfer *6:* 1044
Heat, measurement of. *See* **Calorie**
Heisenberg, Werner *8:* 1609
Heliocentric theory *3:* 574
Helium *7:* 1349
Helminths *8:* 1471 (ill.)
Hemiptera *6:* 1105
Hemodialysis *5:* 841
Henbury Craters *2:* 240
Henry, Joseph *4:* 761, *10:* 1865
Herbal medicine *1:* 120
Herbicides *1:* 54-59
Herculaneum *5:* 828
Heredity *7:* 1246
Hermaphroditism *9:* 1667
Heroin *1:* 32, 34
Herophilus *1:* 138
Héroult, Paul *1:* 124
Herpes *9:* 1737
Herschel, John *2:* 277

Herschel, William *2:* 277, *10:* 1871, 1952
Hertz, Heinrich *6:* 1188, *8:* 1502, 1626
Hess, Henri *3:* 525
Hevelius, Johannes *7:* 1296
Hewish, Antony *7:* 1340
Hibernation *6:* **1046-1048,** 1047 (ill.)
Himalayan Mountains *1:* 194, 197, *7:* 1301
Hindbrain *2:* 340
Hindenburg *1:* 76
Hindu-Arabic number system *1:* 178, *7:* 1396, *10:* 2047
Hippocrates *2:* 348
Histamine *6:* 1085
Histology *1:* 141
Historical concepts *6:* 1186
HIV (human immunodeficiency virus) *1:* 70, 72 (ill.), *8:* 1583
Hodgkin's lymphoma *6:* 1201
Hoffmann, Felix *1:* 6
Hofstadter, Robert *7:* 1339
Hogg, Helen Sawyer *10:* 1964
Holistic medicine *1:* 120
Holland, John *10:* 1835
Hollerith, Herman *3:* 549
Holmium *6:* 1163
Holograms and holography *6:* **1048-1050,** 1049 (ill.)
Homeopathy *1:* 120
Homeostasis *8:* 1516, 1517
Homo erectus *6:* 1058
Homo ergaster *6:* 1058
Homo habilis *6:* 1058
Homo sapiens *6:* 1055, 1058-1059
Homo sapiens sapiens *6:* 1059
Hooke, Robert *1:* 140, *4:* 731
Hooke's law *4:* 731
Hopewell mounds *7:* 1301
Hopkins, Frederick G. *10:* 1982
Hopper, Grace *3:* 551
Hormones *6:* **1050-1053**
Horticulture *6:* **1053-1054,** 1053 (ill.)
HTTP *6:* 1128
Hubble Space Telescope *9:* 1808, *10:* 1873, 1872 (ill.)
Hubble, Edwin *2:* 275, *7:* 1328, *9:* 1655, 1810
Human evolution *6:* **1054-1060,** 1057 (ill.), 1059 (ill.)
Human Genome Project *6:* **1060-**

1068, 1062 (ill.), 1065 (ill.), 1066 (ill.)
Human-dominated biomes *2:* 302
Humanistic psychology *8:* 1596
Humason, Milton *9:* 1655
Hurricanes *3:* 610
Hutton, James *10:* 1947
Huygens, Christiaan *6:* 1187, *9:* 1711
Hybridization *2:* 310
Hydrocarbons *7:* 1430-1431
Hydrogen *6:* **1068-1071,** 1068 (ill.)
Hydrologic cycle *6:* **1071-1075,** 1072 (ill.), 1073 (ill.)
Hydropower *1:* 113
Hydrosphere *2:* 305
Hydrothermal vents *7:* 1418, 1417 (ill.)
Hygrometer *10:* 2020
Hypertension *3:* 484
Hypertext *6:* 1128
Hypnotherapy *1:* 119
Hypotenuse *10:* 1932
Hypothalamus *2:* 342, 343
Hypothesis *9:* 1723

I

Icarus *1:* 74
Ice ages *6:* **1075-1078,** 1077 (ill.)
Icebergs *6:* **1078-1081**, 1080 (ill.), 1081 (ill.)
Idiot savants. *See* **Savants**
IgE *1:* 109
Igneous rock *9:* 1702
Ileum *4:* 656
Imaginary numbers *6:* **1081-1082**
Immune system *1:* 108, *6:* **1082-1087**
Immunization *1:* 161, *10:* 1060-1960
Immunoglobulins *1:* 159
Imprinting *2:* 272
In vitro fertilization *4:* 791
Incandescent light *6:* **1087-1090,** 1089 (ill.)
Inclined plane *6:* 1207
Indian peninsula *1:* 197
Indicator species *6:* **1090-1092,** 1091 (ill.)
Indium *1:* 126
Induction *4:* 760

Industrial minerals *6:* **1092-1097**
Industrial Revolution *1:* 28, *3:* 523, *6:* 1193, **1097-1100,** *7:* 1236, *9:* 1817
  automation *2:* 242
  effect on agriculture *1:* 63
  food preservation *5:* 892
Infantile paralysis. *See* **Poliomyelitis**
Infants, sudden death. *See* **Sudden infant death syndrome (SIDS)**
Inflationary theory *2:* 275, 276
Influenza *4:* 672, *6:* 1084, *10:* 1978, 1979-1981
Infrared Astronomical Satellite *9:* 1808
Infrared astronomy *6:* **1100-1103,** 1102 (ill.)
Infrared telescopes *6:* 1101
Ingestion *4:* 653
Inheritance, laws of. *See* **Mendelian laws of inheritance**
Insecticides *1:* 67
Insects *6:* **1103-1106,** 1104 (ill.)
Insomnia *9:* 1747
Insulin *3:* 474, *4:* 638
Integers *1:* 180
Integral calculus *2:* 372
Integrated circuits *6:* **1106-1109,** 1108 (ill.), 1109 (ill.)
Integumentary system *6:* **1109-1112,** 1111 (ill.)
Interference *6:* **1112-1114,** 1113 (ill.)
Interferometer *6:* 1115 (ill.), 1116
Interferometry *10:* 1874, *6:* **1114-1116,** 1115 (ill.), 1116 (ill.)
Interferon *6:* 1084
Internal-combustion engines *6:* **1117-1119,** 1118 (ill.)
International Space Station *9:* 1788
International System of Units *2:* 376
International Ultraviolet Explorer *10:* 1946, *6:* **1120-1123,** 1122 (ill.)
Internet *6:* **1123-1130,** 1127 (ill.)
Interstellar matter *6:* **1130-1133,** 1132 (ill.)
Invertebrates *6:* **1133-1134,** 1134 (ill.)
Invertebrates, age of *8:* 1461
Io *6:* 1148, 1149
Iodine *6:* 1035
Ionic bonding *3:* 455
Ionization *6:* **1135-1137**
Ionization energy *6:* 1135

Ions   *4:* 733
Iron   *10:* 1915-1918
Iron lung   *8:* 1548 (ill.)
Iron manufacture   *6:* 1098
Irrational numbers   *1:* 180, 181
Isaacs, Alick   *6:* 1084
Islands   *3:* 500, *6:* **1137-1141,** 1139 (ill.)
Isotopes   *6:* **1141-1142,** *7:* 1241
IUE.   *See* **International Ultraviolet Explorer**

J

Jackals   *2:* 385
Jacquet-Droz, Henri   *9:* 1691
Jacquet-Droz, Pierre   *9:* 1691
James, William   *8:* 1594
Jansky, Karl   *8:* 1635
Java man   *6:* 1058
Jefferson, Thomas   *7:* 1300
Jejunum   *4:* 655
Jenner, Edward   *1:* 161, *10:* 1957
Jet engines   *6:* **1143-1146,** 1143 (ill.), 1145 (ill.)
Jet streams   *2:* 221, *4:* 783, *7:* 1293
Jones, John   *8:* 1529
Joule   *6:* 1045
Joule, James   *10:* 1885
Joule-Thomson effect   *3:* 597
Jupiter (planet)   *6:* **1146-1151,** 1147 (ill.), 1150 (ill.)

K

Kangaroos and wallabies   *6:* **1153-1157,** 1155 (ill.)
Kant, Immanuel   *9:* 1765
Kay, John   *6:* 1097
Kelvin scale   *10:* 1882
Kelvin, Lord.   *See* **Thomson, William**
Kenyanthropus platyops   *6:* 1056
Kepler, Johannes   *3:* 425, 574, *7:* 1426
Keratin   *6:* 1110
Kettlewell, Henry Bernard David   *1:* 28
Kidney dialysis   *4:* 645
Kidney stones   *5:* 841
Kilimanjaro, Mount   *5:* 1000
Kinetic theory of matter   *7:* 1243

King, Charles G.   *6:* 1219
Klein bottle   *10:* 1899
Knowing.   *See* **Cognition**
Klein, Felix   *10:* 1899
Koch, Robert   *2:* 292
Köhler, Wolfgang   *8:* 1595
Kraepelin, Emil   *9:* 1718
Krakatoa   *10:* 1998
Krypton   *7:* 1349, 1352
Kuiper Disk   *3:* 530
Kuiper, Gerald   *3:* 530, *7:* 1333
Kwashiorkor   *6:* 1218, *7:* 1403

L

La Niña   *4:* 782
Lacrimal gland   *5:* 852
Lactose   *2:* 388
Lager   *2:* 354
Lake Baikal   *1:* 198
Lake Huron   *6:* 1162 (ill.)
Lake Ladoga   *5:* 824
Lake Michigan   *7:* 1354 (ill.)
Lake Superior   *6:* 1159
Lake Titicaca   *6:* 1159
Lakes   *6:* **1159-1163,** 1161 (ill.), 1162 (ill.)
Lamarck, Jean-Baptiste   *1:* 28
Lambert Glacier   *1:* 149
Laminar flow   *1:* 40
Landfills   *10:* 2007, 2008 (ill.)
Language   *3:* 515
Lanthanides   *6:* **1163-1166**
Lanthanum   *6:* 1163
Laplace, Pierre-Simon   *2:* 323, *9:* 1765
Large intestine   *4:* 656
Laryngitis   *9:* 1681
Laser eye surgery   *8:* 1617
Lasers   *6:* **1166-1168,** 1168 (ill.)
LASIK surgery   *8:* 1617
Laurentian Plateau   *7:* 1355
Lava   *10:* 1995
Lavoisier, Antoine Laurent   *3:* 465, 524, *6:* 1069, *7:* 1444
Law of conservation of energy   *3:* 555, *10:* 1885
Law of conservation of mass/matter   *3:* 554, *5:* 816
Law of conservation of momentum   *7:* 1290

Law of dominance   *7:* 1249
Law of electrical force   *3:* 579
Law of independent assortment   *7:* 1249
Law of planetary motion   *3:* 425
Law of segregation   *7:* 1249
Law of universal gravitation   *3:* 426, *7:* 1427
Lawrence, Ernest Orlando   *8:* 1479
Laws of motion   *3:* 426, *6:* **1169-1171,** *7:* 1235, 1426
Le Verrier, Urbain   *7:* 1330
Lead   *2:* 402-403
Leakey, Louis S. B.   *6:* 1058
Learning disorders   *4:* 690
Leaf   *6:* **1172-1176,** 1172 (ill.), 1174 (ill.)
Leavitt, Henrietta Swan   *10:* 1964
Leclanché, Georges   *2:* 269
LED (light-emitting diode)   *6:* **1176-1179,** 1177 (ill.), 1178 (ill.)
Leeuwenhoek, Anton van   *2:* 253, *6:* 1184, *8:* 1469
Legionella pneumophilia   *6:* 1181, 1182
Legionnaire's disease   *6:* **1179-1184,** 1182 (ill.)
Leibniz, Gottfried Wilhelm   *2:* 371, 372, *7:* 1242
Lemaître, Georges-Henri   *3:* 576
Lemurs   *8:* 1572
Lenoir, Jean-Joseph Éttien   *6:* 1119
Lenses   *6:* **1184-1185,** 1184 (ill.)
Lentic biome   *2:* 298
Leonid meteors   *7:* 1263
Leonov, Alexei   *9:* 1779
Leopards   *5:* 860
Leptons   *10:* 1830
Leucippus   *2:* 226
Leukemia   *2:* 380
Leukocytes   *2:* 328
Lever   *6:* 1205, 1206 (ill.)
Levy, David   *6:* 1151
Lewis, Gilbert Newton   *1:* 15
Liber de Ludo Aleae   *8:* 1576
Lice   *8:* 1474
Life, origin of   *4:* 702
Light   *6:* 1087-1090, **1185-1190**
Light, speed of   *6:* 1190
Light-year   *6:* **1190-1191**
Lightning   *10:* 1889, 1889 (ill.)
Limbic system   *2:* 345
Liming agents   *1:* 66

Lind, James   *6:* 1218, *10:* 1981
Lindenmann, Jean   *6:* 1084
Linear acceleration   *1:* 4
Linear accelerators   *8:* 1477
Linnaeus, Carolus   *2:* 292, 337
Lions   *5:* 860
Lipids   *6:* **1191-1192,** *7:* 1400
Lippershey, Hans   *10:* 1869
Liquid crystals   *7:* 1244-1245
Liquor.   *See* **Alcohol (liquor)**
Lister, Joseph   *1:* 165
Lithium   *1:* 100
Lithosphere   *8:* 1535, 1536
Litmus test   *8:* 1496
Locks (water)   *6:* **1192-1195,** 1193 (ill.)
Logarithms   *6:* **1195**
Long, Crawford W.   *1:* 143
Longisquama insignis   *2:* 312
Longitudinal wave   *10:* 2015
Lord Kelvin.   *See* **Thomson, William**
Lorises   *8:* 1572
Lotic   *2:* 299
Lotic biome   *2:* 299
Lowell, Percival   *8:* 1539
Lowry, Thomas   *1:* 15
LSD   *6:* 1029
Lucy (fossil)   *6:* 1056, 1057 (ill.)
Luminescence   *6:* **1196-1198,** 1196 (ill.)
Luna   *7:* 1296
Lunar eclipses   *4:* 725
Lunar Prospector   *7:* 1297
Lung cancer   *9:* 1682
Lungs   *9:* 1679
Lunisolar calendar   *2:* 374
Lutetium   *6:* 1163
Lymph   *6:* 1199
Lymph nodes   *6:* 1200
Lymphatic system   *6:* **1198-1202**
Lymphocytes   *2:* 329, *6:* 1085, 1200 (ill.)
Lymphoma   *2:* 380, *6:* 1201
Lysergic acid diethylamide.   *See* **LSD**

M

Mach number   *5:* 883
Mach, L.   *6:* 1116
Machines, simple   *6:* **1203-1209,** 1206 (ill.), 1208 (ill.)

Mackenzie, K. R.   *6:* 1035
Magellan   *10:* 1966
Magma   *10:* 1995
Magnesium   *1:* 103
Magnetic fields   *4:* 759
Magnetic fields, stellar.   *See* **Stellar magnetic fields**
Magnetic recording/audiocassette   *6:* **1209-1212,** 1209 (ill.), 1211 (ill.)
Magnetic resonance imaging   *2:* 304
Magnetism   *6:* **1212-1215,** 1214 (ill.)
Malnutrition   *6:* **1216-1222,** 1221 (ill.)
Malpighi, Marcello   *1:* 139
Mammals   *6:* **1222-1224,** 1223 (ill.)
Mammals, age of   *8:* 1462
Mangrove forests   *5:* 909
Manhattan Project   *7:* 1365, 1380
Manic-depressive illness   *4:* 631
Mantle   *4:* 710
Manufacturing.   *See* **Mass production**
MAP (Microwave Anisotroy Probe)   *2:* 276
Maps and mapmaking.   *See* **Cartography**
Marasmus   *6:* 1218
Marconi, Guglielmo   *8:* 1626
Marie-Davy, Edme Hippolyte   *10:* 2021
Marijuana   *6:* **1224-1227,** 1226 (ill.), 1227 (ill.)
Marine biomes   *2:* 299
Mariner 10   *7:* 1250
Mars (planet)   *6:* **1228-1234,** 1228 (ill.), 1231 (ill.), 1232 (ill.)
Mars Global Surveyor   *6:* 1230
Mars Pathfinder   *6:* 1232
Marshes   *10:* 2025
Maslow, Abraham   *8:* 1596
Mass   *7:* **1235-1236**
Mass production   *7:* **1236-1239,** 1238 (ill.)
Mass spectrometry   *7:* **1239-1241,** 1240 (ill.), *8:* 1604
Mastigophora   *8:* 1592
Mathematics   *7:* **1241-1242**
   imaginary numbers   *6:* 1081
   logarithms   *6:* 1195
   multiplication   *7:* 1307
   number theory   *7:* 1393
   probability theory   *8:* 1575
   proofs   *8:* 1578
   statistics   *9:* 1810
   symbolic logic   *10:* 1859
   topology   *10:* 1897-1899
   trigonometry   *10:* 1931-1933
   zero   *10:* 2047
Matter, states of   *7:* **1243-1246,** 1243 (ill.)
Maxwell, James Clerk   *4:* 760, 767, *6:* 1213, *8:* 1626
Maxwell's equations   *4:* 760
McKay, Frederick   *5:* 889
McKinley, Mount   *7:* 1302
McMillan, Edwin   *1:* 24
Measurement.   *See* **Units and standards**
Mechanoreceptors   *8:* 1484
Meditation   *1:* 119
Medulla oblongata   *2:* 340
Meiosis   *9:* 1666
Meissner effect   *10:* 1851 (ill.)
Meitner, Lise   *7:* 1362
Mekong River   *1:* 200
Melanin   *6:* 1110
Melanomas   *2:* 380
Memory   *2:* 344, *3:* 515
Mendel, Gregor   *2:* 337, *4:* 786, *7:* 1247
Mendeleev, Dmitry   *4:* 777, *8:* 1487
Mendelian laws of inheritance   *7:* **1246-1250,** 1248 (ill.)
Meninges   *2:* 342
Menopause   *1:* 59, *2:* 410, *5:* 800, 1020
Menstruation   *1:* 59, *5:* 800, 1020, *8:* 1599
Mental illness, study and treatment of.   *See* **Psychiatry**
Mercalli scale   *4:* 704
Mercalli, Guiseppe   *4:* 704
Mercury   *10:* 1921-1923, 1922 (ill.)
Mercury (planet)   *7:* **1250-1255,** 1251 (ill.), 1252 (ill.)
Mercury barometers   *2:* 265
Méré, Chevalier de   *8:* 1576
Mescaline   *6:* 1029
Mesosphere   *2:* 213
Mesozoic era   *5:* 990, *8:* 1462
Metabolic disorders   *7:* **1254-1255,** 1254 (ill.), 1257
Metabolism   *7:* **1255-1259**
Metalloids   *7:* 1348
Metamorphic rocks   *9:* 1705
Metamorphosis   *7:* **1259-1261**

Meteorograph   *2:* 215
Meteors and meteorites   *7:* **1262-1264**
Methanol   *1:* 89
Metric system   *7:* **1265-1268,** *10:* 1949
Mettauer, John Peter   *8:* 1529
Meyer, Julius Lothar   *4:* 777, *8:* 1487
Michell, John   *2:* 323
Michelson, Albert A.   *6:* 1114, *6:* 1187
Microwave Anisotropy Probe (MAP)
   2: 276
Microwave communication   *7:* **1268-**
   1271, 1270 (ill.)
Microwaves   *4:* 765
Mid-Atlantic Ridge   *7:* 1303, 1409
Midbrain   *2:* 340
Middle East   *1:* 196
Mifepristone   *3:* 565
Migraine   *2:* 349, 350
Migration (animals)   *7:* **1271-1273,**
   1272 (ill.)
Millennium   *2:* 375
Millikan, Robert Andrew   *4:* 771
Minerals   *6:* 1092-1097, *7:* 1401, **1273-**
   1278, 1276 (ill.), 1277 (ill.)
Mining   *7:* **1278-1282,** 1281 (ill.)
Mir   *9:* 1781
Mirages   *2:* 222
Miranda   *10:* 1954
Misch metal   *6:* 1165
Missiles.   *See* **Rockets and missiles**
Mission   *9:* 1787
Mississippi River   *7:* 1355
Mississippian earthern mounds   *7:* 1301
Missouri River   *7:* 1355
Mitchell, Mount   *7:* 1356
Mites   *1:* 170
Mitochondira   *3:* 436
Mitosis   *1:* 133, *9:* 1665
Mobile telephones   *3:* 441
Möbius strip   *10:* 1899
Möbius, Augustus Ferdinand   *10:* 1899
Model T (automobile)   *7:* 1237, 1238
Modulation   *8:* 1627
Moho   *4:* 709
Mohorovičiá discontinuity   *4:* 709
Mohorovičiá, Andrija   *4:* 709
Mohs scale   *1:* 3
Mohs, Friedrich   *1:* 3
Mole (measurement)   *7:* **1282-1283**
Molecular biology   *7:* **1283-1285**
Molecules   *7:* **1285-1288,** 1286 (ill.)

Mollusks   *7:* **1288-1290,** 1289 (ill.)
Momentum   *7:* **1290-1291**
Monkeys   *8:* 1572
Monoclonal antibodies   *1:* 162, *2:* 311
Monocytes   *2:* 329
Monoplacophora   *7:* 1289
Monosaccharides   *2:* 388
Monotremes   *6:* 1224
Monsoons   *7:* **1291-1294**
Mont Blanc   *5:* 827
Montgolfier, Jacques   *2:* 262
Montgolfier, Joseph   *2:* 262
Moon   *7:* **1294-1298,** 1295 (ill.), 1297
   (ill.)
   affect on tides   *10:* 1890
   Apollo 11   *9: 1779*
Morley, Edward D.   *6:* 1187
Morphine   *1:* 32, 33
Morse code   *10:* 1866
Morse, Samuel F. B.   *10:* 1865
Morton, William   *1:* 143
Mosquitoes   *6:* 1106, *8:* 1473
Motion, planetary, laws of   *7:* 1426
Motors, electric.   *See* **Electric motors**
Mounds, earthen   *7:* **1298-1301,** 1299
   (ill.)
Mount Ararat   *1:* 197
Mount Cameroon   *1:* 51
Mount Elbert   *7:* 1357
Mount Elbrus   *5:* 823
Mount Everest   *1:* 194
Mount Kilimanjaro   *1:* 53 (ill.), *5:* 1003,
   7: 1303
Mount McKinley   *7:* 1302, 1354
Mount Mitchell   *7:* 1356
Mount Robson   *7:* 1357
Mount St. Helens   *10:* 1996, 1998
   (ill.)
Mountains   *7:* **1301-1305,** 1304 (ill.)
Movable bridges   *2:* 358
mRNA   *7:* 1285
Müller, Karl Alex   *10:* 1851
Multiple personality disorder   *7:*
   1305-1307
Multiplication   *7:* **1307-1309**
Muscular dystrophy   *7:* 1313, 1337
Muscular system   *7:* **1309-1313,** 1311
   (ill.), 1312 (ill.), 1313 (ill.)
Mushrooms   *6:* 1028
Mutation   *7:* **1314-1317,** 1316 (ill.)
Mysophobia   *8:* 1497

N

Napier, John   6: 1195
Narcolepsy   9: 1748
Narcotics   1: 32
Natural gas   7: **1319-1321**
Natural language processing   1: 189
Natural numbers   1: 180, 7: **1321-1322**
Natural selection   1: 29-30, 2: 292, 5: 834, 837-839
Natural theology   1: 27
Naturopathy   1: 122
Nautical archaeology   7: **1323-1327,** 1325 (ill.), 1326 (ill.)
Nautilus   10: 1835
Navigation (animals)   7: 1273
Neanderthal man   6: 1059
Neap tides   10: 1892
NEAR Shoemaker   1: 203-204, 9: 1787
Nearsightedness   5: 851
Nebula   7: **1327-1330,** 1329 (ill.)
Nebular hypothesis   9: 1765
Negative reinforcement.   *See* **Reinforcement, positive and negative**
Nematodes   8: 1471
Neodymium   6: 1163
Neolithic Age   1: 62
Neon   7: 1349, 1352
Neptune (planet)   7: **1330-1333,** 1331 (ill.)
Nereid   7: 1333
Nerve nets   7: 1333
Nervous system   7: **1333-1337,** 1335 (ill.)
Neurons   7: 1333 (ill.)
Neurotransmitters   1: 128, 2: 350, 4: 631, 7: 1311, 9: 1720
Neutralization   1: 15
Neutrinos   10: 1832, 1833
Neutron   2: 235, 7: **1337-1339,** 10: 1830, 1832
Neutron stars   7: **1339-1341,** 1341 (ill.)
Neutrophils   2: 329
Newcomen, Thomas   9: 1818
Newton, Isaac   1: 4, 5: 1012, 6: 1184, 7: 1242
  calculus   2: 372
  corpsucular theory of light   6: 1187
  laws of motion   6: 1169-1171, 7: 1427

reflector telescope   10: 1871
Ngorongoro Crater   1: 52
Niacin.   *See* **Vitamin B3**
Nicotine   1: 34, 3: 478
Night blindness   6: 1220
Nile River   9: 1686
Nipkow, Paul   10: 1875
Nitrification   7: 1343, 1344
Nitrogen   7: 1344, 1345 (ill.)
Nitrogen cycle   7: **1342-1344,** 1342 (ill.)
Nitrogen family   7: **1344-1349,** 1345 (ill.)
Nitrogen fixation   7: 1342
Nitroglycerin   5: 844
Nitrous oxide   1: 142
Nobel, Alfred   5: 845
Noble gases   7: **1349-1352,** 1350 (ill.)
Non-Hodgkin's lymphoma   6: 1201
Nondestructive testing   10: 2037
North America   7: **1352-1358,** 1353 (ill.), 1354 (ill.), 1357 (ill.)
Novas   7: **1359-1360,** 1359 (ill.)
NSFNET   6: 1127
Nuclear fission   7: **1361-1366,** 1365 (ill.), 1381
Nuclear fusion   7: **1366-1371,** 1370 (ill.)
Nuclear medicine   7: **1372-1374**
Nuclear Non-Proliferation Treaty   7: 1387
Nuclear power   1: 113, 7: **1374-1381,** 1376 (ill.), 1379 (ill.), 10: 1836
Nuclear power plant   7: 1374, 1379 (ill.)
Nuclear reactor   7: 1365
Nuclear waste management   7: 1379
Nuclear weapons   7: **1381-1387**
Nucleic acids   7: **1387-1392,** 1391 (ill.), 1392 (ill.)
Nucleotides   3: 473, 7: 1388
Nucleus (cell)   3: 434
Number theory   7: 1322, **1393-1395**
Numbers, imaginary   6: 1081
Numbers, natural   7: 1321
Numeration systems   7: **1395-1399**
Nutrient cycle   2: 307
Nutrients   7: 1399
Nutrition   6: 1216, 7: **1399-1403,** 1402 (ill.)
Nylon   1: 186, 8: 1533

O

Oberon   *10:* 1954
Obesity   *4:* 716
Obsession   *7:* **1405-1407**
Obsessive-compulsive disorder   *7:* 1405
Obsessive-compulsive personality disorder   *7:* 1406
Occluded fronts   *1:* 82
Ocean   *7:* **1407-1411,** 1407 (ill.)
Ocean currents   *3:* 604-605
Ocean ridges   *7:* 1410 (ill.)
Ocean zones   *7:* **1414-1418**
Oceanic archaeology.   *See* **Nautical archaeology**
Oceanic ridges   *7:* 1409
Oceanography   *7:* **1411-1414,** 1412 (ill.), 1413 (ill.)
Octopus   *7:* 1289
Oersted, Hans Christian   *1:* 124, *4:* 760, 766, *6:* 1212
Offshore drilling   *7:* 1421
Ohio River   *7:* 1355
Ohm (O)   *4:* 738
Ohm, Georg Simon   *4:* 738
Ohm's law   *4:* 740
Oil drilling   *7:* **1418-1422,** 1420 (ill.)
Oil pollution   *7:* 1424
Oil spills   *7:* **1422-1426,** 1422 (ill.), 1425 (ill.)
Oils   *6:* 1191
Olduvai Gorge   *6:* 1058
Olfaction.   *See* **Smell**
On the Origin of Species by Means of Natural Selection   *6:* 1054
On the Structure of the Human Body   *1:* 139
O'Neill, J. A.   *6:* 1211
Onnes, Heike Kamerlingh   *10:* 1850
Oort cloud   *3:* 530
Oort, Jan   *8:* 1637
Open clusters   *9:* 1808
Open ocean biome   *2:* 299
Operant conditioning   *9:* 1658
Ophediophobia   *8:* 1497
Opiates   *1:* 32
Opium   *1:* 32, 33
Orangutans   *8:* 1572, 1574 (ill.)
Orbit   *7:* **1426-1428**
Organ of Corti   *4:* 695
Organic chemistry   *7:* **1428-1431**

Organic families   *7:* 1430
Organic farming   *7:* **1431-1434,** 1433 (ill.)
Origin of life   *4:* 702
Origins of algebra   *1:* 97
Orizaba, Pico de   *7:* 1359
Orthopedics   *7:* **1434-1436**
Oscilloscopes   *10:* 1962
Osmosis   *4:* 652, *7:* **1436-1439,** 1437 (ill.)
Osmotic pressure   *7:* 1436
Osteoarthritis   *1:* 181
Osteoporosis   *9:* 1742
Otitis media   *4:* 697
Otosclerosis   *4:* 697
Ovaries   *5:* 800
Oxbow lakes   *6:* 1160
Oxidation-reduction reactions   *7:* **1439-1442,** *9:* 1648
Oxone layer   *7:* 1452 (ill.)
Oxygen family   *7:* **1442-1450,** 1448 (ill.)
Ozone   *7:* **1450-1455,** 1452 (ill.)
Ozone depletion   *1:* 48, *8:* 1555
Ozone layer   *7:* 1451

P

Packet switching   *6:* 1124
Pain   *7:* 1336
Paleoecology   *8:* **1457-1459,** 1458 (ill.)
Paleontology   *8:* **1459-1462,** 1461 (ill.)
Paleozoic era   *5:* 990, *8:* 1461
Paleozoology   *8:* 1459
Panama Canal   *6:* 1194
Pancreas   *4:* 655, *5:* 798
Pangaea   *8:* 1534, 1536 (ill.)
Pap test   *5:* 1020
Papanicolaou, George   *5:* 1020
Paper   *8:* **1462-1467,** 1464 (ill.), 1465 (ill.), 1466 (ill.)
Papyrus   *8:* 1463
Paracelsus, Philippus Aureolus   *1:* 84
Parasites   *8:* **1467-1475,** 1471 (ill.), 1472 (ill.), 1474 (ill.)
Parasitology   *8:* 1469
Parathyroid glands   *5:* 798
Paré, Ambroise   *8:* 1580, *10:* 1855
Parkinson's disease   *1:* 62
Parsons, Charles A.   *9:* 1820
Particle accelerators   *8:* **1475-1482,**

1478 (ill.), 1480 (ill.)
Particulate radiation   8: 1620
Parturition.   See Birth
Pascal, Blaise   2: 370, 8: 1576
Pascaline   2: 371
Pasteur, Louis   1: 161, 165, 2: 292, 10: 1958, 1990, 1959 (ill.)
Pavlov, Ivan P.   9: 1657, 10: 1990
Pelagic zone   7: 1415
Pellagra   6: 1219
Penicillin   1: 155, 156, 157 (ill.)
Peppered Moth   1: 28
Perception   8: 1482-1485, 1483 (ill.)
Periodic function   8: 1485-1486, 1485 (ill.)
Periodic table   4: 777, 778 (ill.), 8: 1489, 1486-1490, 1489 (ill.), 1490 (ill.)
Periscopes   10: 1835
Perrier, C.   4: 775, 10: 1913
Perseid meteors   7: 1263
Persian Gulf War   3: 462, 7: 1425
Pesticides   1: 67, 67 (ill.), 68 (ill.), 4: 619-622
PET scans   2: 304, 8: 1640
Petroglyphs and pictographs   8: 1491-1492, 1491 (ill.)
Petroleum   7: 1418, 1423, 8: 1492-1495
Peyote   6: 1029
Pfleumer, Fritz   6: 1211
pH   8: 1495-1497
Phaeophyta   1: 95
Phages   10: 1974
Phenothiazine   10: 1906
Phenylketonuria   7: 1254
Phloem   6: 1175, 8: 1523
Phobias   8: 1497-1498
Phobos   6: 1229
Phosphates   6: 1095
Phosphorescence   6: 1197
Phosphorus   7: 1347
Photochemistry   8: 1498-1499
Photocopying   8: 1499-1502, 1500 (ill.), 1501 (ill.)
Photoelectric cell   8: 1504
Photoelectric effect   6: 1188, 8: 1502-1505
Photoelectric theory   8: 1503
Photoreceptors   8: 1484
Photosphere   10: 1846

Photosynthesis   2: 306, 388, 391, 8: 1505-1507
Phototropism   6: 1051, 8: 1508-1510, 1508 (ill.)
Physical therapy   8: 1511-1513, 1511 (ill.)
Physics   8: 1513-1516
Physiology   8: 1516-1518
Phytoplankton   8: 1520, 1521
Pia mater   2: 342
Piazzi, Giuseppe   1: 201
Pico de Orizaba   7: 1359
Pictographs, petroglyphs and   8: 1491-1492
Pigments, dyes and   4: 686-690
Pineal gland   5: 798
PKU (phenylketonuria)   7: 1254
Place value   7: 1397
Plages   10: 1846
Plague   8: 1518-1520, 1519 (ill.)
Planck's constant   8: 1504
Plane   6: 1036 (ill.), 1207
Planetary motion, laws of   7: 1426
Plankton   8: 1520-1522
Plant behavior   2: 270
Plant hormones   6: 1051
Plants   1: 91, 2: 337, 388, 392, 8: 1505, 1522-1527, 1524 (ill.), 1526 (ill.)
Plasma   2: 326, 7: 1246
Plasma membrane   3: 432
Plastic surgery   8: 1527-1531, 1530 (ill.), 10: 1857
Plastics   8: 1532-1534, 1532 (ill.)
Plastids   3: 436
Plate tectonics   8: 1534-1539, 1536 (ill.), 1538 (ill.)
Platelets   2: 329
Platinum   8: 1566, 1569-1570
Pluto (planet)   8: 1539-1542, 1541 (ill.)
Pneumonia   9: 1681
Pneumonic plague   8: 1520
Poisons and toxins   8: 1542-1546, 1545 (ill.)
Polar and nonpolar bonds   3: 456
Poliomyelitis   8: 1546-1549, 1548 (ill.), 10: 1958
Pollination   5: 880-882
Pollution   1: 9, 8: 1549-1558, 1554 (ill.), 1557 (ill.)

Pollution control *8:* **1558-1562,** 1559 (ill.), 1560 (ill.)

Polonium *7:* 1449, 1450

Polygons *8:* **1562-1563,** 1562 (ill.)

Polymers *8:* **1563-1566,** 1565 (ill.)

Polysaccharides *2:* 388

Pompeii *5:* 828, *10:* 1997

Pons, Stanley *7:* 1371

Pontiac Fever *6:* 1181

Pope Gregory XIII *2:* 373

Porpoises *3:* 448

Positive reinforcement. *See* **Reinforcement, positive and negative**

Positron *1:* 163, *4:* 772

Positron-emission tomography. *See* **PET scans**

Positrons *10:* 1832, 1834

Post-it™ notes *1:* 38

Post-traumatic stress disorder *9:* 1826

Potassium *1:* 102

Potassium salts *6:* 1095

Potential difference *4:* 738, 744

Pottery *3:* 447

Praseodymium *6:* 1163

Precambrian era *5:* 988, *8:* 1459

Precious metals *8:* **1566-1570,** 1568 (ill.)

Pregnancy, effect of alcohol on *1:* 87

Pregnancy, Rh factor in *9:* 1684

Pressure *8:* **1570-1571**

Priestley, Joseph *2:* 394, 404, *3:* 525, *7:* 1345, 1444

Primary succession *10:* 1837, 2026

Primates *8:* **1571-1575,** 1573 (ill.), 1574 (ill.)

Probability theory *8:* **1575-1578**

Procaryotae *2:* 253

Progesterone *5:* 800

Projectile motion. *See* **Ballistics**

Prokaryotes *3:* 429

Promethium *6:* 1163

Proof (mathematics) *8:* **1578-1579**

Propanol *1:* 91

Prosthetics *8:* **1579-1583,** 1581 (ill.), 1582 (ill.)

Protease inhibitors *8:* **1583-1586,** 1585 (ill.)

Proteins *7:* 1399, *8:* **1586-1589,** 1588 (ill.)

Protons *10:* 1830, 1832

Protozoa *8:* 1470, **1590-1592,** 1590 (ill.)

Psilocybin *6:* 1029

Psychiatry *8:* **1592-1594**

Psychoanalysis *8:* 1594

Psychology *8:* **1594-1596**

Psychosis *8:* **1596-1598**

Ptolemaic system *3:* 574

Puberty *8:* **1599-1601,** *9:* 1670

Pulley *6:* 1207

Pulsars *7:* 1340

Pyrenees *5:* 826

Pyroclastic flow *10:* 1996

Pyrrophyta *1:* 94

Pythagoras of Samos *8:* 1601

Pythagorean theorem *8:* **1601**

Pytheas *10:* 1890

Q

Qualitative analysis *8:* **1603-1604**

Quantitative analysis *8:* **1604-1607**

Quantum mechanics *8:* **1607-1609**

Quantum number *4:* 772

Quarks *10:* 1830

Quartz *2:* 400

Quasars *8:* **1609-1613,** 1611 (ill.)

R

Rabies *10:* 1958

Radar *8:* **1613-1615,** 1614 (ill.)

Radial keratotomy *8:* **1615-1618,** 1618 (ill.)

Radiation *6:* 1044, *8:* **1619-1621**

Radiation exposure *8:* **1621-1625,** 1623 (ill.), 1625 (ill.)

Radio *8:* **1626-1628,** 1628 (ill.)

Radio astronomy *8:* **1633-1637,** 1635 (ill.)

Radio waves *4:* 765

Radioactive decay dating *4:* 616

Radioactive fallout *7:* 1385, 1386

Radioactive isotopes *6:* 1142, *7:* 1373

Radioactive tracers *8:* **1629-1630**

Radioactivity *8:* **1630-1633**

Radiocarbon dating *1:* 176

Radiology *8:* **1637-1641,** 1640 (ill.)

Radionuclides *7:* 1372

Radiosonde *2:* 216

Radium *1:* 105

Radon   *7:* 1349, 1350
Rain forests   *2:* 295, *8:* **1641-1645,**
   1643 (ill.), 1644 (ill.)
Rainbows   *2:* 222
Rainforests   *8:* 1643 (ill.)
Ramjets   *6:* 1144
Rare earth elements   *6:* 1164
Rat-kangaroos   *6:* 1157
Rational numbers   *1:* 180
Rawinsonde   *2:* 216
Reaction, chemical
Reaction, chemical   *9:* **1647-1649,**
   1649 (ill.)
Reality engine   *10:* 1969, 1970
Reber, Grote   *8:* 1635
Receptor cells   *8:* 1484
Recommended Dietary Allowances
   10: 1984
Reconstructive surgery.   *See* **Plastic
   surgery**
Recycling   *9:* **1650-1653,** 1650 (ill.),
   1651 (ill.), *10:* 2009
Red algae   *1:* 94
Red blood cells   *2:* 327, 328 (ill.)
Red giants   *9:* **1653-1654**
Red tides   *1:* 96
Redox reactions   *7:* 1439, 1441
Redshift   *8:* 1611, *9:* **1654-1656,** 1656
   (ill.)
Reflector telescopes   *10:* 1871
Refractor telescopes   *10:* 1870
Reines, Frederick   *10:* 1833
Reinforcement, positive and negative
   9: **1657-1659**
Reis, Johann Philipp   *10:* 1867
Reitz, Bruce   *10:* 1926
Relative dating   *4:* 616
Relative motion   *9:* 1660
Relativity, theory of   *9:* **1659-1664**
Relaxation techniques   *1:* 118
REM sleep   *9:* 1747
Reproduction   *9:* **1664-1667,** 1664
   (ill.), 1666 (ill.)
Reproductive system   *9:* **1667-1670,**
   1669 (ill.)
Reptiles   *9:* **1670-1672,** 1671 (ill.)
Reptiles, age of   *8:* 1462
Respiration
Respiration   *2:* 392, *9:* **1672-1677**
Respiratory system   *9:* **1677-1683,**
   1679 (ill.), 1682 (ill.)

Retroviruses   *10:* 1978
Reye's syndrome   *1:* 8
Rh factor   *9:* **1683-1685,** 1684 (ill.)
Rheumatoid arthritis   *1:* 183
Rhinoplasty   *8:* 1527
Rhodophyta   *1:* 94
Ribonucleic acid   *7:* 1390, 1392 (ill.)
Rickets   *6:* 1219, *7:* 1403
Riemann, Georg Friedrich Bernhard
   10: 1899
Rift valleys   *7:* 1303
Ritalin   *2:* 238
Rivers   *9:* **1685-1690,** 1687 (ill.), 1689
   (ill.)
RNA   *7:* 1390, 1392 (ill.)
Robert Fulton   *10:* 1835
Robotics   *1:* 189, *9:* **1690-1692,** 1691
   (ill.)
Robson, Mount   *7:* 1357
Rock carvings and paintings   *8:* 1491
Rock cycle   *9:* 1705
Rockets and missiles   *9:* **1693-1701,**
   1695 (ill.), 1697 (ill.), 1780 (ill.)
Rocks   *9:* **1701-1706,** 1701 (ill.), 1703
   (ill.), 1704 (ill.)
Rocky Mountains   *7:* 1301, 1357
Roentgen, William   *10:* 2033
Rogers, Carl   *8:* 1596
Root, Elijah King   *7:* 1237
Ross Ice Shelf   *1:* 149
Roundworms   *8:* 1471
RR Lyrae stars   *10:* 1964
RU-486   *3:* 565
Rubidium   *1:* 102
Rural techno-ecosystems   *2:* 302
Rush, Benjamin   *9:* 1713
Rust   *7:* 1442
Rutherford, Daniel   *7:* 1345
Rutherford, Ernest   *2:* 233, *7:* 1337

S

Sabin vaccine   *8:* 1548
Sabin, Albert   *8:* 1549
Sahara Desert   *1:* 52
St. Helens, Mount   *10:* 1996
Salicylic acid   *1:* 6
Salk vaccine   *8:* 1548
Salk, Jonas   *8:* 1548, *10:* 1959
Salyut 1   *9:* 1781, 1788

Samarium   *6:* 1163

San Andreas Fault   *5:* 854

Sandage, Allan   *8:* 1610

Sarcodina   *8:* 1592

Satellite television   *10:* 1877

Satellites   *9:* **1707-1708,** 1707 (ill.)

Saturn (planet)   *9:* **1708-1712,** 1709 (ill.), 1710 (ill.)

Savanna   *2:* 296

Savants   *9:* **1712-1715**

Saxitoxin   *2:* 288

Scanning Tunneling Microscopy   *10:* 1939

Scaphopoda   *7:* 1289

Scheele, Carl   *7:* 1345, 1444

Scheele, Karl Wilhelm   *3:* 525, *6:* 1032

Schiaparelli, Giovanni   *7:* 1263

Schizophrenia   *8:* 1596, *9:* **1716-1722,** 1718 (ill.), 1721 (ill.)

Schmidt, Maarten   *8:* 1611

Scientific method   *9:* **1722-1726**

Scorpions   *1:* 169

Screw   *6:* 1208

Scurvy   *6:* 1218, *10:* 1981, 1989

Seamounts   *10:* 1994

Seashore biome   *2:* 301

Seasons   *9:* **1726-1729,** 1726 (ill.)

Second law of motion   *6:* 1171, *7:* 1235

Second law of planetary motion   *7:* 1426

Second law of thermodynamics   *10:* 1886

Secondary cells   *2:* 270

Secondary succession   *10:* 1837, *10:* 1838

The Secret of Nature Revealed   *5:* 877

Sedimentary rocks   *9:* 1703

Seeds   *9:* **1729-1733,** 1732 (ill.)

Segré, Emilio   *1:* 163, *4:* 775, *6:* 1035, *10:* 1913

Seismic waves   *4:* 703

Selenium   *7:* 1449

Semaphore   *10:* 1864

Semiconductors   *4:* 666, 734, *10:* 1910, 1910

Semi-evergreen tropical forest   *2:* 298

Senility   *4:* 622

Senses and perception   *8:* 1482

Septicemia plague   *8:* 1519

Serotonin   *2:* 350

Serpentines   *1:* 191

Sertürner, Friedrich   *1:* 33

Set theory   *9:* **1733-1735,** 1734 (ill.), 1735 (ill.)

Sexual reproduction   *9:* 1666

Sexually transmitted diseases   *9:* **1735-1739,** 1737 (ill.), 1738 (ill.)

Shell shock   *9:* 1826

Shepard, Alan   *9:* 1779

Shockley, William   *10:* 1910

Shoemaker, Carolyn   *6:* 1151

Shoemaker-Levy 9 (comet)   *6:* 1151

Shooting stars.   *See* **Meteors and meteorites**

Shumway, Norman   *10:* 1926

SI system   *10:* 1950

Sickle-cell anemia   *2:* 320

SIDS.   *See* **Sudden infant death syndrome (SIDS)**

Significance of relativity theory   *9:* 1663

Silicon   *2:* 400, 401

Silicon carbide   *1:* 2

Silver   *8:* 1566, 1569

Simpson, James Young   *1:* 143

Sitter, Willem de   *3:* 575

Skeletal muscles   *7:* 1310 (ill.), **1311-1313**

Skeletal system   *9:* **1739-1743,** 1740 (ill.), 1742 (ill.)

Skin   *2:* 362

Skylab   *9:* 1781, 1788

Slash-and-burn agriculture   *9:* **1743-1744,** 1744 (ill.)

Sleep and sleep disorders   *9:* **1745-1749,** 1748 (ill.)

Sleep apnea   *9:* 1749, *10:* 1841

Slipher, Vesto Melvin   *9:* 1654

Smallpox   *10:* 1957

Smell   *9:* **1750-1752,** 1750 (ill.)

Smoking   *1:* 34, 119, *3:* 476, *9:* 1682

Smoking (food preservation)   *5:* 890

Smooth muscles   *7:* 1312

Snakes   *9:* **1752-1756,** 1754 (ill.)

Soaps and detergents   *9:* **1756-1758**

Sobrero, Ascanio   *5:* 844

Sodium   *1:* 100, 101 (ill.)

Sodium chloride   *6:* 1096

Software   *3:* 549-554

Soil   *9:* **1758-1762.** 1760 (ill.)

Soil conditioners   *1:* 67

Solar activity cycle   *10:* 1848

Solar cells   *8:* 1504, 1505
Solar eclipses   *4:* 724
Solar flares   *10:* 1846, 1848 (ill.)
Solar power   *1:* 115, 115 (ill.)
Solar system   *9:* **1762-1767,** 1764 (ill.), 1766 (ill.)
Solstice   *9:* 1728
Solution   *9:* **1767-1770**
Somatotropic hormone   *5:* 797
Sonar   *1:* 22, *9:* **1770-1772**
Sørenson, Søren   *8:* 1495
Sound.   *See* **Acoustics**
South America   *9:* **1772-1776,** 1773 (ill.), 1775 (ill.)
South Asia   *1:* 197
Southeast Asia   *1:* 199
Space   *9:* **1776-1777**
Space probes   *9:* **1783-1787,** 1785 (ill.), 1786 (ill.)
Space shuttles   *9:* 1782 (ill.), 1783
Space station, international   *9:* **1788-1792,** 1789 (ill.)
Space stations   *9:* 1781
Space, curvature of   *3:* 575, *7:* 1428
Space-filling model   *7:* 1286, 1286 (ill.)
Space-time continuum   *9:* 1777
Spacecraft, manned   *9:* **1777-1783,** 1780 (ill.), 1782 (ill.)
Spacecraft, unmanned   *9:* 1783
Specific gravity   *4:* 625
Specific heat capacity   *6:* 1045
Spectrometer   *7:* 1239, 1240 (ill.)
Spectroscopes   *9:* 1792
Spectroscopy   *9:* **1792-1794,** 1792 (ill.)
Spectrum   *9:* 1654, **1794-1796**
Speech   *9:* **1796-1799**
Speed of light   *6:* 1190
Sperm   *4:* 785, *5:* 800, *9:* 1667
Spiders   *1:* 169
Spina bifida   *2:* 321, 321 (ill.)
Split-brain research   *2:* 346
Sponges   *9:* **1799-1800,** 1800 (ill.)
Sporozoa   *8:* 1592
Sprengel, Christian Konrad   *5:* 877
Squid   *7:* 1289
Staphylococcus   *2:* 258, 289
Star clusters   *9:* **1808-1810,** 1808 (ill.)
Starburst galaxies   *9:* **1806-1808,** 1806 (ill.)
Stars   *9:* **1801-1806,** 1803 (ill.), 1804 (ill.)

binary stars   *2:* 276-278
brown dwarf   *2:* 358-359
magnetic fields   *9:* 1820
variable stars   *10:* 1963-1964
white dwarf   *10:* 2027-2028
Static electricity   *4:* 742
Stationary fronts   *1:* 82
Statistics   *9:* **1810-1817**
Staudinger, Hermann   *8:* 1565
STDs.   *See* **Sexually transmitted diseases**
Steam engines   *9:* **1817-1820,** 1819 (ill.)
Steel industry   *6:* 1098
Stellar magnetic fields   *9:* **1820-1823,** 1822 (ill.)
Sterilization   *3:* 565
Stomach ulcers   *4:* 656
Stone, Edward   *1:* 6
Stonehenge   *1:* 173, 172 (ill.)
Stoney, George Johnstone   *4:* 771
Storm surges   *9:* **1823-1826,** 1825 (ill.)
Storm tide   *9:* 1824
Strassmann, Fritz   *7:* 1361
Stratosphere   *2:* 213
Streptomycin   *1:* 155
Stress   *9:* **1826-1828**
Strike lines   *5:* 988
Stroke   *2:* 350, 351
Strontium   *1:* 105
Subatomic particles   *10:* **1829-1834,** 1833 (ill.)
Submarine canyons   *3:* 562
Submarines   *10:* **1834-1836,** 1836 (ill.)
Subtropical evergreen forests   *5:* 908
Succession   *10:* **1837-1840,** 1839 (ill.)
Sudden infant death syndrome (SIDS)   *10:* **1840-1844**
Sulfa drugs   *1:* 156
Sulfur   *6:* 1096, *7:* 1446
Sulfur cycle   *7:* 1448, 1448 (ill.)
Sulfuric acid   *7:* 1447
Sun   *10:* **1844-1849,** 1847 (ill.), 1848 (ill.)
   stellar magnetic field   *9:* 1821
Sun dogs   *2:* 224
Sunspots   *6:* 1077
Super Collider   *8:* 1482
Superclusters   *9:* 1809
Superconducting Super Collider   *10:* 1852

Superconductors *4:* 734, *10:* **1849-1852,** 1851 (ill.)
Supernova *9:* 1654, *10:* **1852-1854,** 1854 (ill.)
Supersonic flight *1:* 43
Surgery *8:* 1527-1531, *10:* **1855-1858,** 1857 (ill.), 1858 (ill.)
Swamps *10:* 2024
Swan, Joseph Wilson *6:* 1088
Symbolic logic *10:* **1859-1860**
Synchrotron *8:* 1481
Synchrotron radiation *10:* 2037
Synthesis *9:* 1648
Syphilis *9:* 1736, 1738 (ill.)
Système International d'Unités *10:* 1950
Szent-Györyi, Albert *6:* 1219

T

Tagliacozzi, Gasparo *8:* 1528
Tapeworms *8:* 1472
Tarsiers *8:* 1572, 1573 (ill.)
Tasmania *2:* 241
Taste *10:* **1861-1863,** 1861 (ill.), 1862 (ill.)
Taste buds *10:* 1861 (ill.), 1862
Tay-Sachs disease *2:* 320
TCDD *1:* 54, *4:* 668
TCP/IP *6:* 1126
Tears *5:* 852
Technetium *4:* 775, *10:* 1913
Telegraph *10:* **1863-1866**
Telephone *10:* **1866-1869,** 1867 (ill.)
Telescope *10:* **1869-1875,** 1872 (ill.), 1874 (ill.)
Television *5:* 871, *10:* **1875-1879**
Tellurium *7:* 1449, 1450
Temperate grassland *2:* 296
Temperate forests *2:* 295, *5:* 909, *8:* 1644
Temperature *6:* 1044, *10:* **1879-1882**
Terbium *6:* 1163
Terrestrial biomes *2:* 293
Testes *5:* 800, *8:* 1599, *9:* 1667
Testosterone *8:* 1599
Tetanus *2:* 258
Tetracyclines *1:* 158
Tetrahydrocannabinol *6:* 1224
Textile industry *6:* 1097

Thalamus *2:* 342
Thallium *1:* 126
THC *6:* 1224
Therapy, physical *8:* 1511-1513
Thermal energy *6:* 1044
Thermal expansion *5:* 842-843, *10:* **1883-1884,** 1883 (ill.)
Thermodynamics *10:* **1885-1887**
Thermoluminescence *4:* 618
Thermometers *10:* 1881
Thermonuclear reactions *7:* 1368
Thermoplastic *8:* 1533
Thermosetting plastics *8:* 1533
Thermosphere *2:* 213
Thiamine. *See* **Vitamin B1**
Third law of motion *6:* 1171
Third law of planetary motion *7:* 1426
Thomson, Benjamin *10:* 1885
Thomson, J. J. *2:* 233, *4:* 771
Thomson, William *10:* 1885, 1882
Thorium *1:* 26
Thulium *6:* 1163
Thunder *10:* 1889
Thunderstorms *10:* **1887-1890,** 1889 (ill.)
Thymus *2:* 329, *5:* 798
Thyroxine *6:* 1035
Ticks *1:* 170, *8:* 1475
Tidal and ocean thermal energy *1:* 117
Tides *1:* 117, *10:* **1890-1894,** 1892 (ill.), 1893 (ill.)
Tigers *5:* 859
Time *10:* **1894-1897,** 1896 (ill.)
Tin *2:* 401, 402
TIROS 1 *2:* 217
Titan *9:* 1711
Titania *10:* 1954
Titanic *6:* 1081
Titius, Johann *1:* 201
Tools, hand *6:* 1036
Topology *10:* **1897-1899,** 1898 (ill.), 1899 (ill.)
Tornadoes *10:* **1900-1903,** 1900 (ill.)
Torricelli, Evangelista *2:* 265
Touch *10:* **1903-1905**
Toxins, poisons and *8:* 1542-1546
Tranquilizers *10:* **1905-1908,** 1907 (ill.)
Transformers *10:* **1908-1910,** 1909 (ill.)
Transistors *10:* 1962, **1910-1913,** 1912 (ill.)

Transition elements *10:* **1913-1923,** 1917 (ill.), 1920 (ill.), 1922 (ill.)

Transplants, surgical *10:* **1923-1927,** 1926 (ill.)

Transuranium elements *1:* 24

Transverse wave *10:* 2015

Tree-ring dating *4:* 619

Trees *10:* **1927-1931,** 1928 (ill.)

Trematodes *8:* 1473

Trenches, ocean *7:* 1410

Trevithick, Richard *6:* 1099

Trichomoniasis *9:* 1735

Trigonometric functions *10:* 1931

Trigonometry *10:* **1931-1933**

Triode *10:* 1961

Triton *7:* 1332

Tropical evergreen forests *5:* 908

Tropical grasslands *2:* 296

Tropical rain forests *5:* 908, *8:* 1642

Tropism *2:* 271

Troposphere *2:* 212

Trusses *2:* 356

Ts'ai Lun *8:* 1463

Tularemia *2:* 289

Tumors *10:* **1934-1937,** 1934 (ill.), 1936 (ill.)

Tundra *2:* 293

Tunneling *10:* **1937-1939,** 1937 (ill.)

Turbojets *6:* 1146

Turboprop engines *6:* 1146

Turbulent flow *1:* 40

U

U.S.S. *Nautilus* 10: *1836*

Ulcers (stomach) *4:* 656

Ultrasonics *1:* 23, *10:* **1941-1943,** 1942 (ill.)

Ultrasound *8:* 1640

Ultraviolet astronomy *10:* **1943-1946,** 1945 (ill.)

Ultraviolet radiation *4:* 765

Ultraviolet telescopes *10:* 1945

Uluru *2:* 240

Umbriel *10:* 1954

Uncertainty principle *8:* 1609

Uniformitarianism *10:* **1946-1947**

Units and standards *7:* 1265, *10:* **1948-1952**

Universe, creation of *2:* 273

Uranium *1:* 25, *7:* 1361, 1363

Uranus (planet) *10:* **1952-1955,** 1953 (ill.), 1954 (ill.)

Urban-Industrial techno-ecosystems *2:* 302

Urea *4:* 645

Urethra *5:* 841

Urine *1:* 139, *5:* 840

Urodeles *1:* 137

Ussher, James *10:* 1946

V

Vaccination.*See* **Immunization**

Vaccines *10:* **1957-1960,** 1959 (ill.)

Vacuoles *3:* 436

Vacuum *10:* **1960-1961**

Vacuum tube diode *4:* 666

Vacuum tubes *3:* 416, *10:* **1961-1963**

Vail, Alfred *10:* 1865

Van de Graaff *4:* 742 (ill.), *8:* 1475

Van de Graaff, Robert Jemison *8:* 1475

Van Helmont, Jan Baptista *2:* 337, 393, 404

Variable stars *10:* **1963-1964**

Vasectomy *3:* 565

Venereal disease *9:* 1735

Venter, J. Craig *6:* 1063

Venus (planet) *10:* **1964-1967,** 1965 (ill.), 1966 (ill.)

Vertebrates *10:* **1967-1968,** 1967 (ill.)

Vesalius, Andreas *1:* 139

Vesicles *3:* 433

Vibrations, infrasonic *1:* 18

Video disk recording *10:* 1969

Video recording *10:* **1968-1969**

Vidie, Lucien *2:* 266

Viè, Françoise *1:* 97

Vietnam War *1:* 55, *3:* 460

Virtual reality *10:* **1969-1974,** 1973 (ill.)

Viruses *10:* **1974-1981,** 1976 (ill.), 1979 (ill.)

Visible spectrum *2:* 221

Visualization *1:* 119

Vitamin A *6:* 1220, *10:* 1984

Vitamin B *10:* 1986

Vitamin B_1 *6:* 1219

Vitamin B_3 *6:* 1219

Vitamin C *6:* 1219, *10:* 1981, 1987, 1988 (ill.)

Vitamin D   6: 1219, 10: 1985
Vitamin E   10: 1985
Vitamin K   10: 1986
Vitamins   7: 1401, 10: **1981-1989,**
   1988 (ill.)
Vitreous humor   5: 851
Viviparous animals   2: 317
Vivisection   10: **1989-1992**
Volcanoes   7: 1411, 10: **1992-1999,**
   1997 (ill.), 1998 (ill.)
Volta, Alessandro   4: 752, 10: 1865
Voltaic cells   3: 437
Volume   10: **1999-2002**
Von Graefe, Karl Ferdinand   8: 1527
Vostok   9: 1778
Voyager 2   10: 1953
Vrba, Elisabeth   1: 32

W

Waksman, Selman   1: 157
Wallabies, kangaroos and   6: 1153-1157
Wallace, Alfred Russell   5: 834
War, Peter   10: 1924
Warfare, biological.   2: 287-290
Warm fronts   1: 82
Waste management   7: 1379, 10:
   2003-2010, 2005 (ill.), 2006 (ill.),
   2008 (ill.)
Water   10: **2010-2014,** 2013 (ill.)
Water cycle.   *See* **Hydrologic cycle**
Water pollution   8: 1556, 1561
Watson, James   3: 473, 4: 786, 5: 973,
   980 (ill.), 982, 7: 1389
Watson, John B.   8: 1595
Watt   4: 746
Watt, James   3: 606, 9: 1818
Wave motion   10: **2014-2017**
Wave theory of light   6: 1187
Wavelength   4: 763
Waxes   6: 1191
Weather   3: 608-610, 10: 1887-1890,
   1900-1903, **2017-2020,** 2017 (ill.)
Weather balloons   2: 216 (ill.)
Weather forecasting   10: **2020-2023,**
   2021 (ill.), 2023 (ill.)
Weather, effect of El Niño on   4: 782
Wedge   6: 1207
Wegener, Alfred   8: 1534
Weights and measures.   *See* **Units and
   standards**

Welding   4: 736
Well, Percival   8: 1539
Wells, Horace   1: 142
Went, Frits   6: 1051
Wertheimer, Max   8: 1595
Wetlands   2: 299
Wetlands   10: **2024-2027,** 2024 (ill.)
Whales   3: 448
Wheatstone, Charles   10: 1865
Wheel   6: 1207
White blood cells   2: 328, 1085 (ill.)
White dwarf   10: **2027-2028,** 2027
   (ill.)
Whitney, Eli   6: 1098, 7: 1237
Whole numbers   1: 180
Wiles, Andrew J.   7: 1394
Willis, Thomas   4: 640, 9: 1718
Wilmut, Ian   3: 487
Wilson, Robert   8: 1637
Wind   10: **2028-2031,** 2030 (ill.)
Wind cells   2: 218
Wind power   1: 114, 114 (ill.)
Wind shear   10: 2031
Withdrawal   1: 35
Wöhler, Friedrich   7: 1428
Wöhler, Hans   1: 124
Wolves   2: 383, 383 (ill.)
World Wide Web   6: 1128
WORMs   3: 533
Wright, Orville   1: 75, 77
Wright, Wilbur   1: 77
Wundt, Wilhelm   8: 1594

X

X rays   4: 764, 8: 1639, 10: 1855,
   2033-2038, 2035 (ill.), 2036 (ill.)
X-ray astronomy   10: **2038-2041,** 2040
   (ill.)
X-ray diffraction   4: 650
Xanthophyta   1: 95
Xenon   7: 1349, 1352
Xerography   8: 1502
Xerophthalmia   6: 1220
Xylem   6: 1175, 8: 1523

Y

Yangtze River   1: 199
Yeast   10: **2043-2045,** 2044 (ill.)
Yellow-green algae   1: 95

Yoga   *1:* 119
Young, Thomas   *6:* 1113
Ytterbium   *6:* 1163

Z

Zeeman effect   *9:* 1823
Zeeman-Doppler imaging   *9:* 1823

Zehnder, L.   *6:* 1116
Zeppelin, Ferdinand von   *1:* 75
Zero   *10:* **2047-2048**
Zoophobia   *8:* 1497
Zooplankton   *8:* 1521, 1522
Zosimos of Panopolis   *1:* 84
Zweig, George   *10:* 1829
Zworykin, Vladimir   *10:* 1875
Zygote   *4:* 787